A GUIDE TO THE GREATER LONDON AUTHORITY

AUSTRALIA
LBC Information Services
Sydney

CANADA and USA
Carswell
Toronto

NEW ZEALAND
Brooker's
Auckland

SINGAPORE and MALAYSIA
Sweet & Maxwell Asia
Singapore and Kuala Lumpur

A GUIDE TO THE GREATER LONDON AUTHORITY

by

Arden Chambers, Barristers, London

Chambers Authors: Scott Collins, Iain Colville and Sarah Pengelly

Chambers Editor: Jonathan Manning

LONDON
SWEET & MAXWELL
2000

Published in 2000 by
Sweet & Maxwell Limited
100 Avenue Road
Swiss Cottage
London NW3 3PF
(http://www.sweetandmaxwell.co.uk)

Typeset by Dataword Services Limited, Chilcompton
Printed in Great Britain by MPG Books, Bodmin, Cornwall

No natural forests were destroyed to make this product;
only farmed timber was used and replanted

ISBN 0 421 72700 4

A CIP catalogue record of this book is available from the British Library

Note that some of the material included in this text was first published in Current
Law Statutes as annotations to the Greater London Authority Act 1999. Original
annotations by Scott Collins, Iain Colville Sarah Pengelly and Lydia Challen.

PREFACE

The Greater London Authority is a local authority of a kind never before seen in the United Kingdom. A strategic authority, not responsible for the provision of services, it consists of a directly-elected Mayor with executive powers, together with an Assembly (of which he is not a member) undertaking a primarily monitoring (and to some extent financial) role.

This is worlds away, in both form and substance, from the traditional model of local government in which services are provided to the local community and decisions are taken by an authority's members in full council or, through schemes of delegation, by committees, sub-committees and/or officers. The new form was devised to combat apathy on the part of the public towards local democracy, by rendering the executive — the Mayor — directly accountable to the electorate. The substance, *i.e.* the purely strategic as distinct from service providing role, is an attempt to deal with the perceived weakness of previous London-wide authorities which were criticised for duplicating (or competing with) services already provided by the London boroughs and/or central government.

Thus in this new model, the Mayor is responsible for the Authority's main functions, *i.e.* the development and implementation of sustainable policies and integrated strategies across the area of Greater London. The Assembly has extensive powers to call the Mayor and his staff publicly to account so as to provide an essential "check and balance" to the power of the Mayor, and also enjoys a specific role in relation to the formulation of budgets.

The importance of this new species of local authority and, in particular, the directly-elected mayor — aside from that intrinsic to any new authority for London — is that is may well soon form the basis for local government generally in the twenty-first century. By the Local Government Act 1999, the directly-elected mayor, with either a cabinet or a council manager, is at the forefront of two of the three new constitutional structures that any authority may adopt (the third being a cabinet with a leader).

In the midst of these changes, it is worthy of note that the notion that there should be an authority for London is comparatively recent. Until the twentieth century, Greater London did not exist as a distinct legal and political entity, in spite of the historic importance of London as the national capital and the concentration of populations over many centuries around the ancient city. For centuries, local government in the Greater London area consisted of the Corporation of the City of London and the local borough corporations.

After the sixteenth century and as a result of catastrophic events such as the Great Fire of London, a pattern was established of ad hoc legislation directed at specific problems associated with London's expansion, which pattern continued well into the late nineteenth century. During this period, Greater London was governed by numerous local bodies of trustees and commissioners which provided services that could not be supplied by local authorities.

The transformation of the political and geographical landscape of the Greater London area began to be recognised in the late nineteenth century leading to the creation, then and during the twentieth century, of London-wide entities such as the Metropolitan Board of Works, the London County Council and, finally, the Greater London Council. For a raft of political and economic reasons, however, each in turn was ultimately rejected.

The controversial abolition of the Greater London Council in 1986 led to a period during which there was no real co-ordinated strategic local government for the London area. Supporters of the idea of a London authority identified as the cause of the failures of the previous bodies the fact that they provided services and regulated activities in unnecessary competition with, or in addition to, the London boroughs and central government departments and agencies.

To meet this criticism, when a new Greater London Authority was proposed, its main function was to be the development and implementation of broad policies and strategies in fields which fell outside the jurisdiction of the London boroughs but which affected all residents of the Greater London area. The Government's suggested model was that of a democratically elected body with policy-making powers to tackle what government identified as the main problems of the Greater London: unemployment and poverty; the need for improved infrastructure to enhance London's economic competitiveness; and environmental issues such as traffic congestion, air pollution and noise which undermined the sustainability of London as a city and the quality of life it offered to its people.

In a referendum held on May 7, 1998, a substantial majority of Londoners approved the establishment of the Greater London Authority. The first Mayor (Ken Livingstone) and Assembly members were elected on May 4, 2000.

These are interesting times for local government. Time will tell whether the new Authority, with its novel functions and purposes, will succeed where earlier experiments failed. The aim of this book is to provide a guide to a new form of local government which, given the importance and unusual nature of the Greater London Authority, will be of interest to all practitioners.

Scott Collins
Iain Colville
Jonathan Manning
Sarah Pengelly

CONTENTS

PART A
HISTORICAL AND PROCEDURAL MATTERS

Chapter 1
HISTORY OF LONDON GOVERNMENT AND OUTLINE OF THE GREATER LONDON AUTHORITY ACT 1999

Chapter 2
ELECTIONS

Contents

PART B
FINANCIAL PROVISIONS

Contents

Contents

Chapter 14
HIGHWAYS

Chapter 15
NEW CHARGES AND LEVIES

PART D
MISCELLANEOUS PROVISIONS

Chapter 16
THE LONDON DEVELOPMENT AGENCY

Contents

PART E
PLANNING AND ENVIRONMENTAL FUNCTIONS

TABLE OF CASES

Table of Cases

TABLE OF STATUTES

Table of Statutes

TABLE OF STATUTORY INSTRUMENTS

Table of Statutory Instruments

LIST OF ABBREVIATIONS

1992 Act	Local Government Finance Act 1992
1988 Act	Local Government Finance Act 1988
1999 Act, GLA Act, "the Act"	Greater London Authority Act 1999
EA	Environment Act 1995
EPA	Environmental Protection Act 1990
ESDP	European Spatial Development Perspective
INTERREG	European Community Initiative on Transnational Co-operation on Spatial Planning
IPC	integrated pollution control
GLA	Greater London Authority
LAAPC	London Authority air pollution control
LIP	local implementation plan
LPA	local planning authority
LRT	London Regional Transport
LTUC	London Transport Users' Committee
MPA	Metropolitan Police Authority
MPS	Metropolitan Police Service
PPG	planning policy guidance notes
PPP agreement	public-private partnership agreement
PPP	public private partnership
RPG	regional planning guidance
SDS	Spatial Development Strategy
TCPA	Town and Country Planning Act
TfL	Transport for London

"The White Paper"   "A Mayor and Assembly for London", March 1998 Cm. 3897

"The Green Paper"   "New Leadership for London: the Government's Proposals for a Greater London Authority (Cm. 3724, July 1997)

UDP   Unitary Development Plan

PART A

HISTORICAL AND PROCEDURAL MATTERS

Chapter 1

HISTORY OF LONDON GOVERNMENT AND OUTLINE OF THE GREATER LONDON AUTHORITY ACT 1999

Introduction

There are seven million people living in the Greater London area; 5.5 **1.01** million of them are eligible voters. London contains three million households, a third of whom comprise one person. The total labour force of London is 3.7 million. There are 10 Euro-constituencies, 74 Parliamentary constituencies, 32 London borough councils and the Corporation of the City of London. One hundred and ninety-three languages are spoken in London amongst 33 different national communities of more than 10,000 people born outside the United Kingdom. There are 1,500 cultural events each week and, in 1996, 34 per cent of visitors to London cited the theatre as the sole reason for their visit. It is one of the top three most popular urban tourist destinations in the world. (These statistics were all cited by the Department of the Environment, Transport and the Regions in notes accompanying the White Paper, "A Mayor and Assembly for London", Cm. 3897 (March 1998), referred to in this text as "the 1998 White Paper").

Pre-history of London Government

The idea of London as a distinct geopolitical entity is a late nineteenth- **1.02** century innovation. In 1855 *The Times* declared that "there is no such place as London." London, it claimed, was ". . . rent into an infinity of divisions, districts and areas . . . within the metropolitan limits, the local administration is carried on by no fewer that 300 different bodies deriving from 250 different local Acts" (Wood, House of Lords Research Paper, "The Greater London Authority Bill: A Mayor and Assembly for London" (Research Paper 98/115)). The first statutory attempt to define London geographically was the London Police Act 1829 which established the Metropolitan Police District, defined as an area within a 15 mile radius of Charing Cross. According to the authors of "The New Government of London"

(Travers and Jones, 1997), the term "London" had no particular legal significance until the census of 1851 where, for the first time, London was defined as a full census division, the boundaries of which approximated to modern Inner London.

The first metropolitan London-wide public authority was the Metropolitan Board of Works, created by the Metropolis Local Management Act 1855. This Act created 23 large directly-elected parishes and 15 district boards. The purposes of the Board included the improvement of the city's sewage system, fire protection, slum clearance, the enforcement of building codes and the construction of main roads. Its boundaries corresponded to Inner London. The members of the Board were elected by the parishes and district boards and the Common Council of the City of London.

The London County Council

1.03 The London County Council, created by the Local Government Act 1888, replaced the Metropolitan Board of Works. The Council had more or less the same powers and duties but it had, in addition, other more general powers in the fields of housing, bridges, health and education. According to Young and Garside in "Metropolitan London: Politics and Urban Changes 1837–1981" (1991), the Council was criticised for being too large and powerful and there was a demand for some of its powers to be devolved. This led to the London Government Act 1899, which established 27 metropolitan boroughs in the London County Council area, and the Westminster City Council.

Subsequently, however, London's population increased dramatically. Travis and Jones, in "The New Government of London" (1997) at page 50, write:

> "The vast growth of London, from a population of four million in 1900 to eight million in the 1950s, led to a sprawling expansion well beyond the limits if the Victorian City. At the time of its creation, the LCC covered virtually the whole of the capital's enormous urban area. By the 1950s, the majority of the population of what had become known as Greater London lived beyond the LCC boundaries."

1.04 A Royal Commission in 1921–23 chaired by Lord Ullswater recommended the establishment of a statutory committee to advise the Government about planning, housing and transport issues within an area 25 miles radius from Charing Cross. According to Travis and Jones, there were further inconclusive efforts at reform (such as the Lord Reading Commission set up in 1945 and the committee established by Clement Davies M.P. in 1946) which failed "because of the impossibility of considering the local government of the County of London in isolation from that of the whole built-up area" (*ibid.* page 52). The Clement Davies Committee proposed that there should be a regional authority with executive powers of finance and direction.

The Herbert Royal Commission (1957–60) proposed the creation of the Greater London Council together with 51 borough councils within the area of Greater London. It would be responsible for education, traffic, planning, main roads, waste disposal, and fire protection. It would share functions in housing, recreation and sewerage with the new borough councils but the boroughs would have sole powers with respect to social services, environmental health, libraries and local roads.

The Greater London Council

The Commission's recommendations were largely accepted by the Govern- **1.05** ment, leading to the London Government Act 1963 which established the GLC, the Inner London Education Authority and the 32 boroughs. The City of London was effectively made a borough. The main functions of the GLC under the 1963 Act were in relation to highways, fire services, housing, planning and, from 1970 until 1984, London Transport. The boroughs' functions were broadly similar to those they enjoy today.

According to Barlow ("Metropolitan Government", 1991, at pages 93–4) the GLC had three fundamental "structural weaknesses". These were:

(1) the lack of a substantive and coherent role in the allocation of functions between itself, the Government and the boroughs;

(2) the vague and blurred definition of its functions; and

(3) the lack of subordination of one level of government to the other such that "strong" boroughs tended to undermine the authority of the GLC and to reduce its capacity to perform an effective strategic role.

Even within a few years of its establishment, there were calls for the abolition of the GLC. By the early 1980s, Labour had gained control of the GLC on a comparatively radical socialist manifesto and, as Barlow puts it (at page 97), faced an increasingly hostile Conservative central government bent on reducing public expenditure in general and local authority spending in particular. It was abolished in 1986 by the Local Government Act 1985.

Government in London after the Abolition of the GLC

On abolition, the 32 boroughs and the City of London formed the main **1.06** basis of London government, exercising the customary range of local authority powers and duties. There were efforts amongst the London boroughs to co-ordinate policy across London through bodies such as the Association of London Government. The borough councils also took part in several London-wide joint committees with functions in areas such as the fire service, planning, parking regulation and local authority grants.

5

Otherwise, London was controlled by central government, either through quangos and separate agencies such as London Transport, the London Arts Board, Training and Enterprise Councils, and health authorities; or directly by the Government through agencies under the control of secretary of states for the environment or transport. The Government Office for London was created in 1994 in order to co-ordinate central government's London functions such as the distribution of housing capital allocation and strategic planning. There was also a Cabinet sub-committee for London, chaired by the Secretary of State for the Environment; and a Minister for London.

Proposals for a New London-wide Authority

1.07 The idea of a strategic elected authority for London had been Labour Party policy since 1992 ("An Elected Voice for London", Labour Party, 1992 and "A Voice for the People", 1996). Its basic structure would be unique to local government. There would be a directly elected Mayor; and the main functions of the new authority would be to make and implement policy as opposed to the provision of services.

A green paper, "New Leadership for London: the Government's Proposals for a Greater London Authority", Cm. 3724 (July 1997), (referred to in this text as "the Green Paper") set out the proposed structure of the new authority. At pages 1 to 2, of the Green Paper, the Government identified those problems of London that it considered required a central, democratically elected body with policy-making powers. These were:

". . . concentrations of unemployment and deep poverty, the need for an improved infrastructure in order to enhance London's economic competitiveness, environmental problems such as traffic congestion, air pollution and noise which undermined the sustainability of London as a city and the quality of life offered to its people."

1.08 The Green Paper suggested that the functions of the new authority would fall within the general heading of sustainable development. This was defined as "giving all Londoners an improved and lasting quality of life, combining environmental, economic and social goals". Responses to the Green Paper were generally favourable. At a referendum held on May 7, 1998, pursuant to the Greater London Authority (Referendum) Act 1998, a substantial majority of those who voted approved of the proposal for a new authority.

Meanwhile, the White Paper, "A Mayor And Assembly for London: The Government's proposals for modernising the governance of London", (Cm. 3897), was published in March 1998 and set out in more detail the structure and functions of the Authority which have, to a great extent, been confirmed in the Act. It proposed that the new authority would consist of a Mayor and an Assembly which was, at the time, an entirely novel form of local government. Under the traditional model of local government decision making, all major decisions are made by the members of the authority themselves and, typically, through their committees and sub-committees. Wood, in the House of Lords Research Paper, "The Greater London Authority Bill: A Mayor and Assembly for London" (Research Paper 98/115) notes that a directly elected executive was an arrangement currently unknown to local or central government in the United Kingdom. Until now, the executive at local or central level had been drawn from the ranks of constituency or ward-based elected representatives (at page 21).

Recently, however, critics of the traditional model have put forward an **1.09** alternative model based on a directly-elected mayor, with or without a "cabinet": see, for example, a July 1991 Department of the Environment consultation paper, "The Internal Management of Local Authorities in England". A White Paper, "Modern Local Government: In Touch with the People", Cm. 4014 (July 1998), proposed that councils adopt one of tree broad categories of constitution: replace the committee decision-making process with a directly elected Mayor with a cabinet; a cabinet with a leader, or a directly elected Mayor and council manager. This has now been enshrined in the Local Government Bill 1999.

With regard to the GLA, the Government, in the White Paper, opted for a directly-elected Mayor who would exercise the bulk of its functions, but which would be subject to review and scrutiny by the Assembly. At paragraph 3.11, the White Paper described the Authority as:

". . . an unique new category of local government in which there will be an explicit separation of powers between the executive—the Mayor—and the Assembly and where each will have a separate mandate from the electorate. In these circumstances, the powers and duties which the Mayor and the assembly will exercise on behalf of the GLA, either jointly or separately, must be allocated in an explicit way."

The White Paper, at paragraph 3.6, summarised the Mayor's role as **1.10** "deciding policy and strategic direction for the GLA, setting budgets and ensuring action." The Assembly's job, on the other hand, is " . . . to scrutinise the Mayor's activities, approve budgets and strategies, provide members for new authorities for police and fire, initiate scrutinies on subjects of its choice." In practical terms, "the Mayor will be responsible for developing sustainable and integrated strategies across all of the GLA's functions and the Assembly will provide an essential check and balance to the power of the Mayor."

In this way, a directly elected Mayor would provide "strong leadership" with the elected assembly "to hold the Mayor on account on London's behalf". Given its unique constitutional structure and the London-wide nature of the problems the new authority would have to deal with, the GLA would have a strategic role rather than be a service-provider. At paragraph 1.8 of the White Paper:

"At the heart of our proposals for London is a directly elected executive Mayor with the power to make a real difference to London on issues that matter to Londoners. A Mayor with strategic responsibilities where they are needed, and who will tackle the issues and change things for the better."

1.11 The Authority would have responsibilities to develop strategies in certain specified areas and, at paragraph 3.10, the Authority is:

". . . to be given a remit to address all London-wide issues and play a significant role outside of its specific responsibilities. It will therefore be given a duty to promote the social, economic and environmental well-being of Londoners. This duty will attract the necessary powers to enable the Mayor to fulfil the remit set out in this White Paper."

Hence, while the GLA's main purpose is to develop and implement policy, it is not a legislative body and, unlike ordinary local authorities, it does not provide any services or regulate activities.

Outline of The Greater London Authority Act 1999

Part I—The Greater London Authority

1.12 Part I of the Act establishes the Greater London Authority. It is to comprise of the Mayor and the members of the Assembly. The Mayor is directly elected by all London voters. There are 25 members of the Assembly. There are two types of Assembly member: 14 are "constituency members", one for each of the 14 specially created constituencies; 11 are "London members" who are elected across London, *i.e.* by a list. Subject to modifications, the standard local authority measures with respect to vacancies, franchise, conduct of elections and qualifications apply to the Authority.

Part II—General Functions and Procedure

1.13 Part II deals with the general functions and procedure of the Authority. The Authority's functions are to be exercised according to "principal purposes" of promoting economic development and wealth creation, promoting social development and promoting the improvement of the environment. The Authority is also to have regard to a range of other matters such as the health of persons in Greater London and the achievement of sustainable development in the United Kingdom. It may not exercise any of its functions so as to duplicate the powers of other public bodies, such as those of a local housing authority. In the main, new organisations under the control of the Mayor as well as the London boroughs will carry out the Mayor's policies; in the GLA Act, they are known as "the functional bodies".

The main role of the Authority is that of the Mayor. The Mayor is required to develop, implement and revise strategies with respect to transport, planning and development control, spatial development, biodiversity, waste management, air quality, ambient noise and culture. The Assembly's main function is to review and scrutinise the exercise of the Mayor's functions and to put proposals to him. The Mayor is required to provide the Assembly with periodic reports as to his decisions and proposals and he is required to attend the periodic meetings of the Assembly where he must answer questions about the exercise of his functions. The Mayor is also required to provide the Assembly with an annual report and attend an annual meeting of the Assembly. He must also attend an annual State of London debate and a meeting at which members of the public may ask him questions called the "People's Question Time."

Part III—Financial Provisions

Part III contains provisions concerning finance. They are drawn from the **1.14** existing financing regime of the Local Government Finance Acts 1988 and 1992 and the Local Government and Housing Act 1989. There are specific provisions which reflect the different roles of the Mayor and the Assembly. The major sources of revenue funding for the Authority consist of grants paid by the Secretary of State and redistributed non-domestic rates, and council tax. The Authority is a major precepting authority and the London boroughs are required to collect council tax for the Authority. The Mayor is responsible for setting the budget for the Authority and the functional bodies. The Assembly is required to scrutinise the budget. The budget can be capped by the Secretary of State. The Mayor is also required to develop a capital spending plan. The Authority and the functional bodies are subject to the capital finance provisions of Part IV of the Local Government and Housing Act 1989.

Part IV—Transport

Part IV establishes the transport functions of the GLA in relation to **1.15** transport for Greater London. The general transport duty (section 141) is the underlying theme of Part IV of the Act. The duty sets four standards that must be promoted and encouraged: safe, integrated, efficient and economic transport for London. The transport strategy (section 142) is one of the eight key strategies that the Act requires the Mayor to institute and maintain. The transport strategy must set out the Mayor's proposals for fulfilling the general transport duty. Each London borough council and the Common Council of the City of London must prepare and implement a local implementation plan, or LIP, setting out their proposals for putting the transport strategy into effect in their area (section 145).

A new statutory body, Transport for London (TfL), is the functional body that must implement the Mayor's transport strategy on his behalf (section 154). TfL is also required to facilitate the general transport duty. TfL is the delivering body, whilst policy and budgets are set by the Mayor. TfL runs or manages a wide range of transport services for London. Its responsibilities relate to mass public transport, cabs and taxis and major roads. To do this, TfL will draw together functions relating to transport previously undertaken by a wide range of bodies.

Part V—The London Development Agency

1.16 Part V of the Act contains amendments to amend the Regional Development Agency Act 1998. It establishes the London Development Agency, and amends a number of the provisions of the 1998 Act so that, together with the Greater London Authority, the LDA functions as the regional development chamber for London.

The Mayor is required to prepare a London Development Strategy. He is assisted by the LDA in drawing up the strategy. The strategy must be in line with national policies and there is an overriding power vested in the Secretary of State to direct the Mayor to revise his strategy where there is a conflict or where the strategy will have a detrimental effect, or will be likely to have a detrimental effect.

The Assembly are responsible for scrutinising the Mayor's strategy and examining the effectiveness of the LDA. The London borough councils, whilst retaining their powers to promote economic development in their areas, will work with the Mayor and the LDA to benefit Greater London. This Act also contains substantial amendments to the Regional Development Agencies Act 1998 at least in so far as it concerns Greater London.

Parts VI and VII—the Metropolitan Police and the Fire and Emergency Services

1.17 Parts VI and VII create new authorities for the police and the fire and emergency services. Formerly, the Secretary of State controlled the Metropolitan Police Service. The new authority is modelled closely on the type of police authority found outside London, pursuant to the Police Act 1996. Assembly members may become members of the Metropolitan Police Authority. The Mayor has a role in the appointment of members to the new authority. The London Fire and Emergency Planning Authority is a new body with a constitutional structure similar to that of the Metropolitan Police Authority. It replaces the London Fire and Civil Defence Authority which was a joint committee of the London boroughs.

Part VIII—Planning

1.18 Part VIII deals with planning. It contains extensive amendments to the Town and Country Planning Act 1990 so as to incorporate the planning powers of the Mayor within the planning system and establish his planning functions. The GLA, however, is not a local planning authority.

The Mayor is responsible for producing a Spatial Development Strategy ("SDS") for Greater London: ensuring that any revision of, or amendment to, a unitary development plan by a London borough generally accords with the strategy, directing LPAs to refuse an application on strategic grounds;

and, in consultation with the London boroughs, setting up a scheme to monitor the implementation of the strategy.

The Assembly also has planning functions. It can respond to the draft SDS, carry out investigations into particular planning policy issues, and scrutinise the Mayor's performance in the discharge of his duties and the exercise of his powers.

The powers of the London boroughs have been extended by this part of the Act. They are required to adopt such amendments to, or to replace, the existing plan with a development plan that is in general conformity with the SDS, and consult with the Mayor on applications that are of strategic importance in accordance with the regulations of the Secretary of State.

Finally, the Secretary of State may direct the Mayor to amend the SDS **1.19** to protect national or broader regional interests, and may make regulations which govern the criteria whereby planning applications must be referred to the Mayor for consideration. The Act does not of itself grant the Mayor any powers to control development in Greater London, but the Secretary of State can by development order enable the Mayor in specific circumstances to order a London borough to refuse to grant planning permission. In order to intervene, the Mayor will become a statutory consultee for planning applications of strategic importance. These applications will be set out in secondary legislation which the Government has indicated will cover four broad grounds of development proposals that may give raise to issues of strategic importance. In exercising his functions under this Part of the Act, the Mayor must have regard to the development plan and the SDS.

Part IX—Environmental Functions

Part IX provides the Mayor with functions in respect of the environment. **1.20** In particular, he is required to prepare a wide range of documents relating to environmental policy. These are as follows:

- the state of the environment report;
- the London Biodiversity Action Plan;
- the municipal waste management strategy;
- the London air quality strategy;
- the London ambient noise strategy.

Of these documents, the one likely to receive the highest profile is the state of the environment report as this report draws upon the policies and proposals contained in the strategies and action plan bringing together all the disparate parts of environmental reporting within the city, and providing a central environmental data resource. The separate requirements to produce the strategies and the action plan involve consultation, publishing, promotion of the strategies and revising as required. The Secretary of State has an important role to play in the discharge of the Mayor's functions in this respect, in that he can issue directions, both general and specific, with which the Mayor must comply. Local authorities in Greater London are under a duty to have regard to the strategies in the discharge of their duties under the environmental legislation.

Part X—Culture, Media and Sport

1.21 Part X deals with the Authority's functions with respect to culture, media and sport and Trafalgar and Parliament Squares. There is to be a Culture Strategy Group which is to advise the Mayor as to the formulation of his strategy in this area. The Authority also has functions with respect to London tourism and the control and management of Trafalgar and Parliament Squares.

Establishment of the GLA

1.22 Sections 1 and 2 and Schedule 1 to the GLA Act establish the GLA as a body corporate. All local authorities are bodies corporate: see sections 2(3), 14(2) and 21(2) of the Local Government Act 1972 and have only the functions which are transferred to, conferred, or imposed on them by statute, *e.g. Ashbury Railway Carriage and Iron Co. v. Riche* (1875) 7 H.L. 653; *Baroness Wenlock v. River Dee Co.* (1885) 10 App.Cas. 354; *Hazell v. Hammersmith & Fulham L.B.C.* [1992] 2 A.C. 1

The GLA Act does not define the term, "Greater London" but section 2 of the London Government Act 1963, which is still in force, provides that "the area comprising the areas of the London boroughs, the City and the Temples shall constitute an administrative area to be known as Greater London".

Chapter 2

ELECTIONS

Members

There are approximately five million electors in London and 74 parliamen- **2.01** tary constituencies, 10 Euro-constituencies and 32 London boroughs and the City of London. For the purposes of elections to the Greater London Council, Greater London was divided into electoral divisions, each division returning one councillor. Until 1973, at the first three elections to the GLC, there were 100 councillors and 32 divisions, one for each London borough, each division returning between 2 and 4 councillors for each division but from 1973, there were 92 councillors representing single member divisions.

The White Paper, at paragraph 4.11, states that the method of electing Assembly members ". . . must reflect and support the role envisaged for them". This is described as being required ". . . to think and act strategically, looking at London-wide issues in the round and at the long-term interest of the capital." Accordingly, the Government put forward the proposal of "a small and effective Assembly" of no more than 25 members. Under section 2 of the GLA Act, the Assembly is to have 25 members: fourteen are "constituency members" and eleven are "London members", representing the whole of London. There is to be one constituency member for each Assembly constituency. The constituencies shall be the areas and known by names to be specified in an order of the Secretary of State.

Under subsections (6) to (9) of section 2 of the GLA Act, the Mayor and **2.02** Assembly members are to be returned by the holding of elections for the Mayor, the constituency members and the London members; and by the filling of casual vacancies in these offices. An ordinary election is the election for the return of the Mayor, the London members and the constituency members. The term of office for the Mayor and Assembly members returned at an election shall begin on the second day after the day on which the last of the successful candidates at the ordinary election is declared to be returned and end on the second day after the day on which the last of the successful candidates at the next ordinary election is declared to be returned. If an election is countermanded or abandoned, the day on which the last of the successful candidates at the ordinary election is declared to be returned shall be determined for the purposes of section

2(8) without regard to the return of the Assembly member for that Assembly constituency.

Subsections (10) and (11) of section 2 provide that the validity of proceedings of the Assembly is not affected by any vacancy in its membership. Nor is the validity of anything done by the Authority affected by any vacancy in the office of Mayor or any vacancy in the membership of the Assembly. It is arguable whether this subsection is necessary. There is a similar provision in the Government of Wales Act 1998, section 2(7) and in the Scotland Act 1998, at section 1(4). In the case of the Welsh Assembly, the Solicitor-General said in the House of Lords that the provision was added out of caution, in order to avoid uncertainty which might arises while the issue was being resolved: it was directed at avoiding a situation where there would be ". . . one vacancy in the membership, leading to someone taking this point, thereby providing a cloud over the proceedings of the assembly until the point has been resolved." *Hansard*, H.L. Vol. 591, col. 676.

Ordinary Elections

2.03 Consistently with other provisions of this Act empowering the Secretary of State to make initial arrangements for the Authority, section 3(1) provides that the date of the first election is May 4, 2000 (or such later date as the Secretary of State may determine). Under section 3(3) of the GLA Act, elections for the Authority is subject to a fixed term of four years. Under subs. (2), the poll at every subsequent ordinary election is to be held on the first Thursday in May every four years. Subsections (2) and (3) are subject to an order of the Secretary of State fixing a day other than the first Thursday in May (section 37(2) of the Representation of the People Act 1983). The first elections were held on May 4, 2000. A comparatively low turn-out of electors elected Ken Livingstone, standing as an independent candidate, as Mayor and the majority of Assembly memers were Labour party members.

Under subsection (4) the Secretary of State may make provision for the returning officer to be a person of a description other than those specified in section 35(2C) of the Representation of the People Act 1983. He may also modify the entitlement to vote or registration of electors and prescribe rules with respect to enabling voters to vote at polling stations and other prescribed places and at such times as may be prescribed. Subsection (6) defines "prescribed" as that specified or determined in accordance with an order made under this section.

2.04 Subsections (2) to (3) of section 3 deal with ordinary elections. Ordinary elections to ordinary local authorities take place in one of two ways: there are elections of the whole council; or there are elections of one-third of members at a time. Further, different types of local authority will have elections at different times and in slightly different ways. Elections for county councils take place every four years (as from 1973) (Local Government Act 1972, s.7(1)). Ordinary elections for metropolitan district councils take place in three out of every four years (again, as from 1973) and, under section 7(2) of the 1972 Act, elections were held in 1975 and every year thereafter other than 1977 and every fourth year thereafter, the purpose being to avoid county and district elections in the same year. Non-metropolitan district councils have a choice under section 7(3) of the 1972 Act: they can, by resolution, ask the Secretary of State to provide for a system of whole county elections; or they may resolve to ask for a system of election by thirds. The ordinary election of London borough councils takes place in every fourth year after 1974: Paragraph 6(3), Schedule 2, 1972 Act.

Voting Systems

The Green Paper did not recommend a specific voting system for the **2.05** Mayor or the Assembly. Instead, it put forward a number of different proposals.

In respect of the Mayor, these were: the current system used for local authority elections, the "first-past-the-post" system, the "second ballot" system, and the "alternative vote system". The first-past-the-post system, according to the Green Paper, does not require a candidate to obtain a majority vote over all other candidates as the successful candidate is simply the one with the largest number of votes. Under the second ballot system, there are two rounds of voting. In the first round, only the candidate who secures an overall majority is elected; but, if there is no such candidate, a certain number of candidates will go on to a second vote. Under the "alternative vote" system, voters select any number of candidates, instead of voting for just one; and the winner is the candidate with an overall majority. If there is no such candidate, then the lowest placed candidate drops out and his second preferences are transferred to the other candidates.

The Green Paper considered even more voting systems for the Assembly. **2.06** Unlike the Mayor, it was always considered necessary that Assembly members have some sort of connection with a constituency. There were, however, several constituency models from which to choose. These ranged from single-seat constituencies following borough boundaries through to multi-seat constituencies. The possibility of a single London-wide constituency was considered by the Government but rejected: while it would give members the same strategic outlook as the Mayor, there was a concern that some areas of London would feel under-represented. If there was to be a single London-wide constituency, the only viable electoral options for the Assembly were a first-past-the-post system and the alternative vote system.

Were there to be multi-member constituencies, however, the first-past-the-post system, "the list system" (or "De Hondt" system), "the additional member system" and "the single transferable vote system" were considered to be more appropriate. In the first-past-the-post system for multi-member constituencies, the candidate with the highest number of votes would be elected. Under the list system, electors vote for a party's list, as opposed to voting for an individual, and seats in constituencies would then be allocated amongst the parties according to the proportion of the vote gained in each constituency. The Green Paper suggested that the main problem with the list system was that it would cut out the option of voting for independent candidates. Under the additional member voting system, a proportion of the available seats would be allocated on the first-past-the-post system, with the remainder allocated to parties on an all-London list. The single transferable vote model would require voters to put candidates in an order of preference, and candidates have to reach a minimum of votes in order to be elected and, should they pass it, excess votes are redistributed on the basis of the second preferences.

2.07 The Government Office for London commissioned a report from Patrick Dunleavy and Dr Helen Margetts (Report to the Government Office for London: Electing the London Mayor and the London Assembly, January 20, 1998, Dep 5941: see House of Lords Research Paper 98/188 : "The Greater London Authority Bill: Electoral and Constitutional Aspects", Oonagh Gay and Barry Wintrobe). They worked from simulations of each of the systems and concluded that the most feasible system would be the "supplementary vote system" for elections for the Mayor; and, in respect of the Assembly, they recommended either the "additional member system" with 14 or 16 local seats or the list system. The "supplementary vote" system is a simplified form of the second ballot system in that there is no need to have a second round of voting.

The supplementary voting system was first put forward by the Plant Commission on electoral reform in 1933 and a version of it had been proposed for the Representation of the People (No. 2) Bill (1930-31) but was substituted by the alternative vote system at committee. The authors of the Dunleavy report concluded that, with respect to elections for the Mayor, the supplementary voting system favoured the existing major parties but the second preferences of Liberal Democrats and other voters would be critical in determining the final result. There would, however, be little practical difference between either model as far as the Assembly would be concerned. On the other hand, the difference would be substantial with respect to the Mayoral elections: the supplementary voting system guarantees that only the top two candidates on the first round would emerge as a winner, and restricts voters' abilities to mark preferences, while, under the alternative voting system, a third or fourth placed candidate on first preference could conceivably win (paragraph 2.26 of the Report).

2.08 The Government favoured the supplementary vote system for the Mayor. Lord Irvine of Lairg, in December 1998, said that this was because the Mayor was unique:

"We decided on the supplementary voting system: that is in effect, a system of improved first past the post. We did this because the Mayor will be in a unique position. Never before has so large an electorate voted for a single individual . . . The Mayor's authority will be enhanced by the fact that he will enjoy a broader base of support than might be achieved by first-past-the-post alone." (Government's Programme for Constitutional Reform, December 8, 1998.)

As to the Assembly, the Dunleavy report concluded that a London-wide system with 10 or more list seats would be proportional and stable. The White Paper adopted the recommendations of the report. It proposed the supplementary vote system for the election of the Mayor and the additional member system for the Assembly with 14 individual constituencies and 11 seats from a London wide-list. The Local Government Commission was directed by the Secretary of State (under section 7 of the Greater London Authority (Referendum) Act 1998) to review electoral areas. The results were published in November 1998: Each constituency is to have approximately 330,000 voters. Schedule 1 to the Act deals with further reviews by the Local Government Commission under the Local Government Act 1992 and empowers the Secretary of State, by order, to give effect to the Commissions' recommendations.

Voting for the Mayor

Section 4 of the GLA Act deals with voting at ordinary elections. **2.09** Subsections 4(2) and (3) provide for voting for mayoral candidates. Each voter has one vote for the Mayor and the winner shall be returned under the simple majority system unless there are three or more candidates. If so, then, by virtue of subsection (3), the Mayor shall be returned under the supplementary vote system set out in Schedule 2. Under this voting system, voters mark their first and second choices ("first preference vote" and "second preference vote") for candidates on the ballot paper. Voters' first preferences are counted and if one candidate wins 50 per cent or more of the vote, he or she is elected. If no one candidate wins 50 per cent of the vote, all of the candidates, except the two who received the highest numbers of votes, are eliminated. The second preferences on the ballot papers of the eliminated candidates are examined and any that have been cast for the two remaining candidates are given to those candidates.

Voting for Assembly Members

The Constituency Member is to be returned in the more usual way, by a **2.10** first-past-the-post system for a particular constituency (GLA Act, s.4(4)). Matters become complicated again in respect of the London Members. The election of London Members is further provided for in Part II of Schedule 2. London votes are to be allocated according to the De Hondt system of proportional representation. A registered political party may submit a list of candidates to be London members to the Greater London Returning Officer. When allocating seats in the Assembly on the basis of the London vote, the Greater London Returning Officer considers the listed party affiliation of the constituency candidates who have been returned as members of the Assembly and the number of London votes cast for that party.

He will then divide the party's total London vote by the number of seats that the party has won plus one: this is known as "the London figure": paragraph 6(3)(b), Schedule 2. The first of the seats for London members is then allocated to the party or individual with the highest London figure. When a seat is allocated to a party, its London figure is recalculated on the basis of the new total number of seats plus one. The second and subsequent seats are then allocated on the basis of the highest London figure at that stage, after which the winning party's London figure is recalculated until all 11 seats have been allocated. If two parties tie for the last seat, their figures are recalculated as though each party had one more seat: the one with the highest figure wins the seat. The threshold for allocation of a seat to a particular party, under paragraph 7 of Schedule 2, is at least 5 per cent of the total London votes.

Vacancies—Assembly Members

2.11 Under the GLA Act, a vacancy arises in the following ways:

(1) Resignation: a member resigns under section 5 of the GLA Act. See also section 84(1) of the Local Government Act 1972: a person elected to any office may at any time resign his office by written notice delivered to the proper officer of the council, or in the case of a person elected to a corporate office in a London borough, to the proper officer of the borough. The resignation takes effect on the date the notice is received. This is to be contrasted with the House of Commons where there are no formal procedures allowing a member to resign. The traditional method is to appoint the member to a disqualifying office: see section 4, House of Commons Disqualification Act 1975.

(2) Failure to attend meetings: a member who fails for six consecutive months to attend a meeting of the Assembly, of one of its committees or sub-committees or of an outside body as an Assembly representative is disqualified to be a member (GLA Act, s.6). This section is based on section 85 of the Local Government Act 1972 It has been held that, under section 85 of that Act, once a member has been disqualified due to non-attendance, the disqualification is not removed by subsequent attendance after the six-month period: see *R. v. Hunton, ex p. Hodgson* (1911) 75 J.P. 335. Under subsection (2) of this section (as under section 85(1) of the 1972 Act), non-

attendance will not disqualify a member if the Assembly has approved it. Further, in common with section 85(2) of the 1972 Act, attendance at a meeting of the Assembly is deemed to be attendance on any occasion on which he attended as a member of any committee or sub-committee of the Assembly or attendance as a representative of the Assembly or Authority. Section 6(4) is in the same terms as section 85(3) of the 1972 Act.

(3) Disqualification on electoral grounds: a member who ceases to be qualified as a local government elector for Greater London ceases to be qualified to be a member (see section 20, below).

(4) Automatic disqualification: a member becomes disqualified for any of the reasons set out in section 2, *i.e.* he is a member of staff of the Authority; he is a bankrupt, he has been convicted of a certain category of criminal offence or he has been disqualified under the Representation of the People Act 1983; or he has been disqualified under the Audit Commission Act 1998.

(5) Becoming Mayor: a vacancy shall arise in the Assembly where a person is returned as an Assembly member and as the Mayor at an ordinary election.

Section 7 of the GLA Act provides that a vacancy arising otherwise than on account of death, resignation or automatic disqualification must be declared by an officer of the Authority charged with that function or by the High Court.

The Relevant Date

For the purposes of filling a casual vacancy in the membership of the **2.12** Assembly, section 9 provides that if a vacancy occurs within six months prior to the date of an ordinary election, an election will not be held to fill the vacancy. This section is based on section 87 of the Local Government Act 1972. The relevant date on which the vacancy is deemed to have occurred depends on the nature of the cessation of qualification. Under subs.(2) of section 9, the proper officer must give notice of any casual vacancy among the members of the London members to the Greater London Returning Officer, and give public notice of any casual vacancy among the constituency members. Subsection (3) provides that public notification can be made by posting the notice in a conspicuous place or in any other way the proper officer thinks is desirable for giving publicity to the notice.

Otherwise, for constituency members, where an election is necessary, section 10 of the GLA Act applies. It follows closely section 89 of the Local Government Act 1972. Both sections require that an election be held to fill the vacancy. An election to fill a vacancy declared by the High Court or by the proper officer of the Authority must be held within 35 days from the declaration. A vacancy of which notice in writing has been given must be held within 35 days of notice being given to the proper officer. The date of the election is to be fixed by the constituency returning officer. Where a casual vacancy occurs within the period of 6 months preceding an ordinary election, it is filled at the next ordinary election unless, under subs.(9), the number of unfilled vacancies, along with other vacancies, exceeds one-third of the entire membership of the Assembly.

A different method is required for vacancies among London members. First, if the London member was returned as an individual candidate, the vacancy shall remain unfilled until the next ordinary election. If he was a member of a registered party, the Greater London Returning Officer must notify the Chair of the Assembly of the name of the person who is to fill the vacancy. That person must be a person included in the Part II list of party nominees and willing to serve as a London member.

Vacancies—Mayor

2.13 Sections 12 to 16 of the GLA Act deal with vacancies in the office of the Mayor and are broadly the same as those relating to Assembly members. Section 12 allows for the resignation of the Mayor. As in the case of members of the Assembly, the Mayor may be disqualified if he fails on six consecutive occasions to attend a meeting held under section 52(3) of the Act. These are the monthly meetings of the Assembly and the Mayor at which, *inter alia*, the Mayor's monthly report is scrutinised by the Assembly. As in the case of section 7, section 14 provides that a vacancy arising otherwise than on account of death, resignation or automatic disqualification must be declared by an officer of the Authority charged with that function or by the High Court.

At different stages during the course of the Bill through Parliament, proposals providing for the removal of the Mayor by way of a no confidence motion supported by 19 members were put forward but eventually rejected on the ground that removal on this basis would be for political reasons which would be internal to the Assembly when the Mayor was a directly elected representative. It was also considered that the normal "local authority" rules governing conduct of the Mayor were appropriate (*Hansard*, H.L. Vol. 606 col. 1258; H.C. col. 337, col. 502).

2.14 Where there is a vacancy in the office of Mayor, section 16 provides that, unless it occurs less than six months before the next ordinary election, an election must take place within 35 days after a declaration by the High Court or the proper officer of the GLA that the office is vacant; or 35 days after the giving of notice of the vacancy to the proper officer of the GLA by two or more government electors. The election is to take place in the usual way, as set out in Part I of Schedule 2. Under subsection (10), if a person who is a candidate in an election to fill a vacancy for Mayor is also a candidate in an election to fill a vacancy in an Assembly constituency seat, and that such a person is returned at both elections, then it is deemed that there is still a vacancy in the Assembly constituency.

Special Election Provisions

Section 17 and Schedule 3 make provision for Authority elections by **2.15** amending the Representation of the People Act 1983. The amendments are set out in Schedule 3. Section 203 to the 1983 Act is amended so as to bring GLA elections within the general scope of the 1983 Act. The result is that the normal provisions applying to the local government elections in respect of the entitlement to vote, registration, conduct of election, voting offences, the campaign, questioning a result, and corrupt and illegal practices will apply in respect of Authority elections. Further, Schedule 3 to the GLA Act contains amendments to the 1983 Act which reflect the Authority's different electoral systems.

Paragraph 2 of Schedule 3 enables polling districts for Authority elections to be prescribed by London borough councils and the Common Council. Paragraph 3 makes provision for the returning officers at constituency elections to be designated by the Secretary of State and for the returning officer for the other Authority elections to be an officer appointed by the Authority. Paragraph 5 extends the Secretary of State's power to move the ordinary day for local elections in any year (pursuant to section 37 of the 1983 Act) so that the Authority's elections may be on a day other than the first Thursday in May, while paragraphs 6 and 7 make consequential and technical amendments to sections 39 and 40 of the 1983 Act. Paragraph 9 provides for the returning officer's costs (1983 Act, s.48) and paragraph 10 adds provisions appropriate to the Authority elections to the voting offences in section 61 of the 1983 Act.

Paragraphs 11 to 15 make provision in respect of election agents, in **2.16** particular to deal with the appointment of a single agent for candidates on a registered political party's list. Paragraphs 17 to 20 deal with election expenses in particular to enable the Secretary of State by order to set limits on the election expenses on candidates at Authority elections. Paragraph 21 adds the Authority to section 82 of the 1983 Act dealing with election expenses) and, similarly, paragraph 23 adds Authority members to section 159 (candidates reported guilty of a corrupt or illegal practice). Paragraph 24 and 25 add a number of definitions to sections 202 and 203 of the 1983 Act. Paragraph 18 provides for the Secretary of State to set limits on the election expenses of candidates for Mayor and candidates for the Assembly. Paragraph 22 disapplies section 93 of the 1983 Act as it is impracticable to implement in relation to the new electoral arrangements.

Qualification for Office

Based on Part V of the Local Government Act 1972, sections 20 to 23 of **2.17** the GLA Act deal with the qualification and disqualification of persons elected and holding the office of Mayor or Assembly member or selected to fill a vacancy among London members. Under section 79 of the Local

Government Act 1972, a candidate must be a British subject or a citizen of the Republic of Ireland or a citizen of the Union. Section 20(2) of this Act, on the other hand, refers merely to Commonwealth citizens, citizens of the Republic of Ireland and "relevant citizens of the Union". Section 37 of the 1981 Act defines the term, "Commonwealth citizen" as meaning British citizens and citizens of certain Commonwealth countries.

The term "relevant citizen of the Union", is defined in section 20(8) of this Act as a citizen of the Union who is not a Commonwealth citizen or a citizen of the Republic of Ireland. Under Article 8.1 of the E.C. Treaty every person holding the nationality of a Member State is a citizen of the Union.

Section 20(3) provides for an age qualification of 21 years (which also appears in section 79(1) of the Local Government Act 1972) for candidates for election to the office of Mayor and member of the Assembly. A candidate must have attained the age of 21 on the "relevant day" which is defined in section 20(8) as the day on which he is nominated as a candidate and, if there is a poll, the day of the election; or, if there is no nomination of candidates before the election, the day of the election itself.

2.18 As under section 79(1) of the Local Government Act 1972, in addition to the nationality and age conditions, section 20(4) provides that a person must at the time of the nomination and election also satisfy one of the conditions set out which are intended to demonstrate a relevant connection with London. These are:

(1) registration as a local government elector for Greater London under sections 2 to 7 and 14 to 17 of the Representation of the People Act 1983 which define the entitlement of a person to be an elector at a local government election;

(2) during the last 12 months, he held an interest in land in Greater London;

(3) his principal or only work during the last 12 months has been in Greater London; or,

(4) he has resided in the Greater London area during the last 12 months. The term "resided" has no special legal meaning save that it implies a degree of settled permanence. In *Fox v. Sirk* [1970] 2 Q.B. 463, CA, it was held that students in college residences only during the academic year were entitled to be placed on the electoral register for the district in which the college was situated.

Disqualification from Holding Office

2.19 A person is disqualified from being elected or being the Mayor or an Assembly member if any of the following situations apply:

(1) Staff: a member of staff cannot hold office (GLA Act, s.21(1)(a)). See also section 80 of the Local Government Act 1972. Section

21(1)(a) of the GLA Act refers to any member of staff of the Authority; section 80(1) of the 1972 Act refers to a person who "holds office or paid employment made or confirmed by the local authority or any of their committees". Under the original version of section 80 (s.59(1)(a) of the Local Government Act 1933), it was held that it covered an appointment as a schoolmaster: *Lamb v. Jeffries* [1956] 1 Q.B. 431.

(2) Disqualifying appointment: under section 21(1)(b), a person who holds a post designated by the Secretary of State is disqualified from being a member. Similar provisions exist in respect to the Welsh Assembly and the Scottish Parliament. See also section 1(1) of the House of Commons Disqualification Act 1975: a person is disqualified if he holds certain judicial offices, is employed as a civil servant, is a member of the regular armed forces, is a member of a police authority or is a member of the legislature of any non-Commonwealth country.

(3) Bankruptcy or composition or arrangement with creditors: a bankrupt or person who has made an arrangement whereby his creditors agree to accept less than the full amount of any debts is not qualified (GLA Act, s.21(1)(c)). The term "composition or arrangement with creditors" means an arrangement whereby creditors agree to accept less than the full amount of outstanding debts: *Futcher v. Saunders* (1885) 49 J.P. 424; *Bradfield v. Cheltenham Guardians* [1906] 2 Ch. 371. In *R. v. Cooban* (1886) 18 Q.B. 269, it was held that an assignment of property to a trustee for the benefit of creditors is not a composition with creditors. In the case of an arrangement made by a partnership, every partner is disqualified: *ex p. Atherton* (1886) 2 T.L.R. 631 and *Ward v. Radford* (1895) 59 J.P. 632. Section 21(3) provides that where a person is disqualified under section 21(1) because he has been adjudged a bankrupt, the disqualification shall cease on his discharge; if the bankruptcy order is so annulled, it ceases on the date of the annulment. Similarly, under section 21(4), the disqualification ceases if the person has paid the debt in full but otherwise continues for five years after the date on which the terms of a deed of composition arrangement are fulfilled. A deed by which certain creditors released their debts and others were paid in full did not amount to a payment in full in *Re Keet* [1905] 2 K.B. 666. **2.20**

(4) Relevant convictions: a person is disqualified if he has within five years before the day of the election or since his election been convicted in the United Kingdom, the Channel Islands or the Isle of Man of any offence and has had passed a sentence of imprisonment (whether suspended or not) for a period of not less than three months (GLA Act, s.21(4)(d)). The disqualification may be lifted by a free pardon: *Hay v. Tower Magistrates* (1890) 24 Q.B.D. 561.

(5) Part III of the Representation of the People Act 1983: if the person has been convicted for a corrupt electoral practice under the 1983 Act, he will be disqualified (GLA Act, s.21(1)(e)(i)). **2.21**

(6) Audit Act 1998 offences: a person who has been disqualified under sections 17 or 18 of the Audit Commission Act 1998 will also be disqualified to hold an elected post of the GLA (GLA Act, s.21(1)(e)(ii)).

(7) Officers of other London local authorities: under section 21(2), a person is disqualified if they are a paid officer of a London borough council employed under the direction of the GLA's committees or sub-committees, the membership of which includes the Mayor or persons appointed on the nomination of the Mayor; or under the direction of a joint committee, the membership of which includes one or more members appointed on the nomination of that council and one or more members appointed on the nomination of the Mayor.

Contrast this section with section 80(1) of the Local Government Act 1972 which disqualifies "any member of staff". This subsection may be so wide as to apply to a person who is a party to a contract with the Authority for the provision of services or materials, such as a consultant appointed to advise the committee concerning a special technical matter. An officer of an authority exercising powers delegated to him by another authority where the arrangements include the payment of the whole or part of his salary by the delegating authority might be disqualified from election to or membership of the Authority. See *R. v. Davies, ex. p. Penn* (1932) 96 J.P. 416 where a roadman employed by a district council, his wages being paid by the county council, was disqualified in respect of each authority.

(8) Declaration of Acceptance of Office (section 28), which follows closely the terms of section 83 of the Local Government Act 1972, provides that a member cannot act in office until he has made a declaration of acceptance of office. See *French's Application* [1985] 7 N.I.J.B. 48, where it was held that as this was the only declaration required by statute, it was to be regarded as exhaustive of a council's power to require the making of a declaration as a pre-condition to taking office.

Disqualification Proceedings

2.22 Section 23 provides that section 92 of the Local Government Act 1972 Act will apply in relation to the Authority as it applies to a local authority. Any registered local government elector for Greater London may instigate legal proceedings against any person on the grounds that he acted or claimed to act as Mayor or as an Assembly member, while he was disqualified or failed to meet the qualification criteria of section 20, failed to make a declaration under section 28 or ceased to be Mayor or an Assembly member through resignation or failure to attend meetings.

Proceedings may be brought in the High Court or a magistrates' court. An elector may wish to take proceedings in a magistrates' court, in which case the defendant may be fined; if the elector brings them in the High Court, the court may issue a declaration and an injunction as well as a fine. They must, however, be brought in the High Court if the person against whom they are brought claims to have been entitled to act. Proceedings cannot be brought in respect of an act that took place more than six months before the commencement of the proceedings. If the High Court is satisfied that a person acted while not qualified or disqualified, it has power to not only declare a vacancy in the office but may also order forfeiture of monetary sums; a magistrates' court only has the power to impose a fine. The magistrates have the power to refer proceedings to the High Court and they must be so referred if the defendant requests it.

Salaries and Expenses

Sections 24 to 27 deal with salaries, expenses and pensions. Members of **2.23** local authorities are entitled to allowances as set out in the Local Government and Housing Act 1989 and regulations made under certain of its provisions. Section 18 of the 1989 Act confers on the Secretary of State the power by regulations to authorise any authority to make a scheme providing for payment of allowances to members.

These allowances consist of a basic allowance paid to every member of an authority, an attendance allowance in relation to carrying out certain duties as may be specified in regulations, and a special responsibility allowance in respect of such responsibilities as may be specified and determined. The Secretary of State is empowered to set limits for allowances. Payments may also be made to members for travelling and living expenses necessarily incurred on approved duties inside or outside the United Kingdom and for attending conferences and meetings.

Members of the House of Commons and the Scottish Parliament, on the other hand, receive salaries (see, for example, sections 81 to 83 of the Scotland Act 1998). Section 81 of the 1998 Act empowers the Scottish Parliament to determine the salaries, allowances, pensions and other payments to its members and the Scottish Executive. Section 24 of the GLA Act follows the model set out in the Scotland Act 1998. Under section 24(1), the GLA is to pay to the Mayor and the Assembly members salaries at such levels as it determines. Section 24(2) provides for the payment of allowances. The latter are costs incurred by the Mayor or the Assembly member in the exercise of their functions. Section 24(3) empowers the Authority to pay the Mayor more than an Assembly member; and an Assembly member holding certain offices, may be paid more than one who does not hold such an office. The offices are defined in subsection (4): the Deputy Mayor and the Chair of the Assembly (but not the Deputy Chair). Subsection (5) has a similar effect with respect to allowances.

2.24   For the first year of the Authority's existence, the Secretary of State may make determinations about salaries and allowances, on the basis of recommendations of the Senior Salaries Review Board (sections 24(1)(b) and 24(2)(b)). Subsequently, it will be a matter for the GLA but the Secretary of State's guidance on ethical standards to be issued under section 66 of the GLA Act will contain guidance on this issue to which the GLA must have regard. Further, under section 24(8) of this Act, the Authority's standing orders must provide for publication of every determination (see section 83 of the Scotland Act for a similar provision affecting the Scottish Parliament).

Neither the Scotland Act 1998 nor this Act prohibit a person being a member of other legislative bodies. Therefore, there is no reason why a member of the House of Commons or House of Lords or the European Parliament could not be a member of the Assembly. However, section 25 of this Act prohibits double salaries: if a member of the Assembly is also a salaried member of the European Parliament or the Houses of Parliament, then the Secretary of State (but, in the case of the Scottish Parliament, the Scottish Parliament itself) is required to ensure that there is a reduction in the salary payable to such a person as a member of the Assembly by such proportion as the Secretary of State determine (and subsection (5) empowers the Secretary of State to exercise his discretion and treat different cases differently). The Greater London (Limitations of Salaries) Order 2000 (S.I. 2000 No. 1032) provides that the salary of the Mayor or any member of the Assembly who also receives a salary as a member of either House of Parliament or the European Parliament shall be reduced by one third.

Chapter 3

GENERAL POWERS AND FUNCTIONS OF THE GLA

Local authorities in England and Wales have only the powers conferred **3.01** upon them by parliament. The principle of "general competence", under which an authority can do anything they wish save that which is expressly excluded, has never been a feature of United Kingdom local authority law. Local authorities, as statutory bodies, can only do that which they are given the power to do under a statute; and that which is incidental or ancillary to such a power. The Royal Commission on Local Government in England, Cm. 4040 (Vol. 1 at paragraph 323), was of the view that main local authorities should have a general power to spend money for the benefit of their areas in addition to their expenditure on specific statutory functions. The white paper, "Reform of Local Government in England", Cm. 4276 (at paragraph 69), however, expressed concerns that unconditional powers which were not restricted to a particular financial limit would lead to unnecessary duplication or conflict with central government policy.

Some statutory powers govern the provision of a particular service by a local authority themselves, such as education; while others give a local authority the power to regulate activities which take place in their areas (for example, planning). Some powers, however, are so general that they are more accurately described as "framework" powers. The purpose of such powers is to supplement the more specific powers that are found elsewhere in the same Act (see, for example, the Education Act 1996, s.13 or the Police Act 1996, s.6).

Principle Purposes of the GLA

Section 30 of this Act contains a unique and complicated set of general **3.02** principles within which the GLA must operate. That is, the GLA functions must be exercised so as to conform with, or further, the specified "principal purposes". It is important to note from the outset that, in effect, the general powers of the GLA, will be exercised by the Mayor on behalf of the GLA (GLA Act, s.30(10)). This is consistent with the Authority's fundamental constitutional structure: the Mayor is the executive and his main role is to develop strategies in certain key areas; the Assembly's main role

27

is to scrutinise the exercise by the Mayor of his powers. If the Mayor's main role is to develop strategies, then the general purposes and powers in this section should be understood within the context of, or by reference to, the strategies set out in section 41(1): transport, planning, biodiversity, waste management, air quality, noise and culture.

Under section 30(1), the Authority has the power to do anything which it considers will further any one or more of its principal purposes. These are defined in subsection (2):

(1) promoting economic development and wealth creation in Greater London;

(2) promoting social development in Greater London; and,

(3) promoting the improvement of the environment in Greater London.

3.03 The terms, "promoting economic development and wealth creation", "promoting social development" and "promoting the improvement of the environment" have no particular legal meaning. As a guide to what they mean, it is useful to consider what the Government considered to be Greater London's main problems, for which the GLA was proposed to be the remedy. These are set out in the Green Paper, at pages 1 to 2:

". . . concentrations of unemployment and deep poverty, the need for an improved infrastructure in order to enhance London's economic competitiveness, environmental problems such as traffic congestion, air pollution and noise which undermined the sustainability of London as a city and the quality of life offered to its people."

The Green Paper suggested that the functions of the new authority would fall within the general heading of sustainable development. This was defined as "giving all Londoners an improved and lasting quality of life, combining environmental, economic and social goals". The White Paper restated the Government's position that there should be a directly elected Mayor providing "strong leadership" and an elected assembly "to hold the Mayor to account on London's behalf".

3.04 By the time of the publication of the White Paper, it had already been decided that, given its unique constitutional structure and the London-wide nature of the problems the new authority would deal with, the GLA's role was to be more strategic than that one of providing services. At paragraph 1.8 of the White Paper:

"At the heart of our proposals for London is a directly elected executive Mayor with the power to make a real difference to London on issues that matter to Londoners. A Mayor with strategic responsibilities where they are needed, and who will tackle the issues and change things for the better."

At paragraph 3.6, the White Paper described how the Mayor would be responsible for developing sustainable and integrated strategies across all of the GLA's functions with the Assembly providing an essential check and balance to the power of the Mayor. In this regard, it should be noted that the Assembly's general function is to review the exercise of the Mayor's functions. The Assembly may investigate and provide reports about "matters relating to the principal purposes of the Authority" (GLA Act, s.59(2)).

The GLA, at paragraph 3.10 of the White Paper, was described as "a unique category of local government in which there is to be an explicit separation of powers between the Mayor and the Assembly." It would have responsibilities in those areas (now defined in section 41 and elsewhere in the GLA Act) and, at paragraph 3.10, the GLA is:

". . . to be given a remit to address all London-wide issues and play a significant role outside of its specific responsibilities. It will therefore be given a duty to promote the social, economic and environmental well-being of Londoners. This duty will attract the necessary powers to enable the Mayor to fulfil the remit set out in this White Paper."

During the passage of the Bill through the House of Commons, **3.05** Mr Raynsford, Minister for London and Construction, said:

"The Mayor's strategies will provide the framework within which the authority and its functional bodies operate. They will also provide the framework within which other public bodies and organisations operate within London. It is therefore vital that the strategies should have regard to the authority's own principal purposes and also to wider national and international considerations which will impact on the quality of life of Londoners. The Authority cannot and will not operate in a vacuum." *Hansard*, H.C. Vol. 330, col. 764.

The general powers in section 30, whilst detailed and extensive, are nonetheless framework powers. They also illustrate a fundamental tension in central government's attitude to the Authority (and, perhaps, to local authorities generally). On the one hand, the GLA must have express powers (general and specific). On the other hand, all of its powers must be controlled or restricted in such a way that there is no duplication of activities that could be carried on by other statutory bodies exercising statutory functions Nor must there be conflict with central government policy. Therefore, under section 30(8), the Authority is to have regard to guidance from the Secretary of State about the exercise of its general powers. Further, by section 31(8), below, the Secretary of State may by order impose limits on the expenditure that may be incurred by the Authority under this section. Another control can be found in section 32, below, under which the Authority, before exercising any section 30 powers, must undertake a widespread consultation exercise.

"Promoting Economic Development"

3.06 The term, "promoting economic development" is already known in local government legislation: see section 33 of the Local Government and Housing Act 1989 under which an authority may take such steps as they may from time to time consider appropriate for "promoting the economic development of their area". (Note that the GLA is not subject to this part of the 1989 Act). Under section 33(2)(a) of the 1989 Act, the steps that may be taken include both participation in and the encouragement of the setting up or expansion of any commercial, industrial or public undertaking in the authority's area, or the setting up or expansion of an undertaking which appears likely to increase the opportunities for employment of people living in their area.

Authorities may also participate in and encourage the creation or protection of opportunities for employment with any such undertaking or with any other commercial, industrial or public undertaking with actual or prospective employment opportunities for people living in their areas (1989 Act, s.33(2)(b)). Authorities may also provide financial and other assistance towards the same ends. This power is subject to the power of the Secretary of State to restrict or prohibit steps which authorities might propose to take by making regulations under section 34 of the 1989 Act.

A similar term appears in section 4 of the Regional Development Act 1998. This provides that a regional development agency is required to have certain defined purposes including "the furthering of economic development and regeneration, the promotion of business efficiency, the promotion of employment and to contribute to the achievement of sustainable development". Under section 5 of the 1998 Act, the regional development agency may do anything which is expedient for these purposes.

The Exercise of the General Powers

3.07 Section 30(2) of the GLA Act provides that that, in determining whether or how to exercise the general power in subsection (1) to further any one or more of its principal powers, the Authority must have regard to desirability of so exercising that power (a) to further the other principal purpose or purposes, and (b) to secure, over a period of time, a reasonable balance between furthering each of its principal powers. The assumption is that, but for this subsection, it would be possible for the Authority to further one particular purpose at the expense of the others. For example, it might have been possible for the Mayor to develop a waste management strategy which, while it may be extremely efficient at reducing or recycling waste, is so expensive for, and so burdensome on, London employers that it has a disproportionately adverse effect on economic development. This subsection has the effect of requiring the Mayor at least to consider the economic impact of such a waste management strategy.

Under section 30(4), in determining whether or how to exercise the subsection (1) power, the Authority must consider the effect which the proposed exercise would have both on the health of persons in Greater London and sustainable development in the United Kingdom. Then, in subsection (5), where the Authority exercises a principle section 30 power, it must do so in way which is best calculated (a) to "promote improvements in the health of persons in Greater London, and (b) to contribute towards the achievement of sustainable development in the United Kingdom". It must to do this only to the extent that it considers any action taken under this subsection is reasonably practicable.

Under subsection (6), the term "promoting improvements in health" is **3.08** defined so as to include a reference to mitigating any detriment to health. When it comes to the actual exercise of the power, the Authority, under subs. (5), must likewise do so in the way calculated best to achieve these objects, save so far as it is not reasonably practicable to do so.

The Secretary of State may issue binding guidance to the Authority as to how the general power may be exercised (subsections (7) and (8)). Subsection (9) provides that the Secretary of State may publish his guidance in any way that he considers appropriate.

The general rule is that, while local authorities must have regard to all guidance, formal and general, they are not required to follow it invariably and they may depart from it if there are good reasons to do so: *e.g., R. v. Islington L.B.C., ex p. Rixon* [1997] E.L.R. 66, QBD. A requirement to "have regard to" guidance or a code means that it is a relevant consideration which, if it is departed from, requires an explanation from the authority: *Padfield v. Minister of Agriculture, Farming and Fisheries* [1968] A.C. 997. See also *de Falco, Silvestri v. Crawley* B.C. [1980] Q.B. 460.

Another role for the Secretary of State's guidance was suggested by the **3.09** Minister for London when the Bill was in committee. In reply to a question when the Bill was in committee in the House of Commons as to why this subsection was necessary, the Minister said:

"The answer is that we are dealing with a new type of authority with a strategic remit and a relatively limited number of specific powers. It is, however, being given a wider general power to pursue policies that have a beneficial effect on the economic, social and environmental well-being of London . . . Given the authority's wider remit, there is inevitably scope for it to trample on the toes of other bodies that have specific remits in the areas that I mentioned . . . We are dealing with a new structure of government and are inevitably moving into relatively uncharted waters. In that context, it is perfectly proper for the Secretary of State to issue guidance on how the power in the clauses before us can best be used in the spirit in which we prepared them." *Hansard*, H.C. Standing Committee A, Fourth Sitting, February 2, 1999, col. 212.

Express Limits to the General Power

3.10 Section 31(1) of this Act contains a number of limitations, cutting back the broad powers in section 30 to ensure that the Authority does not act so as to duplicate the powers of Transport for London, the Metropolitan Police Authority, the London Fire and Emergency Planning Authority. It is a little different with respect to the London Development Agency in that, under section 31(2) it must merely "seek" that it does not duplicate the functions of the London Development Agency. The difference in subsection (2) may be because the London Development Agency's activities are less specific than those of the bodies listed in subsection (1). The prohibition on duplication operates by reference to what is actually being done by the London Development Agency, rather than what it has power to do.

A similar restriction exists in section 137(1) of the Local Government Act 1972: a local authority cannot incur expenditure for a purpose for which they are authorised or required to make a payment by or by virtue of any other enactment. That limitation only applies where the authority themselves have other specific powers, as distinct from prohibiting expenditure where other authorities have the power: *Manchester City Council v. Greater Manchester Metropolitan County Council* (1980) 79 L.G.R. 560.

3.11 By virtue of section 31, subsections (4) to (7), there are four special fields in which the Authority cannot take any action at all, by way of incurring expenditure. These are housing, education, social services and health services provided by a London borough, the Common Council or another public body. Housing includes housing management but excludes acquisitions by the Authority of housing accommodation to make it available on a temporary basis for the Authority's own or incidental purposes (subsection (4)) such as, for example, providing temporary accommodation for staff or visitors. Section 31(6), however, allows the Authority to incur expenditure in co-operating with or facilitating or co-ordinating the activities of other authorities exercising housing, education, social services or health services functions. For example, the Authority may organise and conduct a conference about policies to tackle housing problems in London.

Section 31(7) allows the Secretary of State to amend this section, so as to prevent it from doing anything which could be done by a London borough, Common Council or other public body. He may also impose limits on the expenditure that the Authority may incur in exercising the section 30(1) power. Finally, he may amend this section by removing or restricting any prohibitions imposed by this section. The purpose seems to be to allow some flexibility in the Government's approach as to what the Authority may and may not do.

Consultation

3.12 Reflecting both general legal developments, and the policy of this Act, section 32 of the Act puts consultation at the core of the exercise of the

Mayor's functions. Consultation is a fundamental component of the exercise of the Authority's functions: see, for example, sections 30, 32, 36, 42, 47 to 48, 70, 73 and 77. A requirement to consult is now a common statutory prerequisite to the exercise of decision-making powers. See Arden, Manning and Collins, *Local Government Constitutional and Administrative Law* (Sweet & Maxwell, London, 1999) at page 193:

> "The following propositions may be extracted from the cases. The essence of the consultation exercise is the communication of a genuine invitation to the consulted body to give advice, and a genuine receipt of that advice by the consulting body, at a time when proposals are still in their formative stage; accordingly, for there to be sufficient consultation, there must be provided to the consulted body sufficient information to enable it to consider the proposals intelligently and to tender an intelligent response or helpful advice, in sufficient time for it do so, and in sufficient time for the product of consultation to be taken into account before reaching the relevant decision."

A failure to consult, or to consult properly, at common law, will not **3.13** necessarily lead a court to quash the relevant decision. Consultation requirements have been held to be mandatory: *R. v. Secretary of State for Social Services, ex p. Association of Metropolitan Authorities* [1986] 1 W.L.R. 1. See also *R. v. Governors of Small Heath School, ex p. Birmingham C.C., The Times,* May 31, 1989, where it was said that the test as to whether or not there had been adequate consultation was to ask whether or not the consultation exercise as a whole caused unfairness.

As most of the Authority's functions will actually be exercised by the Mayor, section 32(5) provides that the consultation function is exercisable by the Mayor acting on behalf of the Authority. Under section 32(1), the power conferred by section 30(1) is exercisable only after consultation with such persons and bodies as the Authority may consider necessary. Note section 32(1): the persons and bodies which must be consulted include any London borough council, the Common Council and "generic" bodies with particular functions. These last bodies are defined in subs. (3) as bodies representing the interests of different racial and ethnic groups in London, different religious groups and bodies which represent the interests of persons carrying on business in Greater London. Section 32(4) empowers the Authority to make arrangements with the above statutory consultees in order to facilitate the carrying out of any functions under this Act.

Equality of Opportunity and Discrimination

Section 33 of this Act is similar to section 120 of the Government of Wales **3.14** Act 1998, under which the Welsh Assembly is required to make appropriate arrangements with respect to equality of opportunity in the exercise of its functions. Under this section, the GLA must make appropriate arrangements to secure that "due regard" is had to equality of opportunity with respect to both the exercise of its functions and in the formulation of the policies and proposals included in any of the section 41 strategies. This is a function that may be exercised on behalf of the Authority by the Mayor (GLA Act, s.33(3)).

The phrase, "equality of opportunity", may be defined as including the ceasing of discrimination as well as the taking of positive steps to eliminate discrimination: see, for example, the Sex Discrimination Act 1975. Section 55 of the 1975 Act provides for the establishment of the Equal Opportunities Commission whose duties are, *inter alia*, to work towards the elimination of discrimination and to promote equality generally. See also the Code of Practice issued by the Commission in 1985 for the elimination of discrimination and the promotion of equality of opportunity by employers and trade unions. Part 2 of the Code requires employers to formulate an equal opportunities policy. What this means in practice is not defined but it is a requirement that the policy must contain measures which not only eliminate discrimination in the organisation but actively promote anti-discrimination measures such as re-training and positive encouragement for women to apply for management posts.

3.15 In this section, the GLA's duty is to arrange that, in the exercise of any of its main functions, "due regard" is paid to the principle of equal opportunity. There is no express limitation on the type of discrimination towards which this duty is directed. Of course sex, race and disability discrimination would be included, but it is arguable that it could also cover discrimination on the basis of sexuality (compare and contrast section 28 of the Local Government Act 1986, which does not apply to the GLA). Nor is it confined to any particular context such as employment. It appears to range across the entire field of the GLA's activities. Section 33(2) indicates the importance of this principle to the GLA's activities in requiring it to publish, each year, a statement of its arrangements and an assessment of their effectiveness.

Another indication of its importance is the use of the phrase, "due regard" as opposed to the more usual "have regard to". The term "due regard" appears in section 120 of the Government of Wales 1998 Act and section 75 of the Northern Ireland Act 1998. When the phrase was considered in the House of Commons, it was initially proposed that the word "due" should be deleted as the Government were advised that it had no particular legal effect. Supporters of the original phrase in the House of Commons relied on "informal" legal advice to the contrary: and, further, as the term existed in the Wales and Northern Ireland Acts, it was suggested that the courts would attach less weight to this provision if it did not also use the term "due." *Hansard*, H.C. Vol. 337, cols 573 to 576.

3.16 It is also notable that, under section 404 of this Act, the GLA, the Metropolitan Police Service and the London Fire and Emergency Planning Authority are required to "have regard" (but not "due regard") to the need to promote equality of opportunity regardless of race, sex, disability, age, sexual orientation or religion; to eliminate unlawful discrimination; to promote good relations between person of different racial groups, religious beliefs and sexual orientation. This duty, however, is expressly required to be exercised without prejudice to the section 33 duty. Unlike section 33, section 404 expressly refers to sexual orientation (but, again, note section 28 of the Local Government Act 1986).

See also section 391 of this Act: this section provides that the GLA, the Metropolitan Police Authority and the London Fire and Emergency Planning Authority are to be treated as local authorities for the purposes of section 71 of the Race Relations Act 1976. Section 71 provides that it is the duty of every local authority to make appropriate arrangements with a view to securing that their various functions are carried out with due regard to the need to eliminate unlawful discrimination and to promote equality of opportunity and good relations between people of different groups.

Incidental and Ancillary Powers

Section 34(1) of this Act is in the same terms as section 111 of the Local **3.17** Government Act 1972. As already noted, above, local authorities only have those powers which are conferred on them by statute. Under the doctrine of implied powers, such bodies, however, also enjoy an implied power to engage in that which is incidental: "those things which are incident to, and may reasonably and properly be done under the main purpose, though they may not be literally within it, would not be prohibited": *Att.-Gen. v. Great Eastern Railway* (1880) 5 H.L. 473 at 477.

What is to regarded as "calculated to facilitate, conducive or incidental" to a power is to be determined in each case. Section 111 of the 1972 Act, however, cannot be used to circumvent the provisions of other statutes. In *Hazell v. Hammersmith & Fulham L.B.C.* [1992] 2 A.C. 1, the authority sought to justify the use of swap agreements as a tool of debt management; this was rejected in the House of Lords on the ground that Schedule 13 to the 1972 Act already contained a comprehensive code concerning borrowing. See also *Credit Suisse v. Allerdale B.C.* [1997] Q.B. 306: a scheme for time share holiday homes could not be used to facilitate the provision of a swimming pool as recreational powers were governed by their own statutory provisions.

Further, incidental or implied powers are not powers to do anything **3.18** generally but only to do that which "calculated to facilitate or conducive or incidental to" the discharge of other statutory functions. An incidental power is not a function in its own right. See Lord Templeman in *Hazell v. Hammersmith & Fulham L.B.C.* [1991] 2 A.C. 1 at 29, approving Woolf L.J. ([1990] 2 Q.B. 697 at 722–723):

"The subsection does not of itself independently of any other provision authorise the performance of any activity. It only confers, as the side note to the section indicates, a subsidiary power. A subsidiary power which authorises an activity where some other statutory provision has vested a specific function or functions in the council and the performance of the activity will assist in some way in the discharge of that function or those functions."

Specific Commercial Functions

3.19 Section 388 of the GLA Act amends section 1(4) of the Local Authorities (Goods and Services) Act 1970 so that the 1970 Act applies to the Authority and the London Fire and Emergency Planning Authority, Transport for London and the London Development Agency. The Local Authorities (Goods and Services) Act 1970 enables authorities to engage in "municipal trading" activities. They may enter into agreements to provide services, such as the supply of goods or materials, the provision of administrative and professional services and works of maintenance to other public bodies including other local authorities and joint committees and boards.

By virtue of section 394 of the GLA Act, Part V of the Local Government and Housing Act 1989 Act ("the 1989 Act") applies to the GLA. Part V of the 1989 Act regulates the way in which a local authority can control or invest in outside companies. The extent to which a local authority's interest amounts to a controlling interest in the company determines whether or not the company's affairs are to be treated differently from those of the authority or whether they are to be aggregated with those of the authority.

Exercise of the GLA's Functions by the Mayor and/or Assembly

3.20 Functions transferred to, or conferred or imposed on the Authority, whether under this Act or otherwise, are exercisable:

(1) by the Mayor,
(2) by the Assembly, or
(3) by the Mayor and the Assembly acting jointly.

The general rule, under section 35(2), is that, in the absence of a specific provision, functions of the GLA are exercisable by the Mayor. If a function is transferred to or conferred or imposed on the Mayor, it is taken that it is to be exercised by the Mayor acting on behalf of the Authority (GLA Act, s.35(3)). Likewise, a function transferred to or conferred or imposed on the Assembly is taken to be a function exercised by the Assembly acting on behalf of the Authority (GLA Act, s.35(4)).

A function transferred to or conferred or imposed on the Mayor and the Assembly, is to be exercised by them acting jointly on behalf of the Authority (GLA Act, s.35(5)). Accordingly, a reference to both Mayor and Assembly means jointly, to the exclusion of the several responsibility under subsections (3) and (4) (section 35(6)). References to "functions of" one and/or the other are to be construed in the same way (GLA Act, s.35(7)). For the avoidance of doubt, under subsection (10), the power to contract out in Part II of the Deregulation and Contracting Out Act 1994 is preserved, *cf.* section 40, below.

Section 36 of the GLA Act requires the Assembly to adopt standing **3.21** orders concerning procedure (having consulted with the Mayor). Procedure at meetings of a local authority in full council or committee and sub-committee is regulated by an extensive code under section 99 of, and Schedule 12 to, the Local Government Act 1972 and the authority's standing orders (paragraph 42 of Schedule 12 allows the authority to make standing orders for the regulation of procedure at meetings). The London Government (Various Provisions) Order 2000 (S.I. 2000 No. 942) provides that the first meeting of the Assembly will be conducted in accordance with standing orders prepared by the person appointed to be the Head of Paid Service for the Authority.

Section 36(4) of the GLA Act allows the GLA to make provision in standing orders for the procedure to be followed by the Mayor or by the Assembly in discharging their functions, but only to the extent that the functions relate to "consultation or any other interaction or relationship" between the Assembly and the Mayor. Under section 36(9), which is to be read in the light of subsection (3), the standing orders do not apply in respect of the Mayor's specific express powers (see section 38, below) or to those of the Assembly (see section 54, below). Section 36(3) permits standing orders to be made regulating the procedure to be followed by any member of the Assembly or member of staff of the Authority to whom functions of the Authority are delegated.

The Deputy Mayor

Under section 49 of the GLA Act, there is to be a Deputy Mayor who, by **3.22** subsection (2), is to have such other functions as may be conferred upon him by this or any other Act. By subsection (3), the Deputy Mayor is to be appointed by the Mayor from among the Assembly members. Subsection (4) provides that no one person can be Deputy Mayor and Chair of Assembly at the same time. The Mayor may delegate his functions to the Deputy Mayor (*per* section 31 and Schedule 4) and the Deputy Mayor will act as Mayor when there is a vacancy in the Mayor's office or the Mayor is temporarily unable to act. The Mayor can dismiss the Deputy Mayor at any time. A Deputy Mayor can also resign at any time. In either case, the Mayor must appoint a successor.

Under Schedule 4 to the GLA Act, where there is a casual vacancy in the office of Mayor, the proper officer of the Authority is to give notice to the Deputy Mayor. Paragraph 3 of Schedule 4 provides that, during any vacancy in the office, the Deputy Mayor shall exercise the Mayor's functions including those functions which are exercisable by the Mayor and the Assembly acting together. Paragraph 5 requires the Deputy Mayor to make a declaration of acceptance of office and, on making the declaration, the Deputy Mayor must resign as a member of the Metropolitan Police Authority and he may not act as a member of the Assembly.

3.23   In case there is a vacancy and there is no Deputy Mayor, paragraph 7 of Schedule 4 provides that the above shall have effect in relation to the Chair of the Assembly as if there was no Deputy Mayor. Certain functions of the Mayor cannot be exercised by the Deputy Mayor. These are set out in paragraphs 4 and 10 of Schedule 4: any function exercisable under Schedules 5 or 6 to the Act (the preparation of a consolidated budget for the Authority and the functional bodies); the preparation, alteration or replacement of any of the Mayor's strategies; and the appointments to the functional bodies.

The constitutional role of the Deputy Mayor generated controversy during the passage of the Bill through the House of Lords. It was proposed that the Deputy Mayor, rather than being a member of the Assembly, should be directly elected with the Mayor in order to promote a clear separation of powers between the executive and the Assembly. A proposed amendment to this effect was rejected. Lord Whitty, Under-Secretary of State for the Department of the Environment, Transport and the Regions, said:

> "It must be clear that it is the Mayor who has democratic legitimacy: that it is the Mayor for whom people are voting and that it is the Mayor who will have these powers. We have indicated that a Deputy Mayor should be designated by the Mayor and should be a bridge between the Mayor and the Assembly. Far from being foisted upon the people of London they will have democratic legitimacy, having been elected through the Assembly. That provides the flexibility that the Mayor will need as well as the link to the Assembly." *Hansard*, H.L. Vol. 605, col. 223.

General Delegation

3.24   While local authorities are statutory corporations, they can only act through individuals. The general rule is that if Parliament has entrusted a function to a particular body, it is that body and only that body which can discharge it. Accordingly, every decision of a local authority must, prima facie, be taken by them in full council unless there are statutory provisions which require or permit delegation to another. In the case of local authorities, see particularly section 101 of the Local Government Act 1972, permitting delegation to a committee, sub-committee or officer of the authority.

'If a decision has been properly delegated, it becomes the decision of the authority: *Battelley v. Finsbury B.C.* (1958) 56 L.G.R. 165. An improper delegation or an exercise of the powers without delegation is void. The power to delegate a function to an officer did not exist until the 1972 Act. Subject to subsections (5) and (6) of section 101 of the 1972 Act, there are no limits on a local authority's power to delegate the discharge of their functions to an officer.

Where an officer takes action on behalf of an authority but without **3.25**
proper delegation to him, it may be possible for the council to ratify it:
Warwick R.D.C. v. Miller-Mead [1962] Ch. 441; and *Poppett's (Caterers) v.
Maidenhead B.C.* [1971] 1 W.L.R. 69, where it was held that the officer's
actions reflected the council's intentions even though the intentions had
not been formally expressed. See also *Stoke-on-Trent C.C. v. B&Q Retail Ltd*
[1984] Ch. 1, in which a sub-committee caused the commencement of
proceedings in the council's name but the policy committee subsequently
ratified the decision. In *Webb v. Ipswich B.C.* (1989) 21 H.L.R. 325, the court
held that ratification is not effective if an individual's rights had already
been affected by the purported decision. There can be no ratification if the
decision is not within the powers of the authority: *Co-operative Retail Services
Ltd v. Taff-Ely B.C.* (1980) 39 P. & C.R. 223, CA (confirmed on appeal at
(1982) 42 P. & C.R. 1, HL).

Under section 38, sections (1) and (2) of the GLA Act, the Mayor may **3.26**
delegate functions which he can exercise on behalf of the GLA to specified
persons or bodies. These are: the Deputy Mayor, a member of staff of the
Authority, Transport for London, the London Development Agency, the
Common Council and any local authority. Note that delegation to a body
can effectively expand the powers of that body to the full extent of the
Mayor's powers (save as precluded by this section): see section 38(7) of the
GLA Act. The Deputy Mayor's role has already been discussed. Transport
for London and the London Development Agency are specially constituted
functional bodies under this Act and directly implement the Mayor's
strategies on a day-to-day basis and at the direction of the Mayor.

Note that subsections (1) and (2) are exhaustive: the Mayor cannot
delegate any of his functions to anyone else other than those persons listed
in subsection (2). As is the case with other local authorities, the Mayor
cannot delegate his functions to a single member of the Assembly. The
Assembly, in contrast, is able to delegate its functions to a single member:
see section 54, below. Under section 38(3), the Mayor's delegation may
only be granted or varied with the written consent of the authority to
whom the function has been delegated, and ceases to have effect if they
give notice of withdrawal of that consent to the Mayor. These bodies are
the Common Council and a local authority.

The Act therefore makes a distinction between those bodies upon whom **3.27**
a function may be thrust and those who can elect to refuse it. A member of
the Authority's staff would be required as a condition of his employment to
comply with the reasonable orders of his superiors, particularly the Mayor
and, if the Mayor decided to delegate one of his functions to that employee,
it would appear that he must accept it. Other persons or bodies which
cannot refuse to accept a delegated function are the Deputy Mayor,
Transport for London and the London Development Agency.

Section 38(6) of the GLA Act restricts the Mayor's power to delegate
certain functions. These functions are defined as the power to delegate
itself, the power to appoint staff as set out in section 67 of the GLA Act,
and the powers under Part X of this Act concerning the Mayor's Culture

Strategy and the Cultural Strategy Group, in respect of which there is a separate power to delegate in section 380 (below).

Under section 38(7), Transport for London, the London Development Agency, the Common Council and any local authority may exercise functions on behalf of the GLA whether or not these functional bodies would have the power to do so. Therefore, in principle, the powers of these other bodies, including a local authority, can be extended to any of the powers of the Mayor.

3.28   Section 38(8) incorporates subs. (3) and (4) of section 101 of the Local Government Act 1972. Section 101(3) provides that where arrangements are in force under section 101 for the discharge of a local authority's functions by another local authority, that other authority may arrange for the discharge of those functions by a committee, sub-committee or officer. Hence, the Mayor may delegate a function to Transport for London, the London Development Agency, or a local authority, and that body may, if its own powers permit, sub-delegate to a committee, sub-committee or officer.

Section 101(4) provides that any arrangement made by a local authority or committee under section 101 for the discharge of any functions by a committee, sub-committee or officer or other local authority shall not prevent the authority or committee by whom the arrangements are made from exercising those functions. A local authority which appointed a committee and delegated powers to it can revoke the delegation and resume the powers, albeit without prejudice to any action already taken by the delegatee: *Huth v. Clarke* (1890) 25 Q.B.D. 391.

Subsection (4) of section 101 of the 1972 Act allows for the parallel exercise of powers by the delagator and delegatee. If there is a conflict, validity would be a matter of determining priority of notification to persons affected: *R. v. Yeovil B.C., ex p. Trustees of Elim Pentecostal Church* (1972) 23 P.&C.R. 39.

Section 38(9) provides that the Mayor can revoke or vary his authorisation at any time but must do so in writing. A statutory power to delegate will include, expressly or impliedly, a power to revoke or vary the delegation, but the revocation cannot be retrospective: see *Battelley v. Finsbury B.C.* (1958) 56 L.G.R. 165 where it was held that a council could not repudiate an appointment of an employee made by a committee under delegated powers.

Joint Committees

3.29 Section 39(1) of the GLA Act provides for the establishment of joint committees with other local authorities for the joint discharge of functions where the Mayor has delegated his functions under section 38(1) to one or more local authorities. It expressly incorporates section 101(5) of the Local Government Act 1972. That subsection provides that two or more authorities may combine to discharge a function jointly or arrange for discharge either by a joint committee or by an officer employed by one of the authorities; in which case, the joint committee can arrange for discharge by sub-committee or an officer, and a sub-committee can delegate to an officer.

Subsections (2) and (3) of section 39 of the GLA Act provide for the establishment of joint committees with one or more local authorities where they have related or connected interests. Section 39(2)(b) provides that a function exercised by the Mayor might "affect or be affected by" the exercise of a function belonging to a local authority; and, if so, the Mayor and the authority concerned may set up a section 101(5) joint committee for the joint exercise of that function. Subsection (3) defines the meaning of " affect or be affected by" as meaning a Mayoral function will affect a local authority function simply on the basis that they are similar or related to each other or concern the same subject matter.

Under section 39(4) of the GLA Act, where there is a delegation by the **3.30** Mayor to a local authority under section 38, above, and where the exercise of functions are likely to affect both the Mayor and a local authority such that a joint committee is required (as set out in section 39(2)), section 101(5) and sections 102 to 106 of the Local Government Act 1972 are to have effect as if the Authority, acting through the Mayor, were a local authority. These sections deal with appointment, expenses and qualifications of committees and joint committees. Local authorities, under section 102, have the power to appoint committees for the purposes of discharging their functions; two or more authorities may appoint joint committees and committees may appoint sub-committees. The numbers of members, terms of office and other matters are to be fixed by the appointing committee. Apart from the committee appointed to regulate the finances of the authority, members of committees, by virtue of subsection (3), are necessarily members of the appointing authority or authorities. They can include co-opted members.

Section 103 of the 1972 Act deals with the expenses of joint committees. They are to be defrayed by those authorities in such proportions as they may agree or, if there is no agreement, by an arbitrator appointed by the Secretary of State. Section 104 of the 1972 Act provides that a person disqualified from membership of a local authority cannot be a member of a committee or sub-committee of that authority. Nor can he act for that authority on any joint committee of that authority. Section 105 applies sections 94 to 98 of the 1972 Act (dealing with members with disabling interests in contracts) to membership of committees and joint committees. Section 106 provides that standing orders may be made as respects any local authority committee of joint committee concerning quorum, proceedings, and place of meeting.

Deregulation and Contracting Out

Section 40 of the GLA Act amends section 70 of the Deregulation and **3.31** Contracting Out Act 1994 so that the 1994 Act applies to functions of the Authority; secondly, it adds a new subsection to section 70. Under section

70(5) of the 1994 Act, it is an implied term of arrangements made for the purposes of delegation pursuant to section 101 of the 1972 Act that the delegated authority will not authorise the delegation of a function under the 1994 Act without the consent of the delegating authority. The effect of the new subsection 70(6) is that the provisions relating to the term implied by section 70(5) apply also to an authorisation under section 31 of this Act.

The Mayor's Strategies

3.32 Section 41 of the GLA Act deals with the Mayor's duty to devise strategies and action plans. The White Paper, at paragraph 3.16., states that the Mayor will have the following specific powers and duties:

". . . to devise strategies and actions plans; to propose a budget; to co-ordinate action to implement the agreed strategic plans; and to make appointments to functional bodies."

See also paragraph 5.1:

"The Mayor will have a major role to play in improving the economic, social and environmental well-being of Londoners and will be expected to do this by integrating key activities."

Section 41 is a key provision of the Act because it confers these important strategy duties directly and solely on the Mayor. Indeed, it might be said that, in this context, the Authority is the Mayor, as he is the only constituent element of the Authority with independent functions to exercise, whereas the Assembly's main role is to monitor and scrutinise the exercise of those functions. While the Mayor also has other important financial functions and the power to appoint members to functional bodies, his main positive function is to develop and implement these strategies.

3.33 Subsections (1) to (3) of section 41, require the Mayor produce strategies in respect of specified areas:

(1) transport (section 142);
(2) the London Development Agency Strategy (section 7A(2) of the Regional Development Act 1998);
(3) the Spatial Development Plan (Part VIII);
(4) biodiversity (section 352);
(5) municipal waste management (section 353);
(6) air quality (section 362);
(7) ambient noise (section 370); and
(8) culture, media and sport (section 376).

Under section 41(2), the Mayor is required to review these strategies and revise them where necessary, save for the spatial development plan, for which there are separate procedures in section 340, below.

Part V of the Act contains amendments to the Regional Development Agency Act 1998. Under the new section, section 7A, the Mayor is required to prepare a London Development Strategy. He is to be assisted by the London Development Agency in drawing up the strategy. There is also a new section 7B which provides that the strategy must be in line with national policies and the Secretary of State has the power to direct the Mayor to revise his strategy where there is a conflict with national policies or he is of the view that the strategy will have a detrimental effect, or is likely to have a detrimental effect on any area outside Greater London.

3.34 Section 41(4) of the GLA Act refers to the preparation and revision of a strategy, and subsection (6) to revision and implementation. When engaged in any of these activities, the Mayor is required to have regard to certain matters. These are:

(1) the principal purposes of the Authority under section 30, above;
(2) the effect the proposed strategy or revision would have on the health of persons in Greater London and the achievement of sustainable development in the United Kingdom; and,
(3) more specific matters set out in subsection (5), these being:

    (a) consistency with national policy and international obligations;
    (b) consistency with other strategies;
    (c) the resources available for the implementation of the strategy; and,
    (d) the desirability of the promotion and encouragement of the use of the Thames for Transport.

"National Policies"

3.35 Section 424(1) of the GLA Act defines "national policies" as "any policies of Her Majesty's Government which are available in a written form and which have been laid or announced or otherwise presented to either House of Parliament or have been published by a Minister of the Crown." Before the House of Lords in its third reading, it was proposed that the entire phrase "consistent with national policies" be removed on the ground that it was unduly restrictive. The proposal was rejected. It was feared that, but for this consideration, the Mayor would be able to ignore or undermine central government policies. Lord Whitty, Under-Secretary of State for the Department of the Environment. Transport and the Regions said:

> "Whatever government is in power in London, there will have to be a balance, That balance is between the autonomy of the Mayor to deliver the improvements for which Londoners have voted and the responsibilities of central government to ensure that policies pursued in London do not undermine important national policies . . . All we are

asking here is that Mayor should not pursue policies which are inconsistent with national policies." *Hansard*, H.L. Vol. 606, cols 595 to 596.

"International Obligations"

3.36 The term "international obligations" is defined in subsection (10). It means "international obligations of the United Kingdom under any treaty, including Community Treaties." This therefore includes not only directly applicable law such as European Union law but also unincorporated international human rights conventions (save that the Mayor is not bound legally to comply with them but only to consider them).

Other Material Considerations

3.37 Section 41(7) requires the Mayor, when revising or preparing a strategy, to include such policies and proposals relating to the subject matter of the strategy as he considers best calculated both to promote improvements in the health of the persons in Greater London and also to contribute towards sustainable development in the United Kingdom. The obligation applies only when preparing or revising a strategy, and does not apply to the extent that the Mayor considers it would not be reasonably practicable in all the circumstances. Section 41(8) defines the term "promoting improvements in health" as including a reference to mitigating detriment to health which might be caused by the strategy.

The Mayor is also required to set such targets with respect to the implementation of any strategy, having regard to related targets and national objectives and any relevant performance indicators set by the Secretary of State (GLA Act, s.41(9)).

Consultation

3.38 When preparing or revising a strategy under section 41, section 42 of the GLA Act requires the Mayor to carry out a consultation exercise. Section 42(1) sets out the bodies which he must consult: the Assembly, the functional bodies, each London borough council and the Common Council, and any other person or body the Mayor considers it necessary to consult. The last is defined in section 42(2) so as to include the bodies referred to in section 32(3), above. Subsection (4) provides that this duty to consult is without prejudice to any other consultative duties which the Mayor may have.

Subsection (5), unusually, specifies a priority in the order of consultation, the assumption perhaps being that the order of consultation affects the way the consultation exercise is conducted. Here, the Assembly and the functional bodies must be consulted before the London borough councils and the other relevant bodies and persons. However, subsection (6) provides that when the Mayor is simply revising a strategy, and he considers that the revisions are not of any real significance, he is not under any duty to consult. Conversely, he must consult when he preparing a strategy or he is revising a strategy in a substantial way.

Where the Mayor proposes to go through the consultation process, section 43(1) requires him to take such steps as in his opinion will give adequate publicity to each strategy to which section 42 applies. A copy of the proposals are to kept available for inspection to the public at the Mayor's offices and a copy is to be provided for a reasonable fee to any member of the public who requests it.

Directions from the Secretary of State

Where the Mayor has not published a strategy, and the Secretary of State **3.39** considers that the Mayor has not taken adequate steps, he may, under section 44, issue a direction to the Mayor requiring him to prepare and publish the strategy within a specified period. Directions from the Secretary of State which are triggered by a failure of a body to exercise a duty are common in local government law: see, for example, section 496, Education Act 1996.

Commissioner for Local Government Administration

Part III of the Local Government Act 1974 deals with investigations and **3.40** proceedings of the Commissioners for Local Administration. Section 74 of the GLA Act amends Part III of the 1974 Act so that it applies to the GLA and, by section 394 of the GLA Act, the specified functional bodies are subject to investigation by the Commissioner of Local Administration. Section 74(2) of the GLA Act contains further amendments to Part III of the 1974 Act. Section 25 of the 1974 Act now includes the GLA, the Assembly, a committee of the Assembly and any body or person exercising the functions of the GLA (such as a functional body) in the list of bodies subject to scrutiny by the Commissioner for Local Administration.

Section 74(4) adds a new subsection, subsection (2AA), to section 30 of the 1974 Act. By section 30, where the Local Commissioner conducts an investigation or decides not to do so, he shall send a report of the results of his investigation or a statement of his reasons for not doing so to the complainant and the authority concerned. By virtue of this new subsection, where the body under investigation is the GLA or exercising a GLA function, the Commissioners must send the report to the Mayor and the Assembly.

Subsection (5) of section 74 also adds a new subsection (3AA) to section 30 of the 1974 Act. Subsection (3) of section 30 of the 1974 Act provides that the report, other than identifying the authority concerned, shall not mention the name of any person or contain particulars which might make it likely to identify the person unless it is necessary in the public interest to do so. By virtue of this new subsection, this does not apply to anything done by the Mayor or any member of the Assembly.

Chapter 4

REPORTS, MEETINGS AND PROCEEDINGS

Introduction

Consultation, openness and accountability are key components of the **4.01** exercise of by the Authority of its powers. Paragraph 3.4 of the White Paper stated that:

> "The best way of ensuring this accountability is to provide for the maximum public exposure of decisions taken by the Mayor and the Assembly, so that people can see the action and the results. All of the participants, including the public must have as much access as possible to information and the ability to question and interrogate on the basis of that information."

Sections 45 to 48 of the GLA Act are entitled "Public Accountability" and these provisions impose duties which are entirely unique to this Authority. The Mayor must prepare and publish a periodic report (section 45), and an annual report (section 46), for the Assembly. Section 47 requires the Mayor to hold a "State of London" debate and section 48, a "People's Question Time."

Periodic Report and Meeting

Section 45 requires the Mayor to issue a "periodic report" and attend **4.02** "periodic meetings" of the Assembly (of which there are to be 10 a year) at which he must answer questions put to him by the Assembly members. Under subsection (2), the "periodic report" must deal with the Mayor's decisions, his reasons for his decisions and his response to the proposals submitted to him by the Assembly (under section 60, below). This report is to be considered by, *inter alia*, the members of the Assembly and, under subsections (3) and (4), when attending the Assembly's periodic meetings, held pursuant to section 52 of the GLA Act, he must answer any questions put to him by the members.

Under subsection (6), the Mayor need not disclose in a report or meeting advice given to the Mayor by a member of the Authority's staff, a functional body, a member of a functional body or a member of staff of a functional body unless it is advice of a kind referred to in subsections (7) and (8). Subsection (7) refers to advice received by the Mayor from the Metropolitan Police Authority or the London Fire and Emergency Planning Authority, a member of either of these bodies or a member of staff of either of the bodies functional body if it is advice of the kind referred to in subsection (8). Subsection (8) refers to advice disclosed at a meeting of the particular body or at one of its committee or sub-committee meetings which are open to the public under Part VA of the Local Government Act; or contained in a document which is open to inspection by members of the public under Part VA of the 1972 Act.

In this context, see section 58(6), below, which provides that section 100D of the Local Government Act 1972, dealing with disclosure of background papers and other documents, does not apply to matters falling within section 45(6) of this Act.

The Annual Report

4.03 Section 46 of the GLA Act requires the Mayor to issue "an annual report". Subsection (1) requires the Mayor to prepare the report concerning the exercise of his statutory functions as soon as practicable after the end of each financial year. Subsection (2) provides that the annual report is to contain an assessment of his progress in implementing his strategies under this Act or section 7A(2) of the Regional Development Agencies Act 1998, a summary of information about the Authority's performance of their statutory functions and information as required by the Assembly.

As in the case of the periodic report in section 45, above, the Mayor must send a copy of his annual report to the Assembly but, additionally, he must also publish it. The reason for this is that, while the periodic report is prepared for the purpose of the scrutiny and review by the Assembly at its periodic meetings under section 52, above, the annual report will be subject to scrutiny not only by members but also by the public at large and, particularly, at the State of London Debate held under section 47 (see below). Hence, under section 46(5), the annual report must be available for public inspection and, under subsection (6), it must be sent to any person who requests it (at the cost of a reasonable fee). Note also section 47(7), below: the Mayor must hold a "State of London Debate" at least 7 days after the publication of the annual report.

The State of London Debate

4.04 Section 47 makes provision for the "State of London debate" which is open to all members of the public and held once every financial year. Subsections (2) to (5) deal with procedure. The Mayor may determine the form and procedure of the debate, having first consulted the Assembly but he must ensure that there is an opportunity for members of the public to speak. Otherwise, the Act is completely silent as to the form and procedure at the debate. This would appear to be a deliberate omission: it is impossible to predict exactly how large such a debate will be and how members of the public are to be heard. It is likely that it will take more than a few such meetings before procedure can be finalised. The Mayor may also appoint a person to preside at the meeting and that person need not have any connection with the Authority.

Subsections (6) and (7) provide that, until the year 2002, the Mayor is to determine a date for this meeting so that it occurs in April, May or June, and, after 2001, he must make the decision as to when to hold it seven days after the publication of his annual report under section 46, above. Subsection (3) requires the Mayor, at least one month prior to the date for the State of London debate, to determine where it is to take place and to take such steps as he thinks amount to adequate notice to the public about the debate's time and place.

People's Question Time

Section 48 requires the Mayor and the Assembly to meet twice each **4.05** financial year to hold a meeting which is open to the public known as the "People's Question Time." The purpose of this meeting is set out in section 48(2): to afford members of the public an opportunity to put questions to the Mayor and the Assembly members and to enable them to respond. The form and procedure for the People's Question Time is a matter for the Mayor in consultation with the Assembly: subsection (3). Again, it must be presumed that the absence of detailed provisions as to procedure is deliberate.

Under subsection (4), there is no power to appoint a person to preside over the People's Question Time and that person need not have any connection with the Authority. Further, a member of the public who attends or speaks at the People's Question Time, shall only be permitted to do so in accordance with the procedure (although, as yet, no procedure has been formulated or published). The Mayor is to determine when these meetings are to take place so long as it is not less than a month before or after the State of London debate held under section 39. But it is the Mayor who, under section 40(3), is required to determine the place of these meetings and to take steps he thinks are adequate to notify the public as to the date and place of the meetings.

The Assembly's General Functions

Sections 59 to 60 are fundamental provisions. Section 59(1) describes the **4.06** Assembly's general function as that of reviewing the exercise of the Mayor's functions, and, by section 60, they may submit proposals to the

Mayor. Reference has already been made to the scrutinising and monitoring role envisaged by the government in the White Paper. Under section 59(2), the power referred to in section 59(1) is defined so as to include the power to investigate and prepare reports about the following: actions and decisions of the Mayor, actions and decisions of a member of staff of the Authority, matters concerning the "principal purposes" of the Authority, matters in relation to which statutory functions are exercisable by the Mayor; or any other matter the Assembly considers of importance to Greater London. The term "principal purposes" in subsection (2) is a reference to section 30, above.

The other general function of the Assembly is to submit proposals to the Mayor under section 60. This general function cannot be delegated to a committee or sub-committee. The term, "proposals" is not defined in the Act and has no special legal meaning. It would seem that the Assembly has the power to make section 60 proposals about anything which it may review and investigate under section 59. Hence, the Assembly could issue a proposal to the Mayor in respect of anything done or about to be done by the Mayor or a member of staff, anything related to the principal purposes under section 30, above, and any other matter it considers important to Greater London.

The Chair and Deputy Chair

4.07 Sections 50 and 51 of the Act provide for the offices of Chair and Deputy Chair of the Assembly. Similar officers exist in respect of the Scottish Parliament and Welsh Assembly. Under section 19 of the Scotland Act 1998, the Parliament shall elect a presiding officer and two deputies. Under section 52 of the Government of Wales Act 1998, the Welsh Assembly is to elect a Presiding Officer and deputy. The intention of both Acts is that the Presiding Officer, like the speaker of the House of Commons, ensures efficient conduct and administration of parliamentary business and chairs sessions of the Parliament. The function of the Chair of the Assembly under this Act is broadly similar: under section 50(2), the Chair has the functions of chairing meetings of the Assembly and also any other function that may be conferred upon him by this or any other Act.

4.08 In the case of an ordinary local authority, a chairman must be elected annually by the council and from among its members (Local Government Act 1972, s.3(1)). At common law, the duties of the chairman are " . . . to preserve order, to take care that the proceedings are conducted in a proper manner, and that the sense of the meeting is properly ascertained with regard to any question that is properly before the meetings: *National Dwellings Society v. Sykes* [1894] 3 Ch. 159 at 162. Further, he is " . . . to act neutrally, allowing (subject to standing orders) different opinions to be fully and fairly presented and debated." *R. v. Bradford M.C.C., ex p. Wilson* [1990] 2 Q.B. 375 at 380. The chairman's powers to preserve order are usually set out in standing orders. At common law, legislative bodies are

entitled to protect themselves from obstruction, interruption and distur-
bance of their proceedings. These powers are intended to be "self-
protective and self-defensive" rather than punitive: *Keilly v. Carson* (1842) 4
Moo. P.C. 63; *Re McAnulty's Applications* [1985] N.I. 37.

The Deputy Chair is to have the function of chairing meetings of the
Assembly when authorised or required to do so by this or any other Act or
in accordance with the Authority's standing orders and any other functions
that may be conferred on him (section 50(4)).

Under section 51, both posts are to be filled by members of the Assembly
and by way of an election at a meeting of the Assembly. The Deputy Mayor
is not eligible to be considered for either post. The Deputy Mayor's role is
to act as a "bridge" between the Mayor and the Assembly and it would
over-complicate his role were he to take an active part in controlling the
Assembly.

Meetings of the Assembly

Sections 52 and 53 deal with meetings of the Assembly. Under section 99 of **4.09**
the Local Government Act 1972 and Schedule 12 to that Act, the full
council of a local authority must hold an annual meeting in any year in
which there are ordinary elections, on the eighth day after the retirement
of councillors (but not after a by-election) or on such other day within 21
days of such retirement as the authority may fix. In any other year, the
annual meeting must be held in March, April or May, as the authority may
determine (1972 Act, s.99, and Sched.12, para.1). The first order of
business is the election of the chairman (1972 Act, Sched.12, para.1(4)). An
authority may hold any other such meetings as they wish.

Under section 52, like an ordinary authority, the Assembly may, under
subsection (1), hold any meetings as it may determine, but it must, under
subsection (2) hold a meeting to elect the Chair and Deputy Chair and,
under subsection (3), hold 10 periodic meetings each year. The purposes of
the meetings are to allow the Assembly to consider the Mayor's "periodic
report" and for members to be given the opportunity to put questions to
the Mayor, and to transact any other business on the agenda for the
meeting.

Section 56(5) provides that the questions and answers at such meetings **4.10**
are to be treated as minutes of the Assembly. Further, section 57(5)
provides that section 100C of the Local Government Act 1972, dealing with
the right of members of the public to inspect minutes, applies to questions
and answers at Assembly meetings.

Under section 52(8) and (9), the Chair of the Assembly may call
extraordinary meetings (as may the Chairman of a local authority:
paragraph 2 of Schedule 12 of the Local Government Act 1972). Five
members of the Assembly may also require him to call a meeting by
requisition and, if he refuses, or within seven days after presentation of the
requisition, fails to do so, then they themselves may do so forthwith.

Under section 53, like section 46 of the Government of Wales Act 1998, the procedure of the Assembly is regulated by its standing orders. See also section 99 of the Local Government Act 1972 but note, however, that Schedule 12 to the 1972 Act contains more extensive provisions as to procedure at meetings of local authorities. Under section 53, the Assembly may determine its own procedure and that of its committees, including the size and composition of a quorum. This is subject to section 52, above, which requires the Assembly to elect a Chair and Deputy Chair, to hold regular meetings and extraordinary meetings.

Committees, Sub-Committees and Officers

4.11 Local authorities have the power to discharge their functions through a committee by section 102 of the Local Government Act 1972 but have no power to delegate to a single member: *R. v. Secretary of State for Education, ex p. Birmingham C.C.* (1984) 83 L.G.R. 79. Nor is it possible for a local authority to have a committee of one: *R .v. Secretary of State for the Environment, ex p. Hillingdon L.B.C.* [1986] 1 W.L.R. 967 (note, however, *KLF (United Kingdom) Ltd v. Derbyshire C.C., The Times*, August 21, 1985: the statements of a single member may bind the council). Under section 54(1) of the GLA Act, the Assembly may arrange for any of their functions to be exercised either by a committee of the Assembly or by a single Assembly member. Section 54 (3) provides for sub-delegation from a committee to a sub-committee or single member and, under subsection (4), from a sub-committee to a single member.

Committees of ordinary local authorities may delegate (or sub-delegate) a function to a sub-committee or an officer: *Southwark L.B.C. v. Peters* (1971) 70 L.G.R. 41 and section 101(1)(a) of the 1972 Act. The power to delegate to officers did not exist until the 1972 Act. Standing orders may provide for a power to be delegated to an officer acting in consultation with a specified member.

Section 54(2) expressly provides that the Assembly can delegate its functions under sections 67 and 70. Section 67 concerns staff appointments and section 70, terms and conditions of appointment. Section 54(6), on the other hand, prohibits delegation of functions under section 20A of the Police Act 1996. Section 54(5) provides that delegation does not remove the delegator's power to exercise the same function.

4.12 Section 55 deals with different types of Assembly committees and sub-committees. There are two kinds: "ordinary committees" (and "ordinary sub-committees") and "advisory committees" (and "advisory sub-committees"). Ordinary committees are those committees to which functions can be delegated under section 54 and otherwise. Advisory committees are more unusual. Their function is, obviously, to advise and they may not exercise any functions of the Assembly.

Local authorities may also establish advisory committees under section 102(4) of the Local Government Act 1972 (a power which did not exist until the 1972 Act, although the use of such committees was already widespread). A member of an advisory committee need not be a member of the Assembly (GLA Act, s.55(5)).

Section 56 of the GLA Act is in the same terms as paragraph 41 of Schedule 12 to the Local Government Act 1972. It provides for minutes of meetings of the Assembly, Assembly committees and sub-committees to be kept in a form to be determined by the Assembly. It has been held that the signing of minutes is merely evidence of what occurred at a meeting and does not of itself ratify a decision of a meeting of an authority: *Re Indian Zoedone Co.* (1884) 26 Ch.D. 70; *R. v. Mayor of York* (1853) 1 E.&B. 594. Nor are minutes conclusive of everything that takes place at meetings and such matters which have not been recorded but which did take place may be proved by other means: *Re Fireproof Doors Ltd* [1916] 2 Ch. 142; *Re Indian Zoedone Co*, *ibid.* Note that, by virtue of section 56(5), the term "minutes" is defined to include the text of questions put, and answers given, at the periodic meetings held under section 52, above.

Political Balance

Section 57 of the GLA Act deals with the rules relating to the political **4.13** composition of the Assembly's committees. Political balance on committees is a feature of local authority law and is therefore not found in other more "legislative" assemblies: hence, no such provision exists in the Government of Wales Act 1998 or the Scotland Act 1998.

By section 57, sections 15 to 17 of the Local Government and Housing Act 1989, concerning appointments to committees, are incorporated into the GLA Act. The provisions of the 1989 Act regulate committee membership so as to reflect the overall composition of an authority. The general effect is to ensure that the formal activities of an authority, are representative of its overall political composition. Under section 15(1) of the 1989 Act, authorities are under a duty to review committee appointments after a general meeting or when the members divide into different groups or at such times as may be prescribed by the Secretary of State. Each committee or sub-committee must also review the representation of different political groups. Authorities are considered to have political groups when these is at least one such has delivered to the proper officer a written notice signed by at least two members (1989 Act, s.15(2)).

Further, under section 15(5) of the 1989 Act, membership of committees **4.14** and sub-committees must be allocated proportionately between the different political groups so that not all appointments come from the same political party; that the majority group on the council have the same sort of majority on the committee; and all other appointments are allocated proportionately to the membership of the council. Section 16 of the 1989 Act requires the authority or committee to exercise the power to make the appointments as soon as practicable after allocation. Section 17 of the 1989 Act deals with exceptions to, and extensions of, the political balance requirements.

An authority may make different arrangements from those required under sections 15 and 16, if they are the result of a vote in which no member votes against the decision to adopt alternative arrangements and those arrangements have been approved of by the Secretary of State (1989 Act, s.17).

Publicity and Access to Assembly Meetings

4.15   Schedule 12 to the Local Government Act 1972 requires local authorities to hold an annual meeting and any other meetings as they consider necessary. The annual meeting is to be held on the eighth day after the retirement of members or on a day within 21 days immediately following the day of retirement. If there is no election in a given year, the annual meeting must be held in March, April or May. The chairman may call a meeting at any time or he may be required to do so if requested by five members. The chairman or, in the absence of the chairman, the vice-chairman presides a the meeting. Standing orders provide for the meetings and procedure at meetings of committees. Decisions are taken by a majority of votes of members.

Members of local authorities are entitled to attend meetings of the full council and, at common law, they have the right to inspect the books and documents of the authority, so long as their motives in doing so are proper: *R. v. Hampstead B.C., ex p. Woodward* (1917) 116 L.T. 213 at 215; *R. v. Southwold Corp. and Cooper, ex p. Wrightson* (1907) 97 L.T. 431 at 432. A councillor may also attend as a member of the public and additional powers may be conferred upon members by standing orders. Otherwise, the member's entitlement to information and to attend meetings will depend on whether he has a need to know in order properly to carry out his duties as a councillor: *R. v. Birmingham C.C., ex p. O* [1983] 1 A.C. 578, HL.

4.16   Under Part VA of the Local Government Act 1972, added by the Local Government (Access to Information) Act 1985, members have additional rights of access to materials before going to meetings of committees and sub-committees. Documents in the authority's possession or control which contain material relevant to the business of the meeting are open to inspection by any member.

At common law, neither the press nor the public have a right of access to meetings of an authority: *Tenby Corp. v. Mason* [1980] 1 Ch. 457. Under Part VA of the 1972 Act, the authority's meetings must be open to the general public except to the extent that authorities are specifically and statutory entitled to exclude the public from all or part of meetings.

Copies of the agenda for a meeting of an authority must be open to inspection by members of the public at the offices of the authority. The same applies, in general, to copies of any report to a meeting. Agendas and reports to which the public are entitled must be open to inspection at least three clear days before the meeting, except where the meeting is convened at a shorter notice. Section 100A(6)(a) of the 1972 Act requires that public notice of the time and place of a meeting be published at the authority's offices three days before the meeting or, if called at short notice, at the meeting itself. If the meeting is open to the public, the council cannot exclude the public and members of the press must be afforded reasonable facilities for taking a report of the meeting.

At the core of Part VA, however, are two categories of material which **4.17** may be withheld from the press and the public:

(1) Confidential Information: this means information provided to the council by a government body on the condition that it would not be disclosed; and, information which is prohibited from disclosure by statute or by order of the court (see 1. 100A 1972 Act); and,

(2) Exempt Information: the council may resolve to exclude material from the public if it is likely that "exempt information" under Schedule 12A to the 1972 Act will be disclosed. This includes, for example, information about employees, applicants for council services and the business affairs of any person.

Section 58 of the GLA Act applies to the Assembly the rules which apply to local authorities generally requiring them to hold meetings in public, give public notice of meetings and make documents publicly available. By subsection (1), Part VA of the 1972 Act applies to the Assembly, including any committee or sub-committee, as if it were a council subject to the Part VA. Subsection (2) provides that any information furnished to the Authority and available to the Assembly is to be information furnished to the Assembly; likewise, offices belonging to the Authority are offices of the Assembly and the proper officer of the Authority is the proper officer of the Assembly.

Subsections (3) and (4) of section 58 expand the meaning of confidential **4.18** information to include information relating to the financial and business affairs of any person; the amount of expenditure proposed to be incurred by a relevant body under a particular contract (which would give another party or prospective party to the contract an advantage against either the body or someone else, *e.g.* a competitor); terms of negotiations with respect to a contract; and the identity of persons offering a tender for a contract.

Subsection (5) of section 58 refers to section 100C of the 1972 Act which permits inspection by the public of minutes and other documents for six years after a meeting. This subsection defines "minutes" to include questions put to the Mayor by Assembly members at periodic meetings under section 52(3) of this Act and the answers to them. Note that, under section 56(5) of this Act, above, the questions and answers are, in any case, defined as minutes whether made orally or in writing.

Section 58(6) provides that lists of background papers produced by the Authority under section 100D of the 1972 Act are not to include documents which are capable of disclosing advice received by the Mayor from his political advisors, a functional body, a member of the functional body or a member of staff of a functional body. These are also matters which the Mayor is under no duty to disclose at periodic meetings (see section 45).

4.19   Section 58(7) refers to section 100E of the 1972 Act which provides that
Part VA of the 1972 Act is to apply to committees and sub-committees.
Under this subsection, section 100E is to apply to the GLA's committees,
established under section 55 of this Act. Section 100F of the 1972 Act
provides that, in general, members have the right to see any document in
the possession of an authority which contains matters relating to any
business to be transacted at a meeting of the council or committee or sub-
committee. This is subject to section 100F(2): if the proper officer
concludes that the document contains "exempt information", the document need not be disclosed to the member. By virtue of section 58(8)
Assembly members have the same rights with respect to any document in
the control of the Authority on the basis that it is deemed to be a
document in the possession of the Assembly.

   Section 58(9) applies section 110G(1) of the 1972 Act: this requires
authorities to maintain a register of members. The register is to contain
the names and addresses of the members, the wards or divisions they
represent and the names and addresses of every member of each committee or sub-committee. Under section 58(9), the register of Assembly
members shall state whether the member is a London member or a
constituency member and, if a constituency member, of which constituency.

   Section 100H of the 1972 Act is applied to the GLA by section 58(10) of
this Act. Section 100H provides that a document must be made available at
all reasonable hours and the authority may insist on payment of a
reasonable fee for inspecting it. Section 100H(2) permits members of the
public to take copies of the document but, under section 100H(3), this does
not apply if to do so would be a breach of copyright.

Attendance of Witnesses and Production of Documents

4.20 Sections 61 to 64 deal with the attendance of witnesses and production of
documents at Assembly meetings. At common law, local authorities do not
have any powers to call for documents or summon witnesses to meetings. A
member has a prima facie right to inspect documents which are addressed
to his authority on the ground that members must be aware of council
business. They are not, however, entitled to undertake a "fishing expedi-
tion" and can only see documents on a "need to know" basis. If a councillor
is a member of a committee, then he has the right to see documents
relating to the committee's business. If he is not a member of a committee,
he must be able to show that it is necessary for his duties: *R. v. Birmingham
City D.C., ex p. O* [1983] 1 A.C. 578; *R. v. Barnes B.C., ex p. Conlan* [1938] 3
All E.R. 226. In addition, under section 100F of the Local Government Act
1972, a member has the right to inspect any document in the possession or
control of a principal council and which contains material relating to the
business to be transacted at a meeting of the council or of a committee or
sub-committee (unless it is exempt information).

This is to be contrasted with bodies which more legislative than local **4.21** authorities. At common law, legislative bodies have powers similar to the ordinary courts (and have an inherent jurisdiction in respect of offences against the dignity of body or for contempt of it): *Halsburys Laws*, "Parliament", Volume 34, paragraph 1009. The power, though rarely used, can be directed at any person. The Scottish Parliament is a legislative body and under section 23 of the Scotland Act 1998, it is has been given express powers to call any person to give evidence and to produce any documents in his possession but only in connection with any subject for which any member of the Scottish Executive has responsibility. Under subsections (3) to (6) of section 23 of the Scotland Act 1998, the Scottish Parliament has limited power to impose a requirement to give evidence on Ministers of the Crown and their civil servants. The same section recognises the privileges, such as that against self-incrimination, recognised by the courts. Failure to comply is an offence under section 25 of the 1998 Act.

The Welsh Assembly is an assembly which would appear to be more a local authority than a legislative body yet it has been given similar powers under sections 74 and 75 of the Government of Wales Act 1998 to those of the Scottish Parliament. It may use them against any person who is a member of the Assembly or a member of staff and only with respect to the exercise of functions concerning Wales.

The Assembly is a body with no particular legislative powers at all. Its **4.22** main function, however, is to review and scrutinise the Mayor's exercise of his functions. Accordingly, under section 61 of the GLA Act, it has the power to require certain persons to attend meetings for the purpose of giving evidence and to produce any documents in their possession or control. It applies, however, only to certain categories of persons:

(1) members of staff of the Authority or a functional body who may only be required to give evidence and provide documents about the exercise of the Authority's or the functional body's functions;

(2) a person who is the chairman or member of any functional body, and they may only be required to give evidence or provide documents about the exercise of the Authority's or the functional body's functions;

(3) a person who has had, within the last three years, a contractual relationship with the Authority as to the contractual relationship

(4) any member of staff of a body which has had within the last three years had a contractual relationship with the authority, as to that relationship;

(5) a person who has received a grant from the Authority in the last three years, about the grant;

(6) a member of staff who has received a grant from the Authority in the last three years, about that grant;

(7) a member of the Assembly or a person who has been a member of the Assembly within the last three years, as to the exercise by them of functions; and,

(8) any person who has, within the last three years, been the Mayor, as
to his exercise of his functions.

4.23 Under section 61(10), this section does not apply to any staff appointed
under section 67, below, (*i.e.* the Mayor's political advisers) if they would be
required to disclose advice give to the Mayor. Section 61(11) and (12) have
a similar effect with respect to advice to the Mayor given by a member of a
functional body or a member of staff of a functional body. This exemption
does not apply in certain cases: see subsection (6) to (9) of section 45.

The term, "documents" is defined in section 61(11). It means anything
in which information is recorded in any form. Subsection (11) also defines
"member of staff of a body" as including any officer or employee of that
body.

The Assembly's powers under section 61 may be exercised by any
committee or sub-committee of the Assembly so long as it is expressly
authorised to exercise those powers by standing orders or by a simple
majority of those present and voting at a meeting of the whole Assembly.
They may not be exercised by any individual member or by a member of
staff of the GLA. Section 62 sets out the procedures the Assembly is
required to follow when it requires attendance at its meetings. By section
62(3), the Authority's Head of Paid Service must give at least two weeks
notice to a person who is required to attend to give evidence under section
61, setting out the time and place at which he is to give evidence and the
matters about which he is to give evidence or the documents or types of
documents he is to produce. If a person is required to attend proceedings
or produce documents on behalf a body, the notice required to be given to
him under subsection (3) must specify the body.

4.24 Section 62(6) deals with service of the notice. Notice is deemed to have
been given to him if it has been sent by registered post or recorded
delivery. If the person is a member of staff of the Authority, or the
chairman of or member of staff of a functional body, it may be sent to his
place of work. If he is a person representing a body, it may be sent to the
registered or principal office of the body. In the case of any other
individual, the notice may be sent to his usual or last known address.

Under section 64, a person is guilty of an offence and liable to a level 5
fine or imprisonment for three months if (a) he refuses or fails, without a
reasonable excuse, to attend proceedings, (b) he refuses to answer any
question put to him when attending, (c) he refuses or fails, without a
reasonable excuse to produce any document required by the notice, or (d)
he intentionally alters, suppresses, conceals or destroys any document
required to be produced. Under section 64(3), a person is not obliged by
section 61 to answer any question or produce any document which he
would be entitled to refuse to answer or produce for the purposes of
proceedings in a court. The general rule as to privilege is that, in the
absence of an express provision, the relevant Act must be examined as a
whole in order to determine the purpose of the powers in question and

whether that purpose abrogates the privilege. There are no such express provisions, for example, in the Audit Commission Act 1998.

Section 65 applies certain provisions of Part VA of the Local Govern- **4.25** ment Act 1972 to proceedings of the Authority where persons are called to give evidence or provide documents under section 61, above. Under section 65(1), "evidentiary proceedings" and documents concerning them are to be "open" within the meaning of Part VA of the 1972 Act, subject to certain qualifications. Section 65(2) and(3) modify section 100B of Part VA of the 1972 Act which provides for access by members of the public to agendas and reports prepared for meetings. Section 65(2) defines the term "report" to include a reference to any document supplied before and for the purposes of the meeting, and, under subsection (3), copies of those documents are to be available to the public as soon as they are available to Assembly members.

Section 65(4) of the GLA Act defines "minutes" and "reports" as they are used in section 100C of the 1972 Act. Section 100C provides for members of the public to inspect minutes and other documents after meetings. By section 65(4) the term "minutes" includes transcripts or other record of evidence. Note that by section 100C of the 1972 Act, minutes and reports are to be kept available for six years after the meeting.

Section 64 (5) of the GLA Act deals with section 100D of the 1972 Act. **4.26** Section 100D of the 1972 Act provides for access of the public to "background papers" for a report and, by section 64(5) the term "background papers" includes "additional documents supplied by a witness". Hence, the public has the same right to inspect documents produced by the witness as if they were background papers and they are to be kept available for inspection by members of the public after the meeting. The term "additional documents provided by a witness" is itself defined, in section 64(6), as "documents supplied by a witness before, during or after the evidentiary proceedings by a person called to give evidence and for use of Assembly members in the evidentiary proceedings".

Section 65(7) deals with the rights of access of members under section 100F of the 1972 Act. Reference has been made to the common law rule under which members have a right to inspect documents addressed to the council but on a need to know basis only. Section 100F of the 1972 Act improves the non-committee member's right to see documents of a committee so that any member can now see any "open" document which pertains to business to be transacted at a meeting of the council. By section 65(1) of the GLA Act, this applies to Assembly members. Section 65(7), however, provides that section 100F of the 1972 Act is not to have effect in relation to documents which contain material relating to any business to be transacted at the evidentiary proceedings.

Ethical Standards

4.27 Section 31 of the Local Government and Housing Act 1989 empowers the Secretary of State to issue a code of recommended practice for the conduct of members of local authorities. The current code is the National Code of Local Government Conduct (Circular 8/90). Further, under section 31(7) of the 1989 Act, the form of declaration of acceptance of office, under section 83 of the Local Government Act 1972, may include an undertaking from the member that he will be guided by the Code in the performance of his functions. Most of the current Code consists of guidance as to how members are to act when they may have an interest in matters before the council.

Following the recommendation of the Third Report of the Committee on Standards in Public Life, the Government, in a white paper "Modern Local Government: In Touch with the People", Cm. 4014 (July 1998, Chapter 6), proposed the introduction of legislation requiring every council to adopt a Code of Conduct which all members would observe. The new Local Government Bill contains proposed provisions under which each authority is to adopt their own Code of Conduct to replace the current National Code and breaches of the Code will be investigated by an independent standards board. Each Code will contain "General Principles of Conduct" common to all authorities as well as the local rules of conduct adopted by the authorities themselves. Another provision in the Local Government Bill, published in 1999, is that there be a statutory duty to establish and maintain a public registers of interests and a new duty on the part of members to avoid participation in matters before the authority in which members have a direct pecuniary interest or which might be such as to raise a perception of bias.

4.28 Section 66 of the GLA Act empowers the Secretary of State to issue guidance to the Authority about the disclosure and registration of interests, voting in cases where an Assembly member has an interest, the exercise of functions by or on behalf of the Mayor, the Deputy Mayor or any member of the Authority's staff in cases where any such person has an interest; and the prescription of model codes of guidance. The Secretary of State may also provide guidance on the establishment of a committee concerned with ethical standards.

A consultation paper entitled "Ethical Standards for the Greater London Authority" was published by the Government Office for London in October 1999. It sets out a draft code of conduct for members with additional provisions with respect to the Mayor and the Deputy Mayor. In addition, it covers matters such as disclosure, registration and disposal of interests and the establishment of a standards committee. There are special provisions concerning the Mayor. In particular, the Mayor (and the Deputy Mayor) must resign all directorships of companies operating in London and consult the standards committee about appointments they wish to accept during the two years after they have left office.

Staff

Sections 67 to 74 of the GLA Act deal with the Authority's staff. Under **4.29** section 112 of the Local Government Act 1972, local authorities have the power to appoint "such officers as they think necessary for the proper discharge of their functions and on such terms as they think appropriate". They must, however, make certain specified appointments, for example the Director of Social Services (section 6 of the Local Authority Social Services Act 1970) and Chief Education Officer (section 532 of the Education Act 1996). The same authorities are required to ensure that they have a finance officer (section 151 of the Local Government Act 1972), a head of paid service (section 4 of the Local Government and Housing Act 1989) and a monitoring officer (section 5 of the 1989 Act). Otherwise, they may appoint such staff as they decide and on the terms they decide subject to two general but related rules. These are that staff must be appointed on merit; and the authority must observe rules concerning political neutrality in making the appointments.

Under section 67(1) of the GLA Act, the Mayor may appoint two **4.30** political advisers. He may also appoint up to 10 other members of staff.

Under section 67(2), the Authority can appoint such staff as it thinks necessary for assisting the Mayor and the Assembly in the discharge of their functions. By virtue of subsection (3), all appointments under subsection (1) and (2) are employees of the Authority.

None of the Mayor's appointments cannot extend beyond the Mayor's term of office (subsection (4)) and he must notify the Assembly of the appointment, the name of each appointee and the terms of his appointment (subsection (5)).

At each stage during the progress of the Bill through the House of Lords, the issue was raised as to whether the number of Mayoral staff was sufficient. The Government's position was based on the conviction that it was necessary ". . . to ensure the electors of London and the professional staff of the GLA that there will not be significant numbers of political or personal appointees brought in to run the GLA on behalf of the Mayor. In order to reassure them, one needs a limit on the number of such appointments." Lord Whitty, *Hansard*, H.L. Vol. 606, col. 604.

Staff—Appointment and Merit

Section 67(6) of the GLA Act requires that all appointments by the Mayor **4.31** and the Assembly except for the Mayor's political advisers, are to be appointed on merit. Under section 7 of the Local Government and Housing Act 1989, every appointment of a person to a paid office or employment by an authority must made on merit. Thus, an authority must ignore the applicant's political affiliations in making an appointment.

Section 67(7) of the GLA Act requires the Authority to adopt standing orders, as is required pursuant to section 8 of the Local Government and Housing Act 1989. Section 8(1) of the 1989 Act empowers the Secretary of State by regulations to require authorities to incorporate certain provisions into their standing orders relating to their staff and, in particular, with respect to appointment, dismissal or other disciplinary action. The regulations, under section 8(3) of the 1989 Act, can specify the matters which the authority's standing orders must deal with. They may require both selection and appointment to be exercisable only by the authority, a committee or sub-committee or by officers. They may also restrict the power of the authority or any committee or sub-committee to interfere with the persons making the appointment or to require the monitoring officer to prepare a report to the authority about every proposed appointment to "a politically restricted post" (see section 68, below). They may also prohibit the authority or any committee, sub-committee or officer from dismissing or disciplining a member of staff other than in accordance with a recommendation contained in a report by an independent person.

4.32   Section 67(8) of the GLA Act provides that section 9 of the Local Government and Housing Act 1989 is to apply to the appointment of the Mayor's political advisors. Section 9 of the 1989 Act deals with political assistants. Section 9(1) provides that the requirement that appointments must be made on merit (under section 7(1) of the 1989 Act) is not to apply to the appointment of political assistants. Section 9(9) of the 1989 Act provides that ordinary employees shall not be required to work under the direction of political assistants, otherwise than to provide clerical and secretarial services. Hence, the Mayor's political advisers may be appointed with regard to their political affiliations and no other member of the Authority's staff may work under their direction unless it is to provide secretarial or clerical services.

Section 68 of the GLA Act makes provision with reference to "politically restricted posts" by incorporating sections 1 to 3 of the Local Government and Housing Act 1989, applying these provisions to the bodies listed in section 68(2). These are: the GLA, Transport for London, the Metropolitan Police Authority and the London Fire and Emergency Planning Authority. Section 1 of the 1989 Act prevents persons holding a politically restricted post (as defined by section 2) from standing for election as or becoming a member of a local authority or from remaining a member. Under section 2 of the 1989 Act, the politically restricted posts are as follows: head of paid service, statutory chief officers and non-statutory chief officers and deputy chief officers, monitoring officers, political assistants, a person earning more that £19,5000 (or such higher amount as may be prescribed) and persons to whom functions are delegated and who are included in a list maintained by the authority under section 100G(2) of the 1972 Act. Section 100G(1) of the 1972 Act sets out the additional information which authorities are to publish and includes a register of the name and address of every member of the authority. Section 100G(2) requires an authority to publish a list of powers of the authority which are exercisable by the officers of the council except where the arrangements for its discharge by the officer are made for a specified period not exceeding six months.

Section 3 of the 1989 Act requires the Secretary of State to appoint a **4.33** person to give general guidance as to whether or not to include a post on the lists of politically restricted posts due to either the holder's remuneration or the fact that he gives advice to or represents the authority. The authority must also consider applications for an exemption from the political restriction by the office-holder. Hence, in the case of the Authority, persons holding these offices, if any, in any of the bodies listed in section 68(2), above, cannot be members of the Authority as well. Note section 70(7) which deals with the Mayor's staff and the terms and conditions of their employment: any question as to whether a political adviser holds a politically restricted post is to be determined in accordance with sections 2 and 3 of the 1989 Act.

Section 69 of the GLA Act amends section 80 of the Local Government Act 1972. There is now a new subsection (subsection 2AA). Under section 80(1) of the 1972 Act, a person is disqualified for being elected or being a member of a local authority if he holds any paid office or employment in the authority; by section 80(2) a paid officer of a local authority who is employed under the direction of a committee or sub-committee of the authority, any member of which is appointed on the nomination of some other local authority, or a joint board or joint committee on which the authority are represented is also disqualified. This new subsection (2AA) provides that a paid member of staff of the Authority who is employed under the direction of a joint committee whose membership includes Authority nominees or members of London borough councils is disqualified from being elected to, or being a member of, those London boroughs.

Staff—Terms and Conditions

Under section 112(2) of the Local Government Act 1972, officers hold **4.34** office on such reasonable terms and conditions as the authority thinks fit. This provision is repeated with respect to the Mayor's appointments, in 70(1) of the GLA Act, except that the terms and conditions are to be as the Mayor thinks fit and within the financial resources available to the Authority. Section 70(2) is a similar provision with respect to the Assembly's appointments. The Assembly may make such appointments, and on such terms and conditions, as the Assembly thinks fit, but only after consultation with the Mayor.

Section 67(8) of the GLA Act incorporates section 9 of the Local Government and Housing Act 1989 which deals with politically restricted posts. A consequence is that the Mayor's staff are not required to work under the direction of the Assembly's staff. Section 70(3) of the GLA Act further provides that no Mayoral staff are to required to perform work or services for the Assembly or any member of the Assembly. This is subject to subsections (4) and (5) of section 70: these officers must attend the periodic meetings of the Assembly held pursuant to section 52(3) above and answer questions put to them by the Assembly members.

4.35 Section 71 of the GLA Act applies section 117 of the Local Government Act 1972 to employees of the GLA. Under that section, if it comes to the knowledge of an officer employed by an authority that a contract in which he has a pecuniary interest (direct or indirect) has been or is proposed to be entered into by the authority, he shall give notice in writing to the authority of the fact of his interest. Failure to disclose an interest is a summary offence under section 117(3). An interest has been held to include a commission paid to an officer for his superintendence of buildings works: *R. v. Ramsgate B.C.* (1889) 23 Q.B.D. 66. An officer is treated as having an indirect interest, under section 95 of the 1972 Act, if a member would be so treated. Nor may an officer accept any fee or reward whatsoever other than his proper remuneration (1972 Act, s.117(2)). Contravention is also a summary offence. Note also the offences under the Public Bodies Corrupt Practices Act 1889 and the Prevention of Corruption Acts 1906–1916.

Head of Paid Service

4.36 Section 72 establishes the office of the Head of Paid Service. This duty shall be discharged by the Assembly after consultation with the Mayor. Section 4 of the 1989 Act requires local authorities to appoint a Head of Paid Service. It is common for the chief executive to undertake this role. The Head of Paid Service is required to prepare a report whenever he considers it necessary to do so concerning the manner in which the discharge by the authority of their functions is co-ordinated, the number and grades of staff required by the authority, the organisation of the authority's staff and the appointment and management of staff. Each member is to be sent a copy of such a report and the authority must consider it within three months thereafter.

Under section 72(4) of the GLA Act, the duty to make the appointment belongs to the Authority but it must be discharged by the Assembly, in consultation with the Mayor. Provision of staff for the head of paid service is also a duty to be discharged by the Assembly under section 72 (5)(a) but, under section 72 (5)(b), the provision of accommodation for the Head of Paid Service and his staff is to be discharged by the Mayor. When the Head of Paid Service prepares a report, then under section 72(6), it is a report to both the Mayor and the Assembly but the Mayor, under section 72(7), is under a personal duty to consider such a report. The Assembly must consider the report at a meeting and the meeting is not to take place until the Mayor has submitted to the Chair of the Assembly, a statement as to his views about the report (section 72(9)). In considering the report, the Assembly must take into account the Mayor's expressed views about the report (section 72(10)).

Monitoring Officer

Section 73 of the GLA Act establishes the office of monitoring officer. Local **4.37** authorities are required by section 5 of the 1989 Act to create this office. The monitoring officer's duty is to prepare a report to the authority with respect to any proposal, decision or omission of the authority; or a committee, sub-committee or officer or employee of the authority or any joint committee on which the authority are represented, which appears to him to have given rise to or be likely to give rise to a contravention of the law or code of practice or amount to maladministration.

The monitoring officer must, when preparing the report, consult with the head of the paid service and the chief finance officer. The authority must consider the report within 21 days of its delivery to members, pending which the monitoring officer is obliged to ensure that no step is taken to give effect to any proposal or decision to which the report relates during the period of suspension. Under section 73(5) of the GLA Act, the appointment of the monitoring officer is a matter for the Assembly after consultation with the Mayor, and the duty to provide the officer with staff is imposed on the Assembly. The duty to provide him with accommodation is imposed on the Mayor.

By virtue of section 73(6) of the GLA Act, the monitoring officer's duty is **4.38** to prepare a report to the Mayor and Assembly with respect to any proposal, decision or omission made by a "GLA body or person" which would give rise to a contravention of any enactment or rule of, or code of, practice and/or any maladministration. The term "GLA body or person" means the Authority itself, Transport for London, the London Development Agency, the Mayor, the Assembly, a committee of sub-committee of the Assembly, a joint committee to which the Mayor may appoint a member, the Deputy Mayor, any member of the Assembly, any member or member of staff of Transport for London or the London Development Agency; and any member of staff of any of the above bodies.

Under section 73(7) of the GLA Act, the duty to consider the report and to ensure that no steps are taken during the period of suspension is to be discharged by the Mayor if the proposal, decision or omission relates to a function of the Authority exercisable by the Mayor. If it relates to a function of the Assembly, then the duty is imposed on the Assembly; and if with respect to a proposal, omission or decision of a function of both the Mayor and the Assembly, then the Mayor and the Assembly must discharge the duty. Hence, under subsection (10), the Mayor and the Assembly shall take into account, when considering the report, any views about the report which have been expressed by the other in a statement submitted either by the Assembly to the Mayor or by the Mayor to the Chair of the Assembly.

Notices and Documents

4.39 Section 75 of the GLA Act provides that certain provisions of the Local Government Act 1972 are to apply to the Authority. The provisions of the 1972 Act, specified in section 75(2), are to apply to the Authority as if it were an authority under the 1972 Act and to the Mayor, as though he were the chairman of such an authority.

The specified provisions are as follows:

(1) section 224 of the 1972 Act which imposes a duty on an authority to make proper arrangements as to the custody of documents;

(2) section 225 of the 1972 Act, under which the proper officer of a principal council is under duty to receive and retain documents deposited with the council pursuant to the standing orders of either House of Parliament or any statute or instrument;

(3) section 228 of the 1972 Act, to the extent that it is applicable to the GLA allows a local government elector to inspect and make copies of or take extracts from an order for the payment of money by a local authority. Members of any local authority may also inspect and take copies of the accounts of a local authority;

(4) section 229, which provides that if a document is to be kept or made available for inspection, a photocopy is sufficient unless the original was in colour and the copy is such that it is not clear or the document is deposited under the Public Records Act 1958 which refers to the preservation of historic documents (photocopied copies if certified by the proper officer are admissible in legal proceedings);

(5) section 230, requiring every local authority to send to the Secretary of State such reports and returns and give him such information with respect to their functions as may be required;

(6) section 231, under which a notice or document required to be served by any enactment, apart from those concerned with court proceedings, may be served not only at the principal office of an authority but also at any office specified by them;

(7) section 232, which provides that a public notice required to be given by a local authority shall be given by posting it in some conspicuous place or places within the authority's area and in any other manner as appears to the authority to be desirable for giving publicity to the notice; and,

(8) section 233 which contains provisions as to the service of notices on the authority.

Byelaws

4.40 Section 77 of the GLA Act requires the Authority to follow the same procedure as local authorities in respect of the making of byelaws as set out in section 236 of the 1972 Act. Section 236 of the 1972 Act provides that byelaws are to made under the common seal of the Authority. At least one month before the application for confirmation of the byelaw by the Authority, a notice of the intention to apply for confirmation shall be published in local newspapers. The Authority may then confirm or refuse to confirm any byelaw submitted under this section and, if confirmed, may fix a date when it is to come into operation. County council byelaws, under section 236(10), must be sent by the county council proper officer to district councils. The effect of this subsection is to amend section 236 of the 1972 Act by providing a new subsection to section 236, subsection (10), which ensures that that the Authority comes within section 236 and that, copies of the Authority's byelaws are sent to each London borough and to the Common Council.

Promotion of Bills in Parliament

Principal councils and joint authorities have powers under section 239 of **4.41** the Local Government Act 1972 to promote or oppose local or personal Bills in Parliament if they are "satisfied that it is expedient" to do so. They must also comply with the procedure laid down in section 239 of the 1972 Act. A resolution passed by a local authority to promote or oppose a Bill must be passed by a majority of members at a special meeting, the purpose of which has been widely advertised.

Section 70 of the 1972 Act prohibits any local authority from promoting a Bill for forming or abolishing any local government area or for altering the status or electoral arrangements of any local government area. Note, however, that under section 261 of the 1972 Act, local Acts are to continue to apply notwithstanding any changes in the local government area but only with respect to the area or persons to which they applied before April 1974. Under section 254 of the 1972 Act, the Secretary of State may by order amend or modify the application provision of a local Act or extend it to a new area.

Under section 77(1) of the GLA Act, the GLA may promote or oppose a Bill if to do so would be for "the public benefit of the inhabitants of or of any part of Greater London" except for Bills dealing with changes in local government areas (section 77(2)). Under section 77(3), the power to promote or oppose is a function of the Authority exercisable by the Mayor.

Section 77(4) and Schedule 5 set out a procedure for promoting a local **4.42** Bill. The most important paragraphs of Schedule 5 are paragraphs 2 and 4. Under paragraph 2, the Mayor must prepare a draft of the Bill and send copies to the Assembly, and each London borough council and the Common Council. He must also give these bodies an opportunity to make representations to him about the draft Bill. Paragraph 4 requires the Mayor to consider representations made to him about the draft Bill and, if he decides to continue, he must prepare a revised draft. Within 30 days of having issued received the representations, he must send a revised draft of the bill to the same bodies. He may then deposit the Bill in Parliament. If a Bill contains provisions affecting the exercise of functions by a London local authority, then, under paragraph 6, it cannot be deposited in Parliament unless the affected local authority has given its consent or, if more than one London local authority is affected, unless 90 per cent of those affected have consented.

4.43   Under section 87 of the Local Government Act 1985, a local Bill promoted by a London borough council (including the Common Council) or metropolitan district council may include provisions requested by another London local authority or metropolitan district council. The authority making the request must comply with a procedure similar to that of section 239 of the 1972 Act. If the resolution to propose such a Bill is not confirmed, then under section 239(3), the authority must give notice to the authority promoting the Bill and they must take all necessary steps to omit the provisions from the Bill. The authority making the request may make a contribution to the expenses of the promoting authority.

The Authority, under section 78 of the GLA Act, may also request that certain provisions be included in a local Bill promoted by a London local authority but only after it has confirmed the request in writing as soon as practicable after the expiration of 14 days after the Bill has been deposited in Parliament. Under subsection (5), this function is exercisable by the Mayor, but he must first consult the Authority (pursuant to subsection (6). The Authority may also contribute to the expenses of the London local authority in promoting a Bill if the Authority requests the inclusion of the provisions. Subsection (8) amends section 87(3) of the 1985 Act so that it refers to the Authority by including it among the "other councils" which may have made requests for a provision to be included.

4.44   Under section 79 of the GLA Act, a London local authority may promote a Bill which contains provisions affecting the exercise of functions by the Authority or a functional body but only where the Authority gives its consent and then confirms that consent as soon as practicable after 14 days from the date on which the Bill has been deposited. If the Authority does not give its consent, then it must give notice to the London local authority. The London local authority is required "to take all necessary steps to omit the provisions". This function is exercisable by the Mayor after consulting the Assembly.

PART B

FINANCIAL PROVISIONS

INTRODUCTION

The financial provisions in respect of the GLA seek to treat it like other authorities, but take account of the fact its structure is completely different. Thus, the provisions are largely enacted by way of amendments to the existing financial regime in the Local Government Finance Acts 1988 and 1992 and the Local Government and Housing Act 1989, but there are specific provisions to take account of the different roles of the Mayor and the Assembly and the position of the four functional bodies, Transport for London, the London Development Agency, the Metropolitan Police Authority and the London Fire and Emergency Planning Authority.

There are provisions relating to the revenue finance of the GLA, which includes the setting of a budget requirement for the Authority and the functional bodies, capital finance involving capital spending plans and the award and distribution of credit approvals from the Secretary of State, and financial administration.

The General Decision-making Structure

The Mayor, as the executive, takes the principal role in authority-wide financial decisions. He decides the budget requirement, formulates the capital spending plan, allocates credit approvals and decides what action should be taken in respect of reports by the chief finance officer of the Authority or the auditor.

All functions conferred or imposed on the GLA under or by virtue of Part III of the Act are exercisable by the Mayor acting on behalf of the GLA unless the function has been expressly conferred or imposed on the Assembly: section 140.

The Assembly has very little power in relation to financial decisions (except that it can set a budget requirement if the Mayor fails to do so). Rather, its role is to scrutinise the decision of the Mayor. During the debates on the Bill, the government expressed the position as follows:

"The mayor will be the motivating power and the assembly will have the right of scrutiny." (Glenda Jackson, Minister for Transport in London, *Official Report, Standing Committee A*, February 11, 1999, col. 521).

"The entire procedure is based on a different model — one that gives the assembly a strong role in scrutiny, and executive powers to the Mayor. Those powers are not dictatorial but are part of a new structure in a new system." Baroness Farrington of Ribbleton, *Hansard*, H.C. Vol. 603, No. 107, col. 54.

While the Mayor decides strategic priorities in terms of funding, the functional bodies must put these into practice. They must manage their financial affairs independently, but within constraints: the Mayor decides the amount of revenue and capital funds they will have available and the Secretary of State may give the Mayor power to require them to give away some of those resources to another body. Responsibility for their financial affairs remains however with the functional bodies. It is for this reason that there is no provision for an authority-wide financial administration. Rather, the Mayor has a right to information in relation to the financial administration of the functional bodies, but has no right to interfere in it.

Chapter 5

REVENUE FINANCE

Overview

The GLA will have three major sources of revenue: council tax, grant paid **5.01** by the Secretary of State, and redistributed non-domestic rates.

Council Tax: Chapter I of Part III

The GLA is a major precepting authority, which means that it raises **5.02** money indirectly by issuing a precept to the London boroughs in respect of the amount the GLA sets as its council tax. The boroughs are obliged to collect the tax and pass it to the GLA.

There is detailed provision for the procedures to be followed in setting the council tax for the GLA. The principal feature is the setting of the budget requirement for the GLA and each of the functional bodies, which forms the basis of the calculation of the basic amount of council tax. This is the responsibility of the Mayor. The Assembly has two roles: the first is to scrutinise the budget requirement (but not to amend it without a two-thirds majority), and the second is to set the budget requirement if the Mayor fails to do so in time.

The budget requirement set by the Mayor can be "capped" by the Secretary of State under Part IVA of Local Government Finance Act 1992 (the "1992 Act").

Grants: Chapter II of Part III

The grant from the Secretary of State will include a revenue support grant, **5.03** any additional grant awarded under section 85 of the Local Government Finance Act 1988 (the "1988 Act"), a special grant, a general GLA grant, a GLA transport grant paid for the purposes of Transport for London, and a police grant.

Non-domestic Rates: Chapter II of Part III

Non-domestic rates are currently distributed amongst local authorities in **5.04** proportion to their population and are shared between authorities according to the services which they provide. The inclusion of the GLA as a further tier of London government will reduce the amount of non-domestic rates available for distribution to the boroughs. The Government has said, however, that London boroughs will receive further revenue support grants to compensate for such losses.

Council Tax

5.05 Council tax is the domestic charge introduced by the Local Government Finance Act 1992 (the "1992 Act"), with effect from the financial year 1993–94.

Authorities setting and charging council tax in respect of dwellings in their areas are "billing authorities". In London, the billing authorities are the London borough councils and the Common Council of the City of London (1992 Act, s.1(2)).

Billing authorities are subject to "precepts" levied by other authorities and bodies. An authority or body may only issue a precept to those billing authorities that are partly or wholly within their own area (1992 Act, s.39(4)). There are two classes of precepting authority, "major precepting authorities" and "local precepting authorities".

Amount of Council Tax

5.06 Council tax is payable in respect of dwellings (1992 Act, ss.1–3). Dwellings are categorised according to the area of the billing authority and whether there are any special, additional calculations to be carried out: in respect of the GLA, such calculations are made under section 89 of the GLA Act, see below. Dwellings are also "banded" into eight bands—A (lowest) to H (highest)—according to their value on April 1, 1991.

The formula in section 47 of the 1992 Act for calculating the council tax for dwellings in each of the bands is modified in respect of the GLA so that it refers to the GLA provisions (GLA Act ss.88 and 89) and so is different from those applicable to other authorities (1992 Act, ss.44 and 45).

The amount of council tax to be set (1992 Act, section 30(1)) is generally determined by aggregating:

- the amounts most recently set for council tax by the billing authority under the 1992 Act, sections 32–36;
- the amounts calculated by major precepting authorities under sections 43 to 47 of the 1992 Act, and the amounts of precepts most recently issued to the billing authority under the section 40 of the 1992 Act (1992 Act, s.30(2)).

However, in London this regime is modified because of the establishment of the GLA.

Council Tax in Greater London

The principal feature of the council tax regime for the GLA is the **5.07** predominant role of the Mayor. He will set the budget requirement for the GLA and each of the functional bodies. Those budget requirements will form the basis of the calculation of the basic amount of council tax.

The Assembly has two functions in relation to council tax. First, it will scrutinise the budget requirement, although it cannot amend this without a two-thirds majority. Second, in the unlikely event that the Mayor fails to set the budget requirement in time, it will undertake this task.

The GLA as a Major Precepting Authority

The GLA is a major precepting authority (GLA Act, s.82, amending the **5.08** 1992 Act, s.39).

Because of the new role of the GLA, the London Fire and Civil Defence Authority and the Receiver for the Metropolitan Police District are deleted from the list of major precepting authorities (GLA Act, s.82).

A "major precepting authority" (in other words one listed as such in section 39(1) 1992 Act) raises council tax indirectly. As a major precepting authority, the GLA cannot raise its council tax directly from individual council tax payers. Instead, it sets an amount called a "precept" as its council tax. Each London billing authority must then include the precept when they calculate their own council tax bills (GLA Act, s.81). The London boroughs then collect the precept from the council tax payers in their areas and pass it on to the GLA.

As a major precepting authority, the GLA is subject to the provisions of Chapter IV (sections 39 to 52) of the 1992 Act, except where provided otherwise. Those provisions deal with the mechanism for calculating and receiving precepts.

The First GLA Precept: The Financial Year 2000–2001

The GLA will be in existence for only the second part of the financial year **5.09** ending on March 31, 2001. It was therefore necessary for transitional provisions to provide for the first precept to be set by a body other than the Mayor and Assembly. The Secretary of State has undertaken this task in accordance with the transitional provisions set out in The Greater London Authority Act (Commencement No. 3 and Transitional Finance Provisions) Order 1999 (S.I. 1999 No. 3434) and The Greater London Authority Act (Transitional and Consequential Finance Provisions) Order 1999 (S.I. 1999 No. 3435).

Procedure for Issuing a Precept

5.10 The procedure for issuing a precept is set out below. See paragraphs 5.24 *et seq.* below for the way in which the GLA's council tax, and on which the precept is based, should be calculated.

The GLA is required to issue a precept to each billing authority in its area for each financial year, in accordance with the provisions of section 40 of the 1992 Act, as amended by section 83 of the GLA Act. These provisions are outlined below.

A financial year is "a period of twelve months ending with March 31 (GLA Act, s.424(1)) or "any period of twelve months beginning with April 1 (1992 Act, s.116).

Dwellings are categorised according not only to the area of the billing authority but also according to whether there are any special, additional calculations to be carried out in relation to the Metropolitan Police Authority (as to which, see below): section 30(1) to (4) and section 47 of the 1992 Act and sections 85 to 90 of the GLA Act and, for substitute calculations, sections 85, 86 and 88 to 90 and Schedule 7 of the GLA Act.

The precept must state (a) the amount of council tax which the GLA has calculated in respect of each category of dwellings, and (b) the amount it has calculated to be payable by the billing authority for the year (1992 Act, s.40(2)).

The precept cannot be issued until the "prescribed time" has elapsed in relation to the assessment of "council tax base", or the billing authority has actually notified the precepting authority of its calculations in that respect (1992 Act, s.40(6)).

5.11 The "prescribed time" for any given financial year is December 1 to January 31 (1992 Act, s.40(6) as amended and the Local Authorities (Calculation of Council Tax Base) Regulations 1992 (S.I. 1992 No. 612)). That period is the time allowed to the billing authority to notify its calculation to the major precepting authorities.

The "council tax base" is determined in accordance with the Local Authorities (Calculation of Council Tax Base) Regulations 1992 (S.I. 1992 No. 612). Broadly, it is a local authority's assessment of the full amount of council tax that could be recovered for their area.

Although a precept for any given financial year should be issued by March 1 in the preceding financial year, it is not invalid if it is issued after that date (1992 Act, s.40(5)).

The GLA must make its calculations under the modified provisions applicable, which are referred to as the appropriate Greater London provisions (GLA Act, s.81(10)). These are: sections 85 to 90 of the GLA Act and section 47 of the 1992 Act. In respect of substitute calculations (those made after initial calculations, and either made voluntarily or in pursuance of a direction of the Secretary of State), the relevant provisions are sections 85, 86 and 88 to 90 and Schedule 7 of the GLA Act and section 47 of the 1992 Act. These replace those that apply to other authorities and that are found sections 43 to 47 of the 1992 Act.

The Cost of the GLA Precept

The budget requirement set by the Mayor will be subject to the "capping" **5.12** provisions in Part IVA of the 1992 Act, inserted by the Local Government Act 1999. The Secretary of State can limit the budget if it is set too high.

In addition, the GLA, in so far as it exercises its functions through the Mayor (and otherwise by order of the Secretary of State), is a best value authority under the Local Government Act 1999.

During debates in committee, the Minister for London and Construction, Nick Raynsford, gave the assurance that the costs of the Mayor and Assembly would add about 3p per week to the council tax bill of a band D tax payer: *Official Report, Standing Committee A* (February 9, 1999, col. 388). An opposition amendment to put this into the Bill was defeated.

The cost of the GLA as discussed in Parliament is a factor that the Secretary of State could take into account in deciding whether or not to use his capping powers.

Component and Consolidated Budget Requirements

The Authority must calculate its own budget requirement and that of the **5.13** four functional bodies, Transport for London, the London Development Agency, the Metropolitan Police Authority and the London Fire and Emergency Planning Authority—the component budget requirements (GLA Act, s.85). It must then add the five budgets of these "constituent bodies" (GLA Act, s.85(3)) together to obtain the consolidated budget requirement. These calculations must be made for each financial year.

The budget requirement for each body is calculated by determining the difference between projected expenditure and projected income. Insofar as expenditure will exceed income, that amount is the body's component budget requirement for the year (GLA Act, s.85(6)). The budget requirement cannot be negative. If income will exceed expenditure, the budget requirement is nil (GLA Act, section 85(7)). The body can retain any surplus, subject to the GLA's power to redistribute funds between constituent bodies (sections 120 and 121—see below). These calculations are similar to those made by local authorities in calculating their own budget requirements.

The projected expenditure is the aggregate (section 85(4)) of: **5.14**

(a) expenditure the Authority estimates will be incurred by the body in performing its functions and that will be charged to a revenue account for the year, other than expenditure estimated to be incurred in pursuance of regulations made under section 99(3) of the 1988 Act (these relate to payments made — and received — by precepting authorities in respect of deficits — and surpluses — in a billing authority's council tax in a previous financial year, for which, see below);

(b) the Authority's estimate of the appropriate allowance for contingencies to be charged to the revenue account for the year;

(c) the Authority's estimate of the appropriate amount for the body to raise as financial reserves to meet estimated future expenditure (for which, see further below); and

(d) a sufficient amount of the body's financial reserves to meet an amount estimated by the Authority to be a revenue account deficit of the body for any earlier financial year for which there is no existing provision.

5.15 By virtue of section 85(9) of the GLA Act, expenditure is construed in accordance with section 41(3) of the Local Government and Housing Act 1989, which provides that:

"[E]xpenditure incurred by a local authority in any financial year includes the following (whether or not giving rise to actual payments)—

(a) any amount which does not form part of the authority's capital receipts and which is set aside for the year by the authority as provision to meet credit liabilities, otherwise than by virtue of subsections (2) to (4) of section 63 below [certain sums received from the Secretary of State or a Minister of the Crown as commuted payments and certain grants received from Community institutions — other than from any of the Structural Funds — towards the authority's expenditure on capital purposes]; and

(b) any other amount which is set aside for the year by the authority as reasonably necessary for the purpose of providing for any liability or loss which is likely or certain to be incurred but is uncertain as to the amount or the date on which it will arise (or both)."

5.16 The projected income for each year is the aggregate (section 85(5)) of:

(a) sums the Authority estimates will be payable to the body and will be credited to the revenue account, other than (i) certain sums from central government, namely amounts estimated as payable in respect of redistributed non-domestic rates, revenue support grant, relevant special grant, police or general GLA grant, (ii) sums in respect of precept issued by the Authority or (iii) sums relating to deficit or surplus in its collection fund for the year payable in pursuance of regulations made under section 99(3) of the 1988 Act (these relate to payments made — and received — by precepting authorities in respect of deficits — and surpluses — in a billing authority's council tax in a previous financial year, for which, see below); and

(b) the body's financial reserves that the Authority estimates will be used to meet estimated expenditure and contingencies during the year under section 85(4)(a) or (b).

In calculating a body's income or expenditure, the Authority must follow **5.17** the rules set out in section 86:

   (a) Any amount that has been included in the budget requirement of one constituent body should not be included in that of another.

   (b) In estimating the expenditure of the Metropolitan Police Authority, the Authority should take into account any levy actually issued by the National Criminal Intelligence Service and the National Crime Squad.

   (c) In relation to any other constituent body, the Authority should take into account any levy actually issued.

   (d) The Authority should not anticipate a levy unless regulations made under section 74 of the 1988 Act or an order under sections 17 or 62 of the Police Act 1997 allow it to do so.

   (e) A body's "estimated future expenditure" for the purposes of section 85(4)(c) is defined in section 86(4) as

      (i) the GLA's estimate of the expenditure the body will incur in the financial year following the year in question, will charge to a revenue account for the year and will have to defray in the year before the following sums are sufficiently available, namely sums:

         (a) which will be payable to it for the year, and

         (b) in respect of which amounts will be credited to a revenue account; and

      (ii) the GLA's estimate of the expenditure the body will incur in the financial year following the year in question, or any subsequent financial year, in performing its functions and that will be charged to a revenue account for that or any other year.

   (f) The Secretary of State has power to alter the constituents of the calculations for estimated future expenditure or projected income or amend the rules governing the making of those calculations, in the same way that he may amend the equivalent rules for local authorities generally (section 86(5)).

The Authority must calculate the consolidated budget requirement, which **5.18** is the aggregate of the component budget requirements for each constituent body (section 85(8)—for an explanation of the component budget requirement of a constituent body, see above, at paragraphs 5.13 *et seq.*).

It is noteworthy that, in respect of all the calculations, it is the Authority that must estimate the sums to be required and not the functional bodies. Accordingly, the functional bodies must provide the Authority with information at the request of the Mayor and the Assembly (section 110—see paragraph 6.43 below). The Mayor must also consult the functional bodies before preparing their draft component budget requirements: section 87 and Schedule 6, see below.

Procedure for Determining the Budget Requirements

5.19 The procedure to be followed in determining the component and consolidated budget requirements under section 85 is determined by Schedule 6.

The normal rule of local government law that an authority may
discharge its functions through a committee, sub-committee or officer of
the authority (Local Government Act 1972, s.101) is modified in respect of
this important function. Save where Schedule 6 expressly provides, only the
Authority can set the GLA's budget requirement, *i.e.* it can only be set by
the Mayor, the Assembly or the Mayor and Assembly acting jointly (section
108, amending Local Government Finance Act 1992, s.67).

The determination of the component and consolidated budget requirements is expected to take place between December (when central government's provisional financial settlement is published) and the end of
February (when the budget will be finalised (GLA Act, Sched.6, para.8)).
The Mayor, as the executive, makes representations to ministers in
relation to the financial settlement. It is open to the members of the
Assembly to accompany him or even, at the Secretary of State's discretion,
to make representations themselves.

5.20 The Mayor, after consulting the Assembly and the functional bodies,
must prepare a draft component budget for each of the constituent bodies,
i.e. the GLA and the functional bodies (Schedule 6, paragraph 2). After
consulting the Assembly, or any committee or other representative specified in a resolution of the Assembly, he must also prepare a draft
consolidated budget (Schedule 6, paragraph 3). This is the only provision in
Schedule 6 that permits a function to be delegated.

It is envisaged that the Mayor will consult other bodies (such as
representatives of the business community or of different ethnic groups)
before setting the draft budgets. The government resisted an opposition
amendment to require him to do so. In the House of Lords, the Government Whip, Baroness Farrington of Ribbleton, confirmed that the Assembly would also be entitled to test public opinion about the draft budgets
(*Hansard*, H.L. Vol. 603, col. 52).

The draft consolidated budget must be presented to the Assembly at a
public meeting on or before February 1 in the financial year preceding that
to which it relates. This is expected to coincide with the publication of the
final local government financial settlement; the Secretary of State has
power to change this date by Order (Schedule 6, paragraph 10) to
accommodate any delay to the settlement. If the Mayor fails to comply with
these requirements, the Assembly must prepare draft component and
consolidated budgets. If approved, the draft consolidated budget will be the
Authority's consolidated budget for the year in question (Schedule 6,
paragraph 4).

5.21 After the Mayor presents the draft consolidated budget to the Assembly,
the Assembly must approve it, with or without amendment. After approval
of the budget (or after such period as the Mayor considers reasonable
having elapsed without approval), the Mayor must prepare a final draft of
the consolidated budget to be laid before the Assembly. This can be the

draft budget as amended by the Assembly, the draft budget as amended by the Mayor, or the unamended draft budget. In the latter two cases, the Mayor must lay before the Assembly a written statement of his reasons for rejecting any amendments made by the Assembly (Schedule 6, paragraph 6). The Assembly must approve the budget with or without amendment by the end of February. The approved budget is the consolidated budget for the financial year. Any amendments by the Assembly require a two-thirds majority of the members voting (Schedule 6, paragraph 8). The Government resisted a proposed opposition amendment to require only a simple majority of the Assembly to amend the budget on the basis that this would be out of line with the respective roles of the Mayor and Assembly. Baroness Farrington of Ribbleton said:

". . . It is important that there should be a separation of powers between an executive mayor and an assembly. It is entirely right that an executive mayor should be in the lead in deciding the GLA's budget. There needs to be a means of setting the budget in the extremely unlikely event of the mayor failing to set one. Schedule 5 [of the Bill, now Schedule 6] accommodates such factors . . . [I]t is difficult, but not impossible, to get a two-thirds majority." *Hansard* H.L. Vol. 603, col. 56.

If the Assembly fails to approve the budget by the end of February, the **5.22** final draft budget will be the Authority's consolidated budget for the year (Schedule 6, paragraph 9).

If the Mayor, having presented a draft budget, fails to present a final draft budget, the Assembly must meet and agree by simple majority the component budget requirement of each of the constituent bodies; the consolidated budget is deemed to have been agreed accordingly (Schedule 6, paragraph 7).

The Mayor is required to publish the consolidated and component budgets as soon as practicable after they have been set. They must be kept available for inspection free of charge by the public at the principal offices of the GLA for six years after publication (Schedule 6, paragraph 11). Any person may obtain a copy of the document, on payment of a reasonable fee determined by the Mayor (Schedule 6, paragraph 11). These requirements do not apply where the Assembly has set the budget following the Mayor's failure to set either a first or final draft budget (Schedule 6, paragraphs 4(2)(b) and 7(5)). Publication in that case is governed by section 58 of the GLA Act, which subjects the Assembly to the rules, with some modifications, which apply to local authorities generally, requiring them, amongst other things, to make documents publicly available.

Challenge to a Calculation Relating to the Budget Requirements

The GLA's calculation of its budget requirements may not be questioned **5.23** except by way of judicial review (GLA Act, s.107 amending the Local Government Finance Act 1992, s.66). This restriction only applies if the GLA's calculation was made in accordance with sections 85 to 90 of (or, in relation to substitute calculations, for which see below, sections 85, 86 and 88 to 90 of and Schedule 7 to) the GLA Act. This prevents such matters being raised by way of collateral challenge, for example in proceedings to recover arrears of council tax.

Calculation of the Basic Amount of Council Tax

5.24 Although the method of calculating the GLA's council tax is broadly similar to that for other precepting authorities, the method of calculating council tax of precepting authorities set out in sections 44 and 45 of the Local Government Finance Act 1992 does not apply to the GLA. Instead, the GLA's basic amount of council tax is calculated in accordance with sections 88 and 89 of the GLA Act.

The difference between the two methods of calculation is that, for the GLA, the budget requirement in respect of the Metropolitan Police Authority (or "special item") is treated separately from other grants. This is necessary because the GLA is responsible for the police service in the inner and outer London boroughs, but not in the City of London (section 323, see below). Council tax payers in the City of London pay directly for their own policing and should not, therefore, have to pay for policing in the remainder of London: neither, however, should their council tax take into account grants from central government to the GLA in respect of the police services in the rest of London. Accordingly, council tax payers in the City of London will only pay the GLA the amount for non-police services; council tax payers in the inner and outer London boroughs will pay both the police and non-police amounts.

The normal rule of local government law that an authority may discharge its functions through a committee, sub-committee or officer of the authority (Local Government Act 1972, s.101) is modified in respect of the important function of calculating the basic amount of council tax (section 108), amending section 67 of the Local Government Finance Act 1992. There is no provision for this function to be delegated.

5.25 The basic amount of council tax is calculated in accordance with the following formula (GLA Act, s.88):

$$\frac{R-P1-A}{T}$$

Where:

R is the consolidated budget requirement for the year;

P1 is the aggregate of prescribed (for the meaning of which, see below) amounts, which represent the Secretary of State's estimate of the amounts from central government funds which will be payable to the GLA in respect of the following items (but *excluding* the Secretary of State's estimate of the proportion of each item that is paid in respect of the Metropolitan Police):

  (a) redistributed non-domestic rates,
  (b) revenue support grant,
  (c) general GLA grant,
  (d) additional grant,
  (e) relevant special grant;

A is the budget requirement of the Metropolitan Police;
T is the aggregate of the council tax bases of the billing authorities to which the Authority issues precepts. The "council tax base" of a billing authority is determined in accordance with the Local Authorities (Calculation of Council Tax Base) Regulations 1992 (S.I. 1992 No. 612). Broadly, it is a local authority's assessment of the full amount of council tax that could be recovered for their area.

The amount of P1 is prescribed in either: **5.26**

  (a) regulations made by the Secretary of State,
  (b) the local government finance report for the financial year in question in relation to redistributed non-domestic rates or revenue support grant,
  (c) in relation to general GLA grant, the determination under section 100 of the GLA Act for the financial year in question,
  (d) in relation to additional grant, the report under section 85 of the Local Government Finance Act 1988 relating to that item,
  (e) in relation to relevant special grant, the report under section 88B of the Local Government Finance Act 1988 relating to that item.

The amount of P1 is increased by any sums which the GLA estimates will be paid to it by billing authorities in accordance with regulations under section 99(3) of the Local Government Finance Act 1988, and reduced by any sums the GLA estimates it will pay to billing authorities under such regulations (these relate to payments made — and received — by precepting authorities in respect of deficits — and surpluses — in a billing authority's council tax in a previous financial year, for which, see below).

Billing authorities must make the calculation required by item T in **5.27** accordance with rules set out in regulations made by the Secretary of State (section 88(6)). The Secretary of State may also make regulations to ensure T can be determined if a billing authority fails to notify its calculation to the precepting authority within a prescribed time, and for the formula and its constituent parts to be adjusted (section 88(7) and (8)).

The basic amount of council tax cannot be negative: if the formula produces a negative number, the council tax is nil (section 88(9)).

The calculation of the basic amount of council tax is subject to any additional amount in respect of the "special item" (which is calculated to take account of the special expense of the Metropolitan Police Authority)— see below.

Challenge to a Calculation Relating to the Basic Amount

5.28 As is the case with other calculations relating to council tax, a calculation relating to the basic amount that is made in accordance with sections 85, 86 and 88 to 90 may not be questioned except by way of judicial review (GLA Act, s.107 amending the Local Government Finance Act 1992, s.66). This restriction only applies if the GLA's calculation was made in accordance with sections 85 to 90 of (or, in relation to substitute calculations, for which see below, sections 85, 86 and 88 to 90 of and Schedule 7 to) the GLA Act. This prevents such matters being raised by way of collateral challenge, for example in proceedings to recover arrears of council tax.

Additional Calculation: the Special Item and the Special Expense of the Metropolitan Police Authority

5.29 Additional calculations have to be carried out where there are "special items" applicable to part only of an authority's area, requiring recalculation so as to reduce the basic council tax payable by those who are not, and increase the basic council tax payable by those who are, tax payers in relation to the relevant area.

In respect of the GLA, the budget requirement of the Metropolitan Police Authority is referred to as the "special item" (GLA Act, s.90). The principle is that only those areas within the metropolitan police district should pay for the Metropolitan Police Authority. Accordingly, the basic amount of council tax in those areas calculated under section 88 of the GLA Act is increased by an amount representing the cost of that body.
The additional cost is calculated in accordance with the following formula:

$$\frac{S2 - P2}{TP2}$$

Where:

S2 is the special item;

P2 is an aggregate of the same items as P1, except that police grant is now included, but this time including *only* funds paid for the Metropolitan Police;

TP2 is the aggregate of the amounts which are calculated by the billing authorities to which the GLA has power to issue precepts as respects the special item ("the billing authorities concerned") as their council tax bases for the year for their areas and are notified by them to the GLA within the period prescribed by the Secretary of State or by regulations made by him.

5.30 The amount of the items that comprise P2 may be prescribed in the same way as P1, except that additionally in respect of the police grant, it may be prescribed by the police grant report under section 46(3) of the Police Act 1996 for the financial year in question.

Any regulations made in respect of the calculation of T in section 88 of the GLA Act will apply equally to the calculation of TP2. The Secretary of State may also by regulations alter the formula and its constituent parts (GLA Act, s.89(8)).

The special item cannot be negative: if the formula produces a negative number, it is assumed to be nil (GLA Act, s.89(8)).

Deletion of Certain Other Special Items

5.31 Section 46 of the Local Government Finance Act 1992 is amended to remove references to police services, probation and magistrates' court services in London as special items.

Challenge to a Calculation Relating to a Special Item

5.32 As with the GLA's calculations of budget requirements and basic amount, the GLA's calculation of the special item may not be challenged except by way of judicial review (GLA Act, s.107), amending the section 66 of the Local Government Finance Act 1992. Again, this restriction only applies if the GLA's calculation was made in accordance with sections 85 to 90 of (or, in relation to substitute calculations, for which see below, sections 85, 86 and 88 to 90 of and Schedule 7 to) the GLA Act. This prevents such matters being raised by way of collateral challenge, for example in proceedings to recover arrears of council tax.

Calculation of Amount Payable by Each Billing Authority

5.33 The amount that each billing authority must pay to the GLA is calculated in accordance with section 48 of the 1992 Act, as amended by section 93 of the GLA Act. Each billing authority must pay the basic amount of council tax (C), as calculated above, multiplied by the authority's tax base (T), calculated under section 33 of the 1992 Act.

Substitute Precept

5.34 A substitute precept is a precept issued by a local authority to give effect to substitute calculations of budget requirements and/or basic amounts of council tax carried out by the authority in respect of a particular financial year. For substitute calculations, see below.

Section 84 of the GLA Act amends section 42 of the 1992 Act, so that the GLA will be required to follow the procedure set out in that section when it issues a substituted precept.

Substitute Calculations

5.35 A precepting authority may make a substitute calculation of the constituent amounts voluntarily under sections 49 and 51 of the 1992 Act, or may be compelled to do so as a result of designation ("capping") under Part IVA of the 1992 Act, or following a direction from the Secretary of State to increase the Metropolitan Police Authority's budget under section 95 (see below).

Subject to the restrictions described below, substitute calculations may be carried out at any time and without limit of number.

Substitute calculations may not increase the budget requirement or result in a higher basic amount of council tax than under the original calculations unless the original calculations have been quashed for failure to comply with the statutory requirements (s.94(6)) or the Secretary of State has directed an increase in the budget requirement of the Metropolitan Police Authority under section 95 (see below).

Substitute calculations are accordingly available in most cases only if another element of the equation changes. They will usually be made where a new administration reduces the expenditure element of the equation.

When making substitute calculations, the GLA must use the same amounts determined by P1, T, P2 or TP2 in the original calculation, except that P1 and P2 may be increased by the relevant proportion of any additional grant awarded under section 85 (see below).

If the GLA purports to make substitute calculations which do not comply with these conditions, the calculations have no effect.

Challenge to a Substitute Calculation

5.36 A substitute calculation that is made in accordance with sections 85, 86 and 88 to 90 may not be questioned except by way of judicial review (section 107, amending the Local Government Finance Act 1992, s.66). This restriction on the method of challenge also applies to the GLA's calculation of budget requirements, basic amount and special item (for all of which, see above). This prevents such matters being raised by way of collateral challenge, for example in proceedings to recover arrears of council tax.

Minimum Budget for the Metropolitan Police Authority

5.37 If it appears to the Secretary of State that the budget set by the GLA for the Metropolitan Police Authority is too low to restore or maintain an efficient and effective police force for its area, he may direct the GLA to increase the component budget requirement to a level not less than an amount specified by him in the direction (section 95). The amount the Secretary of State directs must be the minimum he considers necessary to restore or maintain an efficient and effective police force for the Metropolitan Police Authority's area. The Secretary of State's direction must be in writing, and may be varied or revoked by him (section 421).

After the Secretary of State has made such a direction, the GLA must make substitute calculations of the budget requirement for either the

Metropolitan Police Authority alone or the Metropolitan Police Authority and any one or more of the other constituent bodies (section 95(4)). If these calculations lead to an increase in the consolidated budget requirement for the year or result in a different basic amount of council tax, the GLA must make substitute calculations in accordance with sections 85, 86 and 88 to 90 (see above) and Schedule 7 (see below).

In making the substitute calculations, the GLA must comply with the **5.38** Secretary of State's direction and may not increase its consolidated budget requirement by more than the amount by which the new budget requirement for the Metropolitan Police Authority exceeds its original budget requirement (section 95(7)). In addition, the GLA must use the same values for P1, P2, T and TP2 as in the previous calculations, except that the amounts of P1 and P2 may be increased by the relevant proportion of any additional grant awarded under section 85 of the Local Government Finance Act 1988. Thus, the portion of additional grant relating to the budget requirement of the Metropolitan Police Authority (the "special item") is to be attributed (as prescribed by the Secretary of State) to P2 and the remainder to P1.

Period of Restriction

Where a direction has been given to the GLA to increase the Metropolitan **5.39** Police Authority budget, the GLA has 35 days from receipt of the direction to make its substitute calculations. If the GLA fails to do so within this time, the authorities to which it has power to issue a precept (*i.e.* the London borough councils and the Common Council of the City of London, even though the latter does not contribute to the special item) lose the power to pay the GLA anything in respect of any precept issued in that year until it complies. In effect, therefore, the GLA's income is cut off until it makes substitute calculations.

This is similar to the period of restriction that is imposed under sections 52K or 52V of the Local Government Finance Act 1992 where substitute calculations are required pursuant to the Secretary of State's capping powers.

Procedure for making substitute calculations

The calculations must be made in accordance with the procedure set out in **5.40** Schedule 7.

The Mayor, after consulting the Assembly and the functional bodies affected, must prepare draft proposals for the substitute calculations, which he must lay before the Assembly (Schedule 7, paragraph 2).

If the Mayor fails to comply with these requirements before the beginning of any period of restriction (for which, see above), the Assembly must prepare their own draft proposals. If approved by the Assembly, these are the Authority's substitute calculations for the year in question (Schedule 7, paragraph 3).

Where the Mayor presents the draft proposals to the Assembly, the Assembly must approve them, with or without amendment.

After approval of the proposals (or after such period as the Mayor considers reasonable having elapsed without approval), the Mayor must prepare a final draft of the proposals to be laid before the Assembly. This can be the original draft proposals as amended by the Assembly, the draft proposals as amended by the Mayor, or the unamended draft proposals. In the latter two cases the Mayor must lay before the Assembly a written statement of his reasons for rejecting any amendments made by the Assembly (Schedule 7, paragraph 5).

5.41   The Assembly must approve the final draft with or without amendment (which requires a two-thirds majority of the members voting) within 21 days of the day on which the Mayor presented the final draft. The approved proposals are the Authority's substitute calculations (Schedule 7, paragraph 7). If the Assembly fails to approve the proposals within 21 days, the final draft proposals will be the GLA's substitute calculations for the financial year (Schedule 7, paragraph 8).

If the Mayor, having presented draft proposals, fails to present a final draft of the proposals, the Assembly must meet and agree the substitute calculations, which are deemed to be agreed accordingly (Schedule 7, paragraph 6).

Where substitute calculations are made, the Mayor must publish them in a document to be kept available for inspection by the public free of charge at the offices of the GLA for six years. Any person may obtain a copy of the document, on payment of a reasonable fee determined by the Mayor (Schedule 7, paragraph 9). These requirements do not apply not apply where the Assembly has set the substitute calculations, following the Mayor's failure to prepare first or final draft proposals (Schedule 7, paragraphs 3(3)(b) and 6(4)). Publication in that case is governed by section 58 of the GLA Act, which subjects the Assembly to the rules, with some modifications, which apply to local authorities generally requiring them, amongst other things, to make documents publicly available. (See above.)

Financial Information

Information to be Provided to the Secretary of State

5.42   Each functional body must make a return to the Secretary of State, for the year ending on March 31, of its income and expenditure. The Secretary of State may give binding directions as to the form of the returns, the particulars they must contain, the date for their submission and the way in which they must be certified: section 109 of the GLA Act, modifying section 168 of the Local Government Act 1972.

Where the Secretary of State serves a notice on a functional body or a relevant officer (*i.e* a "proper officer" within the meaning of the Local Government Act 1972) requiring it or him to supply specified information which is required by the Secretary of State for the purposes of deciding whether to exercise his powers or how to perform his functions under the Local Government Finance Act 1988, and the information is not personal information, the functional body or officer must provide the information in such form and manner as specified by the Secretary of State (GLA Act, s.109), modifying section 139A of the Local Government Finance Act 1988. Information is defined in section 146(5A) of the 1988 Act to include accounts, estimates and returns, but is probably not restricted to such.

The same duties are imposed on a functional body and relevant officers in respect of requests by the Secretary of State for information in relation to his functions under the Local Government Finance Act 1992 (GLA Act, s.109), modifying section 68 of the Local Government Finance Act 1992.

Information to be Provided to the GLA, Assembly and Mayor

The functional bodies must, at the request of the Mayor or the Assembly, **5.43** provide such information relating to the financial affairs of the body as is required by the GLA for the purpose of any functions of the Mayor or Assembly (GLA Act, s.110). The information must be provided in the form and manner, and within such time, as is specified in the request. Information is defined in section 110(4) to include information which the body has or can reasonably obtain, and information about the body's plans or proposals relating to the finances or expenditure of the body or of any company in which the body has an interest. This, however, is probably not an exhaustive definition.

The Assembly also has power to require attendance at its meetings and the production of documents (GLA Act, s.61—see above).

The Mayor has power to require a functional body or the London Pensions Fund Authority (which was established under the London Government Reorganisation (Pensions, etc.) Order 1989 (S.I. 1989 No. 1815)) to provide information relating to its accounts to the GLA for the purpose of preparing the summary statement of accounts (GLA Act, s.135—see below).

Grants

General GLA Grant

The Secretary of State must pay a general GLA grant to the GLA for each **5.44** financial year (GLA Act, s.100). This grant is paid for the purposes of the GLA itself and the four functional bodies, Transport for London, the London Development Agency, the Metropolitan Police Authority and the London Fire and Emergency Planning Authority.

The Secretary of State must determine, having consulted the Mayor and with the consent of the Treasury, the amount of the grant, the timing of payment, and whether or not the grant is to be paid in instalments. The Minister for Transport in London, Glenda Jackson, indicated that this grant would be paid around the same time as that for other local authorities.

The Secretary of State is not required to reveal the costs assumptions on which the grant is based. In response to an opposition proposal that such a duty be included in the Act, the Minister for Transport in London, the Minister for Transport in London, Glenda Jackson, said,

"The Secretary of State will be obliged to consult the mayor before determining the amount of grant to pay to the GLA. I would expect the mayor's transport strategy for London to form the basis of the consultation on transport grant. I would be very surprised if the mayor did not make public the content of the consultations. I would also be surprised if London Members of Parliament did not table parliamentary questions asking about the basis for the determinations." (*Official Report, Standing Committee A*, February 9, 1999, col. 431).

GLA Transport Grant

5.45 The Secretary of State must pay a GLA transport grant to the GLA for each financial year (GLA Act, s.101). This grant is paid for the purposes of Transport for London. The Secretary of State must determine the same matters as to amount, instalments and timing as for the general GLA grant, and the same issues in relation to consultation of the Mayor and consent of the Treasury arise (see above).

After consulting the Mayor, the Secretary of State may vary the amount of the grant or any terms relating to its payment.

Revenue Support Grant

5.46 Revenue support grant is the principal means by which central government subsidises local government. As a major precepting authority, the GLA will be one of the "receiving authorities" for this grant (Local Government Finance Act 1988, s.76).

The revenue support grant process starts with a determination by the Secretary of State, following consultation with local authority representatives, and with the consent of the Treasury, stating the total amount of grant for the year, the amount proposed for receiving authorities and the amount proposed for specified bodies (1988 Act, s.78). This determination is to be specified in a local government finance report, which also includes the proposed distribution of non-domestic rate. The general nature of the basis of distribution must be notified to local government representatives before the report is made, and once it has been laid before the House of Commons, copies must be sent to each receiving authority.

Once the House of Commons has approved the report, the amount proposed must be paid to the receiving authorities and specified bodies. Payments are in such instalments, and at such times, as the Secretary of State determines (with Treasury consent) but payments to receiving authorities must be within the financial year concerned.

5.47 As soon as reasonably practicable after the House of Commons has approved the local government finance report for a financial year, the Secretary of State must calculate the amounts payable to each receiving authority in accordance with the basis of distribution in the report (1988 Act, s.88(1)). Unless the House of Commons has approved an amending report, the Secretary of State is entitled (at any time before the end of the financial year following that to which the calculation relates) to make one further calculation of this amount.

In making the calculation, the Secretary of State may leave out of account any information relevant to the calculation which is received by him after a specified date, provided he has notified the authorities in writing of the classes of information to be provided by them and the dates by which they must be received by him (1988 Act, s.82).

As soon as reasonably practicable after the calculation has been carried out, the Secretary of State notifies each authority of the amount he calculates is payable to them for the year, even if that amount is nil (1988 Act, s.82).

Amending report

The Secretary of State may put one amending report before the House of **5.48** Commons for approval (1988 Act, s.84A), before the financial year following that to which it applies, which alters the basis for distribution (following consultation with local authority representatives). The amending report must be copied to each receiving authority as soon as reasonably practicable after it has been laid before the House (1988 Act, s.84A). As soon as reasonably practicable following approval, the Secretary of State must recalculate each authority's entitlement, subject to the same requirements as apply to an initial calculation. The Secretary of State may make a single recalculation in the same circumstances as he may do so for an original report (see above).

Additional Grant

As an addition, or alternative, to an amending report (see above), the **5.49** Secretary of State may lay a further report before the House of Commons, where "the Secretary of State forms the view that fresh circumstances affecting the finances of local authorities have arisen since the approval" of the local government finance report (1988 Act, s.85(1)).

In such a case, the Secretary of State may make an additional amount of revenue support grant available (1988 Act, s.85(2)). Before doing so, he must make a determination as to both the amount and its basis of distribution, and obtain the consent of the Treasury (1988 Act, s.85(3)–(5)). As soon as reasonably practicable after the further report has been laid before the House of Commons, copies are to be sent to each of the receiving authorities (1988 Act, s.85(7)). Once approved, the Secretary of State must make payments according to its basis of distribution, which payments may be within or after the financial year concerned (section 85(6)).

An additional grant will affect the amount, and may affect the basis for distribution of, grant. The power to pay additional grant during a given financial year is a tool which central government may wish to use to increase, as a matter of policy, public spending in that year.

Relevant Special Grant

5.50 In addition to revenue support grant, the Secretary of State may, with the consent of the Treasury, pay a relevant special grant to major precepting authorities, which include the GLA. The first stage is for the Secretary of State to make a determination stating to which authority it is to be paid, for what purpose, and the amount (or method of calculation) (1988 Act, s.88B(2)). The determination requires the consent of the Treasury, and must be specified in a special grant report containing such explanation of its main features as the Secretary of State considers desirable. The special grant report must be laid before the House of Commons and, as soon as practicable thereafter, sent to the authority in question (1988 Act, s.88B(4)–(5)). The special grant can be paid only if the House of Commons has approved the report. The report may (with the consent of the Treasury) specify conditions, including conditions as to the provision of returns or other information, or relating to use of the money or its repayment in certain specified circumstances (1988 Act, s.88B(7)). The special grant is paid in instalments at such times as the Secretary of State may, with the consent of the Treasury, determine (section 88B(8)). These provisions are adapted to allow for the approval of more than one special grant at one time, for more than one authority (1988 Act, s.88B(3)).

5.51 A relevant special grant is defined (GLA Act, s.99 and the Local Government Finance Act 1992, s.32(12)) as either:

(a) the special grant payable in accordance with paragraphs 4 and 6 of the special grant report for England (Special Grant Report (No. 31)) approved by a resolution of the House of Commons pursuant to section 88B of the Local Government Finance Act 1992 on February 5, 1998, or

(b) the special grant payable in accordance with paragraphs 5 and 7 of that Report.

Redistributed Non-domestic Rates

5.52 The central government funds to be received by the GLA include sums in respect of redistributed non-domestic rates. Currently, non-domestic rates are distributed among local authorities, none being retained by central government. Accordingly, the creation of the GLA increases the number of bodies to which these sums are to be distributed. The Parliamentary Under-Secretary of State, Lord Whitty, confirmed during the passage of the Bill through the Lords that this will not have an effect on authorities outside London. Within London, there will be a corresponding reduction in the amount of non-domestic rates received by local authorities, but there will also be compensating changes in the revenue support grant received by those authorities (*Hansard,* H.L. Vol. 603, col. 568).

Collection and Distribution of Non-domestic Rates

The Local Government Finance Act 1988 replaced local powers relating to **5.53** taxation for the use of business and other non-domestic hereditaments with a central system, under the direct control of central government. Authorities no longer have powers to set and levy non-domestic rates and, in effect, operate as mere collection agents on behalf of central government. Each authority are allocated only part of the central pool of non-domestic rates which the government then takes into account as part of its overall determination of how much central funding each authority should have, and pay over any excess to central government (1988 Act, s.60).

The Secretary of State maintains a pool into which collected non-domestic rates and various other sums are paid and out of which receiving authorities will receive their share of the distributable amount. The GLA is included among the receiving authorities by virtue of being a major precepting authority (1988 Act, s.76(2)).

The annual local government finance report identifies the amount to be distributed and a basis for distribution, decided by the Secretary of State after consulting with local authority representatives (1988 Act, Sched. 8, para.10). The House of Commons must also approve the method of distribution (1988 Act, Sched. 8, para.11(1)).

As soon as reasonably practicable after the report has been approved, **5.54** the Secretary of State calculates the distribution of the non-domestic rating pool in accordance with the terms of the report. He may leave out of account any information relevant to the calculation which he receives from the authorities concerned after a specified date, provided that he has notified them of the classes of information which they must provide, and the date(s) by which they must provide such information (1988 Act, Sched. 8, para.11(3), (6) and (7)). As soon as reasonably practicable after the calculation has been carried out, the Secretary of State must notify each authority of its share of the distributable amount for the year.

The sums the GLA receives from the central pool will be credited to the general fund.

Subject to the possibility of making an amending report, the Secretary of State has power to make one further calculation of the distribution for each financial year. The receiving authority must be notified of the revised amount.

The Secretary of State also has power to put one amending report before **5.55** the House of Commons for approval, again before the financial year following that to which the report is applicable, which alters the basis of distribution (following consultation with the local authority representatives), and which must be copied to each receiving authority as soon as reasonably practicable after it has been laid before the House. Following approval, the Secretary of State must recalculate each authority's entitlement, subject to the same detailed provisions relevant to an initial calculation (1988 Act, Sched. 8, para.14(1)).

Provision is again made for a single subsequent recalculation, subject to the deadline formed by the end of the financial year following that to which the report relates, but capable of being extended to up to three months following approval by the House of Commons of the amending report. Thus, if the amending report is not laid or approved until late in the following year, the further recalculation may extend into the financial year following that, *i.e.* two years after that to which it relates.

Distribution of Grants, etc., to the Functional Bodies

5.56 The GLA must distribute to each of the functional bodies its share of certain sums received from central government, by way of council tax precepts or in accordance with regulations under section 99(3) of the Local Government Finance Act 1988 (these relate to payments made — and received — by precepting authorities in respect of deficits — and surpluses — in a billing authority's council tax in a previous financial year (for which, see below) (GLA Act, s.102). Those sums are:

(a) revenue support grant (1988 Act, ss.69(1) and 78(1)) (see above);

(b) additional grant (1988 Act, s.85—see above);

(c) relevant special grant (Local Government Finance Act 1992, s.32(12)—see above);

(d) general GLA grant (s.100—see above);

(e) redistributed non-domestic rates (1988 Act, s.69(1) and Sched. 8— see above);

(f) any precept issued by the GLA (1988 Act, ss.39-40 and 42, as amended by the GLA Act, ss.82–84—see above); and

(g) payments to the GLA by billing authorities in accordance with regulations under section 99(3) of the 1988 Act (see below).

The share distributed to each functional body must be allocated in accordance with the component budget requirement of that body (see above).

5.57 The payments must be made by instalments, which must be of such amounts and at such times as to enable the body to meet it budgeted expenditure (*i.e.* expenditure within the body's budget requirement) for the year as it falls due. This contrasts with the Secretary of State's duty in relation to revenue support grant, which he must pay in such instalments or amounts as he determines with the consent of the Treasury (Local Government Finance Act 1988, s.83(2)). In *R v. Secretary of State for the Environment, ex p. Brent L.B.C.* [1982] Q.B. 593, DC, the court held that the effect of wording equivalent to that used in section 83(2) of the 1988 Act was to give the decision as to the timing and amount of any instalments to the Secretary of State and the Treasury. The court did, however, go on to say:

"We have no doubt that if the Secretary of State refused or delayed making the rate support grants to the local authorities . . . for no good reason, so as to frustrate the purpose of this part of the legislation, then this court could intervene by way of judicial review and grant whatever relief was required."

By contrast, section 102 of the GLA Act requires the GLA to pay instalments "punctually". Although that word is not defined, if the GLA should fail to make payments so that functional bodies were unable to meet their budgeted expenditure, its default could be open to challenge by way of judicial review.

Although the GLA must pay instalments punctually, provision is made for the (unlikely) situation in which the Secretary of State has not yet paid a sum to the GLA that the GLA is due to pay to a functional body: the GLA is only required to pay sums to the functional bodies in so far as those sums have been *received* by the GLA (GLA Act, ss.102(1) and (2)).

Regulations under Section 99(3) of the 1988 Act, Payments to and by the GLA

As a major precepting authority, the GLA may be required to make **5.58** payments to a billing authority in respect of any deficit in council tax in the latter authority's collection fund for the previous year. Conversely, the billing authorities are obliged to make payments from their collections funds to the GLA as a major precepting authority in respect of its share of any prior year surplus, being a surplus in the billing authority's collection fund for the preceding year.

These liabilities are determined in accordance with The Local Authorities (Funds) (England) Regulations 1992 (S.I. 1992 No. 2428) (as amended).

Duty to Account to Functional Bodies for Their Grants

The GLA must account for and pay over to a functional body any grant or **5.59** other payment made only for the purposes, or particular purposes, of that body. This would apply, for example, to GLA transport grant (above) or emergency financial assistance under section 155 of the Local Government and Housing Act 1989, as amended by section 104 of the GLA Act (see below).

Funds of the Authority

General Fund of the Authority

The GLA must establish a general fund from a date to be specified by the **5.60** Secretary of State in regulations (section 106, amending the Local Government and Housing Act 1989, s.91).

The general fund is the central fund of a local authority. All payments made, or received, by the authority must be paid into or out of it, unless they are to be paid to or from a collection fund (which the GLA does not have since it is not a billing authority) or a trust fund.

In so far as relevant to the GLA, the Secretary of State has power to make regulations governing general funds, including the liability to make transfers relating to payments made — and received — by precepting authorities in respect of deficits — and surpluses — in a billing authority's council tax in a previous financial year (for which, see above—1988 Act, s.99(3)).

Chapter 6

REVENUE ACCOUNTS AND CAPITAL FINANCE

The Mayor is required, before each financial year, to develop a capital **6.01** spending plan, having consulted the Assembly and the functional bodies. The plan must analyse each body's likely capital resources and expenditure during the year and the way in which such expenditure is likely to be met (GLA Act, ss.122 to 124).

The provisions of Part IV (sections 39 to 66) of the Local Government and Housing Act 1989 are generally applied to the GLA and the four functional bodies, Transport for London, the London Development Agency, the Metropolitan Police Authority and the London Fire and Emergency Planning Authority (GLA Act, s.111).

In place of the basic and supplementary credit approvals that are used by other local authorities, however, the GLA Act introduces aggregate and additional credit approvals (for details of which, see below at paragraphs 6.08 *et seq.* and 6.10 *et seq.* respectively). An aggregate credit approval has the same effect as a basic approval, and an additional approval has the same effect as a supplementary approval. The two categories of aggregate and additional credit approvals are themselves both split further into four categories of amount, to be allocated by the Secretary of State or the Mayor. The Secretary of State may allocate to any of the functional bodies amounts for general or specific capital purposes. The Mayor may allocate further amounts to whichever functional body and for whatever purposes (within those specified by the Secretary of State) he thinks fit. The Secretary of State may also specify an amount for specific purposes, but which the Mayor can allocate to whichever of the functional bodies he thinks fit.

The Authority and functional bodies may pay grants to each other for capital or revenue purposes. This is aimed at allowing capital and revenue resources to be concentrated where they are most needed. The Secretary of State may make regulations to allow the Mayor to direct redistribution of the capital receipts of the functional bodies.

Revenue Accounts

The provisions of Part IV of the Local Government and Housing Act 1989 **6.02** that relate to revenue accounts are applied to the GLA and the functional bodies (GLA Act, s.111).

The GLA and the functional bodies are required to charge all expenditure to a revenue account in the year in which it is incurred unless it falls within the exceptions in section 42 of the Local Government and Housing Act 1989. The exceptions include expenditure:

(a) for capital purposes (defined in 1989 Act, s.40);
(b) made in reliance on a credit approval issued by the Secretary of State or Minister of the Crown;
(c) made out of the usable part of capital receipts; or,
(d) to be met out of money provided by any other person, such as government grants.

A revenue account is an account kept in accordance with any statutory requirements, with proper practices (1989 Act, s.66(4)) or voluntarily (1989 Act, s.41(2)). Unless, by reference to proper practices, it is appropriate to charge an item to a revenue account for an earlier or later year, the item must be charged to a revenue account for the year in which the expenditure was incurred (1989 Act, s.41(1)).

Borrowing

6.03 The provisions of Part IV of the Local Government and Housing Act 1989 that relate to borrowing are applied to the GLA and the functional bodies by including them among the authorities to which section 39 of the 1989 Act applies (GLA Act, s.111).

The GLA and the functional bodies may not borrow so as to exceed their aggregate credit limits, nor in contravention of regulations made by the Secretary of State (Local Government and Housing Act 1989, ss.43 and 44).

The aggregate credit limit of an authority is determined by adding the authority's level of permitted temporary borrowing (1989 Act, s.62) to the authority's credit ceiling, which is a measure of the difference between the authority's total liabilities in respect of capital expenditure financed by credit and the provision that has been made to meet those liabilities.

All money borrowed by an authority is charged indifferently on all its revenues (1989 Act, s.47). Whenever an authority borrows, it must make annual provision from its revenue account (minimum revenue provision) for its liabilities.

An authority may borrow by overdraft or short-term loan from certain substantial financial institutions without the consent of the Secretary of State (1989 Act, s.43). In all other cases, the Secretary of State, with the consent of the Treasury, must approve the borrowing.

Credit Arrangements

6.04 The provisions of Part IV of the Local Government and Housing Act 1989 that relate to credit arrangements are applied to the GLA and the functional bodies by including them in the authorities to which section 39 of the 1989 Act applies (GLA Act, s.111).

The 1989 Act recognises that other mechanisms are in effect equivalent to borrowing. These mechanisms include leases of land, buildings and property and contracts under which capital assets are acquired but payment is significantly deferred. The provisions are designed to encourage authorities to use such credit arrangements only when they represent better value for money than borrowing (1989 Act, ss.50–52).

Credit Approvals

Credit approvals are the principal means of imposing central government **6.05** control on local authority borrowing, or credit. The effect of credit approvals as it relates to all authorities is described below. See paragraphs 6.08 *et seq.* below for the special regime that applies to the GLA and the functional bodies (aggregate and additional credit approvals).

A credit approval acts as permission not to charge capital expenditure to a revenue account or as permission to enter into or agree to a variation of a credit arrangement (Local Government and Housing Act 1989, s.56).

Authorities that do not use their credit approvals may transfer them to another authority, which may use them as if issued to it in the first place.

Each credit approval may be used only once. Credit approvals are also treated as extinguished in other circumstances such as when certain types of capital receipt are received in relation to the same purposes as specified in the credit approval (1989 Act, s.57).

A credit approval issued to a body under the Act is, for the purposes of Part IV of the 1989 Act, treated as if it were issued to the body under that part. The effect of using the credit approval is the same as using a basic or supplementary credit approval under the 1989 Act (section 118(3)). Thus, the credit approval operates as permission to the authority (a) not to charge the expenditure to a revenue account or (b) to enter into a credit arrangement, such as a lease, or (c) to enter into a variation of a credit arrangement. The body may transfer the credit approval to another body or a local authority for use by them (1989 Act, s.56(2)). When the credit approval is used, the body's credit ceiling will be increased (1989 Act, s.63, Sched. 3, Pt III, para.11).

The Modified Regime for the GLA and the Functional Bodies

Subject to the exceptions set out below, the Secretary of State or other **6.06** Minister can have regard to any factors that appear appropriate when issuing a credit approval to the GLA or a functional body (GLA Act, s.117).

In particular, he may have regard to:

(a) the amount of grants or contributions that the relevant authority (for which, see below) has received or is likely to receive in respect of expenditure incurred by the authority or to be incurred by it before the expiration of the period for which the credit approval is to have effect; and

(b) the amount of capital receipts which the relevant authority has received, might reasonably be expected to receive or is likely to receive before the period for which the credit approval is to have effect has expired, subject to those factors of which he is not entitled to take account.

When determining the amount of the credit approval, the Secretary of State or other Minister is not permitted to take account of capital receipts:

(a) to the extent that a relevant authority is required to set aside the receipts as provision for credit liabilities;

(b) which have been received by the authority as trustee of a charitable trust (1989 Act, s.59(7));

(c) which are required to repay any government monies used to acquire the asset being disposed of (1989 Act, s.59(8)).

(d) used by the authority to defray the administrative costs of and incidental to disposals of land held for the purposes of Part II of the Housing Act 1985 or under the Right to Buy (1989 Act, s.59(9)).

6.07 When determining the amount to be specified in an additional credit approval, the Secretary of State or other Minister cannot take account of the extent to which the authority is or is likely to be able to finance the capital expenditure from a revenue account.

The relevant authority in the case of a Category A or B (for which, see below) approval is the body specified in the approval. For a Category C or D approval, it is any body to which the Mayor may allocate an amount in accordance with the approval.

A category A or B approval is treated as a credit approval issued to the body specified in the approval. Where an amount is allocated to a body from a category C or D approval, the notice of allocation and so much of the credit approval as relates to the allocation is treated as a credit approval issued to the body (GLA Act, s.118).

Aggregate Credit Approval

6.08 The Secretary of State may issue to the Mayor aggregate credit approvals in respect of the credit arrangements and capital expenditure of the GLA and the functional bodies (GLA Act, s.113). These are the equivalent of basic credit approvals for other authorities issued under section 53 of the 1989 Act. Although each aggregate credit approval will be issued to the Mayor, the functional bodies will receive a copy.

The credit approvals must specify amounts in relation to the financial year concerned in four categories:

Category A: an amount for the specified body with respect to its credit arrangements and expenditure for general capital purposes;

Category B: an amount for the specified body with respect to specified credit arrangements and expenditure for capital purposes;

Category C: an amount to be distributed by the Mayor to the bodies and for such purposes as he thinks fit;

Category D: an amount for purposes specified by the Secretary of State, but for the Mayor to distribute to whichever of the bodies and for such purposes, within the Secretary of State's specified purposes, as he thinks fit.

An aggregate credit approval may be nil.   **6.09**

The purpose of Category C and D approvals is to enable the Mayor to have some control over the amounts payable to each body for capital expenditure and the purposes to which those sums should be put. The Secretary of State, however, retains a significant amount of control.

Where the Mayor makes an allocation to the GLA or a functional body from a Category C or D amount under an aggregate credit approval, he must notify each of the functional bodies (GLA Act, s.115). Where such an allocation is to a functional body, the notice must be given by including the amount and the purposes for which it is allocated in the capital spending plan that the Mayor is required to prepare for each financial year (GLA Act, s.122—see paragraphs 6.15 *et seq.* below).

Although there is no provision as to when in the preceding year the approval must be issued, it must be envisaged that it will be issued before January 15, because the Mayor is under a duty to prepare a capital spending plan (GLA Act, ss.122 and 123—see below) after the issue of the approval but before January 15 in the preceding financial year.

Additional Credit Approval

Any Minister of the Crown may issue to the Mayor additional credit **6.10** approvals in respect of the credit arrangements and capital expenditure of the GLA and the functional bodies (GLA Act, s.114). These are the equivalent of supplementary credit approvals for other authorities issued under section 54 of the Local Government and Housing Act 1989.

Each additional credit approval must fall into one of the four categories, A to D, referred to above.

They have effect for a specified period and may be retrospective to the previous financial year if issued within the first six months of the following financial year (GLA Act, s.114(2) and (3)).

Although each approval will be issued to the Mayor, the functional bodies will receive a copy. Where the Mayor makes an allocation to the GLA or a functional body from a Category C or D amount under an additional credit approval, he must notify each of the functional bodies: GLA Act, section 115.

Amortisation

Where regulations so require, a credit approval will state an amortisation **6.11** period during which the authority is required to set aside from a revenue account, as provision to meet credit liabilities, amounts determined in accordance with the regulations (GLA Act, s.116).

Different provisions may be made in relation to expenditure for capital purposes of different descriptions, and different periods may be specified in relation to different amounts specified in the approval.

In respect of an additional credit approval, as is the case with regard to supplementary credit approvals, the Secretary of State may order that certain types of expenditure are to be treated as capital expenditure (Local Government and Housing Act 1989, s.40(6)). The main purpose of this provision is to allow authorities that are having difficulties in meeting their revenue liabilities to treat those liabilities as capital and take advantage of the ability to borrow in respect of them. Where a credit approval is directed to a particular functional body or the GLA and relates to such an amount (a Category B credit approval), the Minister is not required to specify an amortisation period. In committee, the Minister for London and Construction, Nick Raynsford, said:

"... [w]e would only issue such a credit approval to an authority facing severe revenue pressures ... We thought it better to allow each case to be tested on its merits. If no amortisation period is specified, the authority is still required by other rules in the system to make provision out of revenue at the rate of 4 per cent of the net outstanding debt to be set aside annually. That, of course, is when no specific provision is made. The Secretary of State may make provision if he feels that it is appropriate to do so ... When the Secretary of State determines the amortisation period, the authority will be informed of the reasons for it." *Official Report, Standing Committee A,* February 11, 1999, col. 481.

It is noteworthy that the Minister committed the Secretary of State to providing reasons even though the GLA Act imposes no duty to give reasons.

Mayor's Power to Require Information

6.12 In exercising his functions under the provisions of Chapter IV of Part III of the GLA Act (relating to revenue accounts and capital finance), the Mayor may require the functional bodies to provide him with information by serving a notice on them. The functional bodies must provide the information as required by the notice (which may provide for the form, manner and timing of the information) to the extent that it is in their possession or under their control. The information must be certified by the chief finance officer, or by any person specified in the notice, or under arrangements made by the Audit Commission (GLA Act, s.125).

There is no statutory restriction on the type of information which the Mayor may require, by contrast with the position under the Local Government Finance Act 1992, where information is defined as including "accounts, estimates and returns" (1992 Act, s.116). The information that the chief finance officer is required to certify is likely to be financial information, but the notice may require other information to be certified by another officer of the functional body.

If the functional body fails to comply with the requirements in the notice, the Mayor may decide (a) whether to exercise his powers, and how to perform his functions, under Chapter IV of Part III of the GLA Act; or (b) whether the body has acted, or is likely to act, in accordance with that Chapter, on the basis of such assumptions and estimates as he thinks fit. It is likely that the functional bodies would have no right to disclosure of these assumptions, estimates or other information to challenge a decision of the Mayor: *R. v. Secretary of State for the Environment, ex p. Greater London Council and Inner London Education Authority*, CA, March 1, 1985, unreported.

The Mayor may also, when making such decisions, take into account any **6.13** other information which is available to him, whatever its source. In *R. v. Secretary of State for the Environment, ex p. Hammersmith and Fulham L.B.C.* [1991] 1 A.C. 521, which involved a challenge to the Secretary of State's decision to designate (in other words, "cap") the applicant authority under the community charge legislation, Lord Bridge stated at 601:

> "In the nature of the case the Secretary of State is bound to receive representations as to how he should exercise his power of capping from many quarters. Bodies speaking for community charge payers and political opponents of those who have set the budget to be capped are likely to urge one view, political supporters and bodies speaking for consumers of local services or employees engaged in the provision of those services are likely to urge another. These representations may be factual, argumentative or both. Against this background to read into the statute a legal obligation on the Secretary of State to disclose to an authority challenging his proposed cap all relevant information before him and then to give the authority the opportunity to comment upon or counter that information (which would be the only purpose to be served by requiring disclosure) would introduce such delays into a procedure which is meant to operate with the greatest expedition that I cannot believe that this is what Parliament intended. ... The important objective of the procedure is that the information on which the Secretary of State acts should be both full and accurate."

It is likely that the same reasoning would apply to the Mayor and the functional bodies.

Capital Receipts

Capital receipts are defined in section 58 of the 1989 Act, and include sums **6.14** in respect of the disposal of any capital asset, the disposal of any investment other than approved investments and the repayment of capital grants and loans made for capital purposes. Local authorities are required to set aside a percentage of their capital receipts as provision for credit liabilities (the reserved part), although at present this requirement only applies to receipts in respect of assets within the authority's housing revenue account, which will not apply to the GLA or any of the functional bodies. The balance of the capital receipts after the reserved part has been deducted (and various limited deductions under 1989 Act, s.59) is called the usable part of the body's capital receipts (1989 Act, s.60).

Where a body receives consideration for a capital asset which is not wholly in money, a value is ascribed to the non-monetary consideration of the difference between the amount which would have been paid in respect of the asset had the consideration been in money and any money actually received. A body is required to set aside sums equivalent to the reserved part of this "notional capital receipt" from either usable credit receipts or a revenue account (1989 Act, s.61). Under the Local Authorities (Capital Finance) (Amendment No. 3) Regulations 1998 (S.I. 1998 No. 1937) the requirement to set aside sums in respect of non-housing capital receipts has been effectively removed.

The Mayor's Capital Spending Plan

6.15 The Mayor must prepare a capital spending plan for the functional bodies: section 122 of the GLA Act.

The capital spending plan is divided into four sections.

Section A must contain a statement for each functional body of the amounts which will be available for capital spending not deriving from the GLA. This includes capital grants, the amount of usable capital receipts at the beginning of the financial year and the amount by which those receipts are likely to increase during the year.

Section B must contain a statement for each functional body of the amounts that will be available for capital spending either by way of a grant from the GLA or by means of credit approval from central government.

Section C must contain a statement for each functional body of the body's "total capital spending". This is the total amount of capital expenditure which the Mayor expects the body to incur in the year plus the total amount of credit cover (for which, see above) which the Mayor expects the body to have available with respect to credit arrangements entered into or varied during the year.

Section D must consist of an analysis of each body's total capital spending for the year, showing how much the Mayor expects the body to meet (a) out of capital grants, (b) from the usable part of capital receipts, (c) by using the aggregate credit approval, and (d) by making a charge to the revenue account.

The Mayor may take into account such factors as appear to him appropri- **6.16**
ate in drawing up the plan (GLA Act, s.124).

The Mayor makes the final assessment of the body's likely capital
spending, although the Assembly and each functional body will have an
opportunity to comment on the draft (GLA Act, s.123). In addition, he may,
by notice, require the body to give him information (GLA Act, s.125—see
above).

In response to an opposition proposal that the capital spending plan
should include a comparison between each functional body's capital
spending plan for the previous year and the amount which the Mayor had
expected it to spend, the Minister for London and Construction, Nick
Raynsford, said:

> "The mayor will draw up the capital spending plan in consultation with
> the functional bodies for the benefit of those bodies and of the GLA as a
> whole. Clearly, it is important that each of those bodies should stick to
> its plan for incurring capital expenditure. The role of the plan is not,
> however, to put the new bodies into a straightjacket regarding their
> capital spending. A functional body's actual spending and the way in
> which it is met out of the credit and grants that are made available have
> to be decided by the body concerned. It is, after all, responsible for the
> discharge of its functions and has to respond during the financial year to
> changes of circumstances. It might, for example, be in a position to
> spend more than expected because it unexpectedly obtains a large
> capital receipt.
>
> Accordingly, clause 108 [now section 123] is intended to confer on the
> mayor a flexible discretion, for the purpose of preparing the capital
> spending plan, to take account of such factors as appear appropriate to
> him or her. That includes the extent to which capital spending by a
> functional body departs from the mayor's expectation." *Official Report,
> Standing Committee A*, February 11, 1999, cols. 493–4.

Procedure for Formulating the Capital Spending Plan

The Mayor must prepare a draft of the plan in time for a copy to be sent to **6.17**
the Assembly and each functional body before January 15 in the financial
year preceding that to which the plan relates (GLA Act, s.123). It will not
be possible for the Mayor to formulate the draft plan until the Secretary of
State has issued the aggregate credit approval (GLA Act, s.113—see
above).

The Assembly's only role is to submit comments to the Mayor within 21
days. This contrasts with the procedure for determining the budget
requirements of the GLA and the functional bodies, where the Assembly
has the opportunity to vote on the proposals (GLA Act, s.87 and Sched. 6—
see above). The Minister for London and Construction, Nick Raynsford,
said:

> ". . . [T]he implications of the capital programme will be seen in the
> revenue budget, and that will be the appropriate opportunity for the

assembly to vote on the programme, if it so wishes. It will have an opportunity to comment on the capital programme, and the mayor will have to make it clear why he or she does not accept the assembly's comments. At the next monthly meeting the assembly will have full opportunity to question the mayor on his or her reasons for departing from its recommendations." *Official Report, Standing Committee A*, February 11, 1999, col. 506.

6.18 The Mayor must consider the Assembly's and functional bodies' comments, if any, and revise the draft accordingly, if he thinks fit.

The Mayor must then send the plan to the Secretary of State, and a copy to the Assembly and each functional body, before February 28 (GLA Act, s.123(4)). The Secretary of State has no power to extend the date by which the Mayor must submit the plan. However, the plan is not invalidated by being submitted late: this contrasts with the consolidated budget requirement (see above).

A copy of the plan must be kept available for public inspection free of charge at the principal offices of the GLA at reasonable hours, and kept available for six years until the sixth anniversary of its publication. Any person may obtain a copy of the plan, on payment of a reasonable fee determined by the Mayor (GLA Act, s.123(7)).

Factors to be Considered in Preparing the Capital Spending Plan

6.19 When the Mayor prepares a capital spending plan he must decide, amongst other things, what, if any, grant the GLA will pay to each functional body and how much will be allocated to it out of the category C and D amounts in the aggregate credit approval for the year (GLA Act, s.124).

The Mayor may take into account the factors that appear appropriate when preparing a capital spending plan (GLA Act, s.124). In particular, he may take account of capital spending plans for any previous financial years and the way in which each functional body's capital spending (set out in section C of those plans) was met out of:

(a) capital grants made to the body;
(b) the usable part of the body's capital receipts;
(c) using the aggregate credit approval or any additional credit approvals; and
(d) charges to a revenue account.

These ways of meeting expenditure will have been set out in section D of the capital spending plan for the year prior to that which the Mayor is considering. In effect, the Mayor may analyse the extent to which the functional body departed from the pattern of capital expenditure set in the prior year's capital spending plan and about which it was consulted.

6.20 Although the weight to be attributed to any factor is a matter for the Mayor, and there is no requirement for the Mayor to give reasons for his decision, the capital spending plan will be a significant decision. As such, it should be included in the Mayor' periodic report to the Assembly (GLA Act, s.45—see above). The Mayor is required to give reasons for all decisions contained in the periodic report. While the strategic decisions as to allocation of funding are matters for the Mayor, an irrational decision would be subject to challenge by way of judicial review. It is likely, however, that as is the case with decisions to cap an authority's council tax (and consistently with the court's reluctance to interfere in financial matters), a challenge to the Mayor's decision would have to be directed to the objective reasonableness of the decision and not a subjective examination of it; accordingly, the functional body will have no right under section 125 of the GLA Act to disclosure of any assumptions, estimates or other information taken into account by the Mayor: *R. v. Secretary of State for the Environment, ex p. Greater London Council and Inner London Education Authority*, CA, March 1, 1985, unreported.

Redistribution of Capital Receipts by the Mayor

As the budgets of the GLA and the functional bodies are all treated **6.21** separately, there needs to be provision for capital receipts to be redistributed among those bodies.

The Secretary of State may make regulations enabling the Mayor to direct any functional body to pay a percentage of its capital receipts to the GLA, for the GLA itself to use or for it to redistribute to another functional body (GLA Act, s.119). Any such amount can only be applied towards meeting expenditure for capital purposes (section 119(2)).

The regulations may prescribe a percentage or maximum percentage that may be specified in a Mayor's direction, or the portion of the usable part of a body's capital receipts in respect of which a direction may be issued. The regulations may also enable the Mayor to specify the capital purposes to which the sums received must be applied.

The Minister for Transport in London, Glenda Jackson, described this power as a "reserve power". She stated:

"There are no immediate plans to make such regulations and there may never be a need for them. Clauses 104 and 105 [now sections 119 and 120] enable the bodies to redistribute resources between themselves by voluntary agreement, subject to the mayor's consent. If these arrangements are used responsibly it may never be necessary to invoke the power in clause 103 [now section 118]. But clause 103 ensures that the mayor can be empowered, if necessary, to secure an efficient distribution of capital resources, thus enhancing his or her ability to decide priorities and improve efficiency and value for money for the GLA and the functional bodies as a whole . . . Each body's capital receipts will remain ring-fenced for its own use until regulations, if any, are made. If this power was conferred on the mayor it would not allow him or her to take away from the functional body capital receipts derived from particular disposals of assets." *Official Report, Standing Committee A*, February 11, 1999, cols 483–4.

Mutual Grants

Capital Grants

6.22 The GLA may pay grants to a functional body towards meeting expenditure for capital purposes in connection with the discharge of the body's functions; the functional bodies may make grants for the same purposes between themselves if the Mayor consents (GLA Act, s.120). Such grants must not be made subject to any limitation in respect of the capital purposes to which they may be applied, but must be applied by the recipient body solely towards meeting expenditure for capital purposes. The powers to make grants may be exercised at any point in the financial year.

The Mayor, acting on behalf of the GLA, may make such a GLA capital grant (GLA Act, s.140).

The Minister for Transport in London, Glenda Jackson, described this power as follows:

> "One of the main benefits of the grant-making powers in clauses 104 and 105 [now sections 119 and 120 of the GLA Act] will be that surplus capital resources or revenue resources of one functional body do not have to lie idle if they can be used by the GLA or any of the other functional bodies. One body might have surplus capital resources but be in urgent need of revenue expenditure. A second body might have surplus revenue resources that it had planned to use for capital spending. Using these powers, the bodies could agree to swap their resources, subject always, of course, to the mayor's consent." *Official Report, Standing Committee A,* February 11, 1999, col. 484.

Revenue Grants

6.23 The GLA may pay grants to a functional body towards meeting expenditure other than for capital purposes in connection with the discharge of the body's functions; the functional bodies may make grants for the same purposes between themselves if the Mayor consents (GLA Act, s.121). Such grants must not be made subject to any limitation in respect of the non-capital purposes to which they may be applied, but must be applied by the recipient body solely towards meeting expenditure for revenue purposes. The powers to make grants may be exercised at any point in the financial year.

The provisions relating to road user charging schemes (GLA Act, s.295) and workplace parking levies (GLA Act, s.296) make separate provision for the way in which the net proceeds may be applied and distributed by the GLA, Transport for London, a London borough council or the Common Council of the City of London. See below.

The Mayor, acting on behalf of the GLA, may make such a GLA revenue grant (GLA Act, s.140).

Chapter 7

FINANCIAL ADMINISTRATION, ACCOUNTS AND AUDIT, AND MISCELLANEOUS FINANCIAL MATTERS

Overview

The GLA, the functional bodies and the London Pension Funds Authority **7.01** are subject to the provisions of the Local Government Finance Act 1988 that deal with financial administration (Part VIII of the 1988 Act) (GLA Act, s.128).

The GLA and the functional bodies are each required to arrange for the proper administration of their financial affairs (GLA Act, s.127).

The GLA and the functional bodies must each have a chief financial officer to be responsible for that administration. His duties include reporting to the GLA or the body concerned when it appears to him that unlawful or improper expenditure has been or will be made (1988 Act, ss.112 and 113).

The provisions of the Audit Commission Act 1998 also apply to the GLA and the functional bodies, with procedural amendments.

Chief Finance Officers

Under Part VIII of the 1988 Act, every local authority must have a chief **7.02** finance officer (1988 Act, s.112).

The Authority and each of the functional bodies are now included among the authorities that are required to appoint their own chief finance officer to be responsible for the administration of their financial affairs (1988 Act, s.127). Subject to the transitional arrangements described below, the Assembly must appoint the Authority's chief finance officer after consulting the Mayor.

Preliminary Financial Arrangements

The GLA will be in existence only for part of the financial year ending on **7.03** March 31, 2001. It is therefore necessary for transitional provisions to provide for initial financial management to be established by a person or body other than the Mayor and Assembly. The Secretary of State has undertaken this task in accordance with his power to appoint persons to secure that provisions of the GLA Act operate satisfactorily when they come into force (GLA Act, s.407) and the transitional provisions are set out in The London Government (Various Provisions) Order 2000 (S.I. 2000 No. 942).

Certain arrangements made by a chief finance officer in relation to the GLA or the London Development Agency (the "relevant bodies") before May 8, 2000 and July 3, 2000 respectively will continue to have effect after those dates until replaced or altered by the relevant body in question (art.2 of the Order). The chief finance officer may make preliminary financial arrangements for the matters that are set out in the Schedule to the Order, namely:

7.04   1. the allocation and delegation of financial functions to persons appointed for the purposes of the relevant body:

   (a) in pursuance of section 407 of the GLA Act, or
   (b) on or after May 8, 2000 in relation to the GLA and July 3, 2000 in relation to the London Development Agency;

   2. access to records of the relevant body;
   3. the preparation of capital and revenue budgets for the relevant body, and arrangements for monitoring and control of budgeted expenditure;
   4. the treatment of any income for the time being receivable for the purposes of any functions of the relevant body;
   5. arrangements for banking accounts in the name of the relevant body;
   6. arrangements for ordering goods and services, and for making payment accordingly;
   7. arrangements for securing tenders for contracts;
   8. the treatment of any payments to members of the relevant body's staff, and of any deductions from such payments;
   9. the handling, and recording, of physical assets held for the purposes of the relevant body, and the disposal of such assets or other assets;
   10. arrangements for the receipt and payment of grants;
   11. the taking of decisions to write off debts;
   12. day to day management, accounting and investment of surplus funds of the relevant body;
   13. arrangements for internal audit; and
   14. the treatment of financial irregularities.

Persons Who May Hold the Post of Chief Finance Officer

7.05 Each chief finance officer must be suitably qualified through membership of one of the professional accountancy bodies set out in the 1988 Act (1988 Act, s.113). A chief finance officer of one body cannot also be a chief financial officer of another body, nor can he hold the post of monitoring officer (GLA Act, s.127(3); 1988 Act, ss.62 and 117; Local Government and Housing Act 1989, s.5).

The chief finance officer of Transport for London and of the London Development Agency may be a member of that body, although the Mayor is not permitted to take on this role. In all other cases, the chief finance officer will be an officer of the body, so that a member of staff or an employee but not the Mayor may take on this role (section 127(4), (5) and (7)).

As a statutory officer (as defined by section 2(1)(b) and (6)(d) of the Local Government and Housing Act 1989), the post of chief finance officer is a "politically restricted" post, which means that he may not become or remain a member of any local authority in Great Britain (1989 Act, s.1(1)).

Functions of the Chief Finance Officer

The current guidance from The Chartered Institute of Public Finance and **7.06** Accountancy in relation to the role of the chief finance officer is that contained in *A Statement on the Role of the Finance Director in Local Government*. Although the statutory title "Chief Finance Officer" is not used in the *Statement*, it is clear that the role of the Chief Finance Officer is included within the roles envisaged for the Finance Director referred to in the *Statement* (paragraph 4.1 *et seq.*). The *Statement* cites the following ten activities as involved in the fulfilment of the statutory duties of financial administration and stewardship by the Finance Director:

1. Advising on corporate risk profiling and management, including safeguarding assets, risk avoidance and insurance.
2. Advising on effective systems of internal control.
3. Ensuring there is an effective system of internal control.
4. Advising on anti-fraud and anti-corruption strategies and measures.
5. Preparing statutory and other accounts and associated grant claims.
6. Ensuring there is an effective internal audit function and assisting management in providing effective arrangements for financial scrutiny.
7. Securing effective systems of financial administration.
8. Securing effective arrangements for treasury management, pensions and trust funds.
9. Ensuring a prudential financial framework is in place.
10. Ensuring that financial management arrangements are in line with broad policy objectives and the authority's overall management.

The chief finance officer is required to make reports as described below, **7.07** and has detailed duties under the Accounts and Audit Regulations 1996 (S.I. 1996 No. 590) as the responsible financial officer of the authority. At the time of writing, he is liable to surcharge under section 18 of the Audit Commission Act 1998 for any loss to the authority caused by his wilful misconduct. However, the Local Government Act 2000 will repeal the current surcharging provisions from a day to be appointed by a statutory instrument (sections 90 and 108(3)(a)).

The chief finance officer may delegate his duties, except for the duty to report under section 114 of the Local Government Finance Act 1988 (for which, see below): *Provident Mutual Life Assurance Association v. Derby C.C.* (1981) 79 L.G.R. 297, HL. This duty may only be delegated if, on account of absence or illness, the chief finance officer is unable to act, in which case delegation may be to a deputy nominated from amongst the chief finance officer's staff.

Chief Finance Officer's Reports

7.08 The chief finance officer's reporting functions are defined in section 114 of the Local Government Finance Act 1988.

In the following circumstances, he must make a report and send it to the body's auditor and the persons set out below:

(a) If it appears to him that the body, a committee of the body, a person holding office or employment under the body, a police force maintained by the body, or a joint committee on which the body is represented—

  (i) has made or is about to make a decision which would lead to unlawful expenditure;
  (ii) has taken or is about to take a course of action which would be unlawful and likely to cause loss to the body;
  (iii) is about to enter an unlawful item of account
    where the

(b) body's expenditure is likely to exceed its available resources.

7.09 Where a report is made in relation to the GLA itself, the report must be sent to the Mayor and each member of the Assembly. If a report is made in relation to one of the functional bodies, the report must be sent to the Mayor, the Chair of the Assembly and each member of the functional body concerned. Although the Mayor and the Assembly are thereby informed about the report, the functional body must deal with the report itself (1988 Act, ss.114 and 115).

The chief finance officer must consult the head of paid service and the monitoring officer before making a report about the GLA, the Metropolitan Police Authority or the London Fire and Emergency Planning Authority. In the case of the London Development Agency, the chief executive is consulted. In the case of Transport for London, a designated member or member of staff is consulted (1988 Act, s.114).

Consideration of the report

Except in the case of the GLA (for which, see below), when a functional **7.10** body receives a report from the chief finance officer, it must consider the report in a meeting of the whole body within 21 days of the report being sent out (1988 Act, s.115). It must decide whether or not it agrees with the report. This duty to consider the report cannot be delegated (1988 Act, s.115).

During the "prohibition period", which lasts from the date the report is sent until the functional body has concluded its deliberations, the body may not pursue the course of conduct that led to the report being made. Any payment made in breach of that prohibition is unlawful. If the report is made because the body's expenditure is likely to exceed its available resources, it may not enter any new agreements during the prohibition period that might involve expenditure.

The body's auditor must be informed of the holding of the meeting and of any decision made at it (1988 Act, s.116).

In the case of a report by the chief finance officer of the GLA itself, the **7.11** procedure is modified as follows (1988 Act, ss.115 and 115A). The Assembly must hold a meeting within 21 days of the report being sent, at which it must consider whether or not it agrees with the report and what action, if any, it recommends the Mayor to take in consequence. The Assembly cannot delegate this duty.

The Mayor must attend the Assembly's meeting. He must also, within 14 days of the conclusion of the meeting, decide whether or not he agrees with the report and what action, if any, he proposes to take. The views of the Assembly must be taken into account. The Mayor may not delegate these duties.

The prohibition period lasts until the first business day after the Mayor's decision about the action to be taken in response to the report. The prohibition extends to all activities, whether those of the Mayor, the Assembly or both acting together.

Accounts and Audit

The provisions of the Audit Commission Act 1998 apply to the GLA, the **7.12** four functional bodies (Transport for London, the London Development Agency, the Metropolitan Police Authority and the London Fire and Emergency Planning Authority) and the London Pensions Fund Authority, with appropriate modifications (GLA Act, s.133).

Annual Accounts

The GLA, the four functional bodies and the London Pensions Fund **7.13** Authority must prepare annual accounts in accordance with the requirements of the Accounts and Audit Regulations 1996 (S.I. 1996 No. 590).

Summary Accounts

7.14 In addition to the annual accounts, the GLA must prepare summary statements of accounts for itself, the functional bodies and the London Pensions Fund Authority in accordance with regulations made by the Secretary of State under section 27 of the 1998 Act. Any GLA elector may inspect these accounts (1998 Act, s.14) but the other rights of public access and the powers of the auditor (for which, see below) do not apply to them (GLA Act, s.134).

The four functional bodies and the London Pensions Fund Authority must, at the request of the Mayor, provide the GLA with information to enable it to compile the summary accounts (GLA Act, s.135).

External Audit

7.15 The accounts of the GLA, the four functional bodies and the London Pensions Fund Authority are subject to audit by an independent external auditor appointed by the Audit Commission after consultation with the body concerned (1998 Act, s.2).

The appointed auditor may be a member of the Commission, an individual or a firm of individuals (*e.g.* an accountancy firm operating as a partnership), or two or more persons.

The auditor will conduct the audit according to the Code of Audit Practice published by the Audit Commission and the Auditing Standards published by the Accounting Practice Board (1998 Act, s.5(2)).

The auditor must satisfy himself that the accounts comply with the appropriate regulations and any statutory requirements, that proper practices were observed to compile them, and that the body has made arrangements for securing economy, efficiency and effectiveness in its use of resources and has published information in relation to this (1998 Act, s.5).

The auditor may require documents, information, explanations and facilities to be provided in order to carry out his duties (1998 Act, s.6). Officers or members of the body may be required to attend before him to give any information or explanation he considers necessary. A person who fails to comply with a requirement of an auditor commits a criminal offence. The maximum penalty in the magistrates' court is a fine of level 3 on the standard scale (currently £1,000 under the Criminal Justice Act 1982, s.37 (as amended)), and an additional fine of £20 for each day the offence continues after conviction.

7.16 In order to discharge his responsibility, the auditor utilises the following means of formally communicating his views (Code, para. 27):

    (a) certificate of completion;

    (b) an opinion on the statement of accounts;

    (c) a statutory report on the audit of the best value performance plan (but in relation to the GLA, this applies only to functions it exercises through the Mayor);

(d) public interest report;
(e) reports to officers and, where appropriate, members on matters arising from the regularity audit (being, in substance, a catch-all for all additional observations either which do not fall within one of the foregoing, or may be in greater detail than is required in any of the foregoing);
(f) annual audit letter.

In addition, the Local Government Act 2000 will amend the Audit Commission Act 1998 to introduce a new system of advisory notices where an auditor considers that a body subject to audit is contemplating a decision or course of action that would result in unlawful expenditure or other financial loss from a day to be appointed by a statutory instrument (sections 91 and 108(3)(a)). See further paragraph 7.22 below.

Public Interest Reports and Auditor's Recommendations

By section 8 of the 1998 Act, the auditor, "shall consider whether, in the **7.17** public interest, he should make a report on any matter coming to his notice in the course of the audit in order that it may be considered by the body concerned or brought to the attention of the public". He must also consider whether the report needs to be made immediately or at the conclusion of the audit.

Schedule 1 to the Code (paragraph S1.24–5) describes the matters that auditors should consider when deciding whether to make a report:

> "A report in the public interest should be made only where auditors consider a matter sufficiently important to be brought to the notice of the audited body or the public . . . Auditors should not be deflected from making a report because its subject matter is critical or unwelcome, if it is considered in the public interest to do so. . . It is not, however, the function of auditors to express an opinion as to the wisdom of particular decisions taken by authorities in the lawful exercise of their discretion."

A public interest report must be sent forthwith to the body and the **7.18** Secretary of State, in the case of an immediate report, otherwise within 14 days of the conclusion of the audit. In the case of a functional body or the London Pensions Fund Authority, the Mayor must also be sent the report (1998 Act, s.10, as amended by the GLA Act, Sched. 8, para. 2).

Where the auditor makes a public interest report or a written recommendation which the auditor states should be considered by the body under section 11 of the 1998 Act, the body must consider the report or recommendation at a meeting held within four months (which period may be extended by the auditor) of the report or recommendation being sent to the body. The body must decide whether to accept the report or recommendation and what action to take in response.

Where the auditor makes a written recommendation to a functional body or the London Pensions Fund Authority, he must also send a copy to the Mayor (GLA Act Sched. 8, para. 2(2)).

7.19   Where a public interest report relates to the GLA itself, the Mayor must consider the report. The Assembly must also consider it at a meeting at which the Mayor is present. The meeting must be advertised in a local newspaper and held in public (1998 Act, s.7).

The Assembly then makes recommendations to the Mayor as to whether the report requires the body to take any action or whether the recommendation is to be accepted and what action, if any, is required. The Mayor must take these recommendations into account when making these decisions (1998 Act, s.11A, inserted by GLA Act, Sched. 8, para. 4).

Neither the Assembly nor the Mayor may delegate these duties.

The auditor must be informed of the Mayor's decisions as soon as practicable after they are taken, and a notice containing a summary of the decisions that has been approved by him must be published in a local newspaper (1998 Act, s.12(2)).

General Report

7.20   At the conclusion of the audit, the auditor must issue a certificate that the audit has been completed and give his opinion on the statement of accounts. Both the certificate and the opinion must be entered on the accounts (1998 Act, s.9(1)). If a public interest report has been made, the certificate and opinion may be entered on that report instead. If the auditor disagrees with the treatment or disclosure of a matter in the statement of accounts and considers it may be material to the statement, a qualified opinion is expressed. In most cases, the qualification will simply be a "subject to" or "except" opinion but, as a last resort, this will be a disclaimer of opinion or an adverse opinion.

Public Access to Information

7.21 A person who is a local government elector for the area of the body subject to audit is entitled to inspect and make copies of the body's accounts and of any report by the auditor, except an immediate report (1998 Act, s.14).

At the audit itself, any interested person is entitled to inspect the accounts and all the documentation that relates to them. Any local government elector may question the auditor about the accounts (1998 Act, s.15) or object in relation to any item of account which the auditor could declare unlawful or in respect of which he could impose a surcharge on members or officers of the body, or as to any matter in respect of which the auditor could make a public interest report (1998 Act, s.16). Note, however, that surcharge will be abolished by the Local Government Act 2000 (see above, paragraph 7.07).

Replacement of the Current Regime in Relation to Unlawful Items of Account

The Local Government Act 2000 amends the Audit Commission Act 1998 **7.22**
to introduce a new system of advisory notices where an auditor considers
that a body subject to audit is contemplating a decision or course of action
that would result in unlawful expenditure or other financial loss. These
provisions come into force from a day to be appointed by a statutory
instrument (sections 91 and 108(3)(a)). Once an advisory notice is issued,
the body will be prevented from proceeding with the activity for a period of
up to 21 days, during which time the auditor may seek the opinion of the
court as to the legality of the activity.

The new system of advisory notices will entirely replace the regime of
declaration, surcharge and prohibition orders that is described below.

The Auditor's Powers

Declaration That an Item of Account Is Contrary to Law

The auditor may apply to the court for a declaration that an item of **7.23**
account is contrary to law, unless the item has been sanctioned by the
Secretary of State (1998 Act, s.17). If the court grants the declaration, it
may order the accounts to be rectified, that any person responsible for
incurring some or all of the expenditure should repay some or all of it to
the body, unless that person acted in the belief the expenditure was lawful,
or if the expenditure exceeded £2,000 and the person responsible was a
member of a local authority (which for this purpose includes the GLA and
the Metropolitan Police Authority), that the person is disqualified from
being a member of a local authority for a specified period.

The auditor is not obliged to use the powers under section 17 rather
than those under section 18 (for which, see below): *Porter v. Magill* (1999) 1
L.G.L.R. 523, CA.

Surcharge

The auditor must certify that a person must pay a sum or amount of a loss **7.24**
if he has reason to believe that person has (a) failed to bring an item into
account which ought to have been brought into account, unless the item
has been sanctioned by the Secretary of State, or (b) has caused loss or
deficiency to the body by wilful misconduct (1998 Act, s.18). The issuing of
a certificate under section 18 is referred to as "surcharging". Although a
surcharge can impose an obligation to pay a very large sum of money the
provisions take no account of the ability of the person surcharged to pay
the sum certified. A person who is surcharged has six weeks to appeal to
the High Court.

Prohibition Orders

7.25 Where the auditor has reason to believe that expenditure would be unlawful or an item of account would be likely to cause a loss or deficiency, he may issue an order to a body that it must desist from making or implementing such decisions, taking such action or entering such items of account as are specified (1998 Act, s.20).

Applications for Judicial Review

7.26 The auditor may apply for judicial review of any decision of a body or any failure to act which it is reasonable to believe would have an effect on the accounts of the body. This provision merely establishes that the auditor has sufficient interest in the matter to apply for judicial review: he must nevertheless obtain the court's permission for the application (1998 Act, s.24).

Requests for the Audit Commission to Carry out Studies

7.27 The Mayor may ask the Audit Commission to promote or undertake studies designed to improve the economy, efficiency and effectiveness in the management or operation of the GLA, the four functional bodies and the London Pensions Fund Authority. Before making such a request in relation to the GLA, the Mayor must consult the Assembly, and before making a request in relation to the five other bodies, he must consult the body itself, the Assembly and any employees' associations which appear to him appropriate (1998 Act, s.34(2A), inserted by the GLA Act, Sched. 8, paras 9 and 10).

The bodies themselves may also make such a request.

Miscellaneous Issues Relating to the Financial Status of the GLA and the Functional Bodies

Council Tax

7.28 Section 19 of the Local Government Finance Act 1992 removes the Crown immunity of specified authorities in respect of liability for the council tax relating to dwellings provided by them for purposes connected with administration of justice, police purposes and other Crown purposes.

The GLA and each of the four functional bodies are therefore not exempt from council tax for these purposes by virtue of being included in the list of specified authorities (GLA Act, s.137, amending the 1992 Act, s.19).

Discretionary Rate Relief

Billing authorities are permitted to give discretionary relief from rates in **7.29** respect of certain charitable and other premises (the Local Government Finance Act 1988, s.47). As a precepting authority, there is no discretion to extend such relief to the GLA. The functional bodies are also excluded from such relief by section 138 of the GLA Act, amending section 47 of the Local Government Finance Act 1992.

Loans to the Functional Bodies

The Public Works Loans Commissioners have power to lend money to the **7.30** functional bodies (GLA Act, s.139, amending the National Loans Act 1968, Sched.4, para.1(a) and the Public Works Loans Act 1965, s.2(1)(a)). Such loans are secured by a charge on the revenue of the functional body concerned.

Emergency Financial Assistance

Recalculation of Budget

Where there has been an emergency or disaster involving destruction of or **7.31** danger to life or property and, as a result, the Mayor considers that the component budget requirements should be recalculated, the GLA may make substitute calculations: GLA Act, s.97. These must be in accordance with the provisions of Schedule 7.

The calculations must not increase the consolidated budget requirement. Accordingly, they must have effect as a redistribution among the functional bodies. For example, the London Fire and Emergency Planning Authority's budget could be increased if a compensating decrease in the budgets of one or more of the other three functional bodies was made (GLA Act, s.102).

The only funds that may be redistributed are those received either from central government or from billing authorities pursuant to regulations under section 99(3) of the Local Government Finance Act 1988 (these relate to payments made — and received — by precepting authorities in respect of deficits — and surpluses — in a billing authority's council tax in a previous financial year, for which, see above). Other sums such as those raised through council tax may not be redistributed (of the GLA Act, ss.97(2) and 102(2)).

Assistance from the Secretary of State

The Secretary of State may give financial assistance to any local authority **7.32** which has incurred expenditure as the result of an emergency or disaster involving destruction of or danger to life or property (Local Government and Housing Act 1989, s.155). The Greater London Authority is treated as a local authority for the purposes of that section, and so may receive assistance (GLA Act, s.104).

Expenditure incurred by the London Fire and Emergency Planning Authority, the Metropolitan Police Authority or Transport for London is also treated as being incurred by a local authority, and they are thereby eligible for financial assistance (GLA Act, s.104). Any sums paid to the GLA that are referable to expenditure incurred by a functional body are treated as having been made to the GLA for the purposes of the body concerned. Such payments therefore fall within the GLA's duty to account to that functional body for grants or payments received for the purposes of that body (GLA Act, s.103—see above).

PART C

THE TRANSPORT FUNCTIONS
OF THE GLA

INTRODUCTION

The functions of the GLA in relation to transport for Greater London are established by Part IV GLA Act. The general transport duty (section 141) is the underlying theme of Part IV of the GLA Act. The duty sets four standards that must be promoted and encouraged: safe, integrated, efficient and economic transport for London.

The transport strategy (section 142) is one of the eight key strategies that the GLA Act requires the Mayor to institute and maintain. The transport strategy must set out the Mayor's proposals for fulfilling the general transport duty.

Each London borough council and the Common Council of the City of London must prepare and implement a local implementation plan, or LIP, setting out their proposals for putting the transport strategy into effect in their area (section 145).

A new statutory body, Transport for London (TfL), is the functional body that must implement the Mayor's transport strategy on his behalf (section 154). TfL is also required to facilitate the general transport duty. TfL is the delivering body, whilst policy and budgets are set by the Mayor. TfL will run or manage a wide range of transport services for London. Its responsibilities relate to mass public transport, cabs and taxis and major roads. To do this, TfL will draw together functions relating to transport previously undertaken by a wide range of bodies.

A new regime is created for a new type of agreement in relation to the London Underground: Public-Private Partnership Agreements, or "PPP agreements" (Chapter VII of Part IV). These agreements are intended to attract private sector investment and expertise into the London Underground without an outright transfer of assets to the private sector.

TfL, the London borough councils and the Common Council of the City of London are given the power to impose two new charges and levies in Greater London: a charge for the use of roads (section 295 and Schedule 23), and a levy for parking at workplaces (section 296 and Schedule 24). Any profits from either type of scheme generated in the first ten years may only be spent on transport.

Chapter 8

TRANSPORT FUNCTIONS

The General Transport Duty

The general transport duty (section 141) is the underlying theme of the **8.01** transport provisions of the GLA Act (Part IV). The Mayor has a duty to, "develop and implement policies for the promotion and encouragement of safe, integrated, efficient and economic transport facilities and services to, from and within Greater London" (section 141(1)). The Authority must exercise its powers under Part IV for the same ends (section 141(2)).

The transport duty will be discharged through the transport strategy: section 142, see below.

At the time of writing, the provisions relating to the general transport duty (section 141) had not been brought into force, nor had a date been set for this.

Transport

The transport facilities and services to which the transport duty relates are **8.02** those required to meet the needs of persons living or working in, or visiting London and those required for the transportation of freight (section 141(3)).

The whole range of modes of transport is covered by the general transport duty: the movement of people, freight, vehicles, cycles and pedestrians are all included. During the course of the GLA Act through Parliament, the government repeatedly emphasised that cycling is included in the term "transport". For example, Lord Whitty, Under-Secretary of State for the Department of the Environment, Transport and the Regions, said that, "Cycling is already included in the term 'transport facilities and services'" *Hansard* H.L. Vol. 603, col. 146. In contrast, pedestrians are not automatically included in the term "transport": if they are to be included, they must be specifically mentioned (as they, are in the general transport duty (section 141(3))).

Safe, Integrated, Efficient and Economic

If the four targets set by the transport duty are achieved, London's **8.03** transport will improve. The white paper, "A Mayor and Assembly for London: The Government's proposals for modernising the governance of

London," Cm. 3897 (March 1998), paragraph 5.6, recognised problems with London's transport: "[T]he capital's public transport is under heavy strain. Services are poorly co-ordinated and the system suffers from years of under-investment in some areas."

Integration should be easier to achieve when a single body is co-ordinating transport. A new body, Transport for London (TfL) will undertake this task (section 154, see below).

Some improvements in efficiency and economy should arise naturally from the rationalisation of the structures for financing transport. Rather than fund transport piecemeal, financial support from central government that is earmarked for transport will be paid in a single block grant (section 101, see above). The Mayor can then adjust spending priorities in order to improve London's transport.

The Transport Strategy

8.04 The Mayor is required to prepare a transport strategy for Greater London (section 142). The transport strategy must set out the Mayor's policies and proposals for fulfilling the general transport duty (for which, see above) and other proposals the Mayor considers appropriate.

The result should be a plan that will provide for safe, integrated, efficient and economic transport for London.

The Mayor must publish the transport strategy and, when revisions are made, must publish it as revised (section 142(1) and (3)). Any reference to the transport strategy includes, unless the context requires otherwise, a reference to the transport strategy as last revised (section 142(5)). The Mayor must make available, and give publicity to, the transport strategy as last published (section 43, see above).

At the time of writing, none of the provisions relating to the transport strategy (section 144) had been brought into force, nor had a date been set for this.

Special Provision for People with Mobility Problems

8.05 The transport strategy must contain proposals for providing accessible transport for people with mobility problems, and a timetable for their implementation (section 142(2)). The Mayor must consult persons or bodies representing the interests of persons with mobility problems when preparing or revising the transport strategy.

Implementation of the Transport Strategy

8.06 Transport for London (TfL) will be the principal body that implements the transport strategy (see below, section 154). The London borough councils and the Common Council of the City of London also play a vital part. They will prepare their own plans for implementing the transport strategy (local implementation plans, or LIPs), and then act on them (see below, sections 145–153).

General Duties Relevant to the Transport Strategy

The transport strategy is one of the eight key strategies that the GLA Act **8.07** requires the Mayor to institute and maintain. It is subject to the provisions of the GLA Act which control the general process by which all the strategies will be prepared and published. For example, there are provisions relating to timing, consultation, review and revision (see above, sections 41–48).

The government made clear that consultation on transport issues must be comprehensive:

"[W]here a general power is exercised in the preparation or revision of any strategy, the authority must—and I emphasise that word—consult those people whose interests are affected or bodies who represent those interests or a mixture of the two. . . . The most appropriate consultees are the people whose interests are affected and those representing them. Therefore, in all those contexts, the authority must—I emphasise 'must'—consult, among others, organisations representing the disabled, the elderly, education, training services, the Environment Agency and other statutory bodies in those situations where their interests are affected by the use of the general power or by the use of the strategies which are developed." Lord Whitty, Under-Secretary of State for the Department of the Environment, Transport and the Regions, *Hansard* H.L. Vol. 602, col. 746.

Effects outside London: the Secretary of State's Involvement in the Transport Strategy

The Secretary of State may act to protect the rest of the country from **8.08** adverse effects caused by the transport strategy (section 143). The Secretary of State may direct the Mayor to change the transport strategy if two conditions are fulfilled: the Secretary of State must consider that: (1) the transport strategy is inconsistent with a government policy presented to either House of Parliament or published by a Minister of the Crown, and (2) the strategy has an adverse effect outside Greater London.

The Secretary of State is not obliged to exercise this power. Even if the Secretary of State does so, however, the damaging effects of a transport strategy may not be quickly remedied. Although the Mayor is obliged to revise the transport duty in accordance with the Secretary of State's direction (section 143(2)), revision of the transport strategy is potentially a slow process. For example, sections 42 and 142 require the Mayor to consult a number of bodies when revising the transport strategy. Until the transport strategy is revised, every London borough council and the Common Council of the City of London must still have regard to a transport strategy that is considered incompatible with national transport strategy and detrimental to an area outside Greater London (section 144). Instead, if the council wishes to ignore the discredited strategy, it will have to rely on its discretion to give very little weight to the strategy. There is no provision to allow the Secretary of State to "short circuit" the process by giving directions straight to a London authority requiring it to have regard to the Secretary of State's direction rather than the strategy. The Secretary of State does, however, have power under section 44 to direct the Mayor to speed up the process of preparing and publishing the strategy. It remains to be seen whether this power will prove adequate to protect the rest of the country from a transport strategy that is, in the opinion of the Secretary of State, damaging.

The Effect of the Transport Strategy on Other Bodies

8.09 The London borough councils, the Common Council of the City of London and any other person or body exercising statutory functions in relation to Greater London will be required to have regard to the transport strategy. They are also required to have regard to any written guidance issued by the Mayor about the implementation of the transport strategy (section 144).

Even the Secretary of State is required to have regard to the transport strategy in certain circumstances: in exercising any functions in relation to the management of roads and traffic in a Royal Park in Greater London (section 144(4)).

Replacement of Secretary of State's Guidance, Traffic Director for London's Plans and Borough Plans

8.10 Any guidance given by the Secretary of State under paragraph 53 of Schedule 4 to the Local Government Act 1985, Part II of Schedule 5 to the Local Government Act 1985 or sections 50 to 63 and 80 of, and Schedule 5 to, the Road Traffic Act 1991 (priority routes, local plans, trunk road plans and the Traffic Director for London) will, until superseded by the transport strategy, continue in force and have effect as if it were part of that strategy. The Mayor may modify or revoke such guidance in accordance with the provisions relating to modification and revocation of the transport strategy (section 294(2)—see below).

Similarly, the following plans continue in force until superseded by the transport strategy as if prepared as part of that strategy: the Traffic Director for London's network plan (under the Road Traffic Act 1991, s.52) to the extent that it relates to GLA roads or side roads; any trunk road local plans (under the 1991 Act, s.56); and, to the extent that they relate to GLA roads or side roads, local plans prepared by a London borough council or the Common Council of the City of London (under the 1991 Act, s.54): section 294(3), (4) and (6). See below, paragraphs 13.02 and 14.02 for an explanation of GLA roads.

Local Implementation Plans (LIPs)

8.11 Each London borough council (for this purpose, the Common Council of the City of London is treated as a London borough council: section 145(4)) is required to prepare a plan setting out its proposals for putting the transport strategy into effect in its area (section 145). The plan must include a timetable for implementing the various proposals contained in it and the date for implementing the whole plan (section 145(3)). Such a plan will be called a local implementation plan (LIP).

The councils must prepare these plans as soon as reasonably practicable after the Mayor's transport strategy is published. This will require advance preparation by the councils. The councils will, however, be aware of the Mayor's proposals before the transport strategy is published. They will have been consulted about the transport strategy and any revisions (sections 42 and 142).

At the time of writing, none of the provisions relating to LIPs (sections 145–153) had been brought into force, nor had a date been set for this.

Local Implementation Plan Consultation

Councils are required to consult various bodies when preparing their LIPs **8.12** (section 145(2) and (5)). A London borough council must consult the Commissioner of Police of the Metropolis and, if it considers it appropriate, the Commissioner of Police for the City of London, Transport for London, such organisations representative of disabled persons as it considers appropriate, other London borough councils it considers likely to be affected by the plan, and any person or body it has been directed to consult by the Mayor under section 153. The Common Council of the City of London must consult the same bodies except that it must consult the Commissioner of Police for the City of London but may also consult the Commissioner of Police of the Metropolis if it considers it appropriate.

The same persons and bodies must be consulted when a LIP is being revised (section 149).

Approval of Local Implementation Plans

The London borough councils and the Common Council of the City of **8.13** London are required to submit their LIP to the Mayor for approval (section 146).

To be approved, each LIP must (section 146(3)):

(a) be consistent with the transport strategy;
(b) contain proposals adequate for the purposes of the implementation of the transport strategy; and
(c) have a timetable and a date for implementing those proposals adequate for those purposes.

The Mayor's Default Powers

The Mayor enjoys wide reserve powers to ensure that each LIP (1) **8.14** complies with the requirements of section 145 (as to content, timetable and consultation), (2) is submitted to him for approval under section 146, and (3) complies with the requirements of section 146 set out above.

If a LIP has not been prepared properly or has not been submitted to the Mayor for approval, he can direct the London borough council or the Common Council of the City of London to do so within a specified period (section 147(1) and section 153). If the council fails to comply with that direction within a reasonable time, the Mayor may prepare the LIP on behalf of the council (section147(2)).

If the Mayor refuses to approve a plan under section 146, the council must prepare a new plan. Alternatively, the Mayor can serve a notice on the council to inform it that he intends to write the plan himself (section 147(3)). If the Mayor decides to write the plan himself, he must consult the council on whose behalf he is preparing the plan and the other bodies that the council would have had to consult (section 147(5)—see above).

If the Mayor prepares a LIP, he may recover his reasonable expenses from the council (section 147(7)).

Reviews and Revisions of Local Implementation Plans

8.15 The London borough councils and the Common Council of the City of London are able to prepare revisions to their LIPs voluntarily at any time (section 148(1)).

If the Mayor revises the transport strategy (section 41(2)), these authorities are required to prepare such revisions as they consider necessary and, if they consider no revisions are required, they must notify the Mayor in writing accordingly (section 148(2) and (3)).

The procedure for making revisions to a LIP (see above and sections 145 and 146) is the same as for the first such plan (section 149, and see above).

The Mayor has wide reserve powers to ensure LIPs are revised in accordance with section 145 and comply with the requirements of section 146 (section 150). These powers mirror the default powers of the Mayor in relation to initial LIPs under section 147 (see above).

Implementing a Local Implementation Plan

8.16 Each London borough council and the Common Council of the City of London must implement its LIP according to the timetable contained in the plan, whether the plan is one that was prepared by the council or the Mayor (under section 147 or section 150—section 151).

Section 152 provides the Mayor with wide reserve powers to ensure LIPs are implemented fully and on time. In effect, if the Mayor considers that a council has not carried out any proposal in the LIP satisfactorily and in accordance with the timetable, he may exercise the powers that the council should have exercised for itself. The Mayor may exercise the same powers when a council fails to comply with his direction under section 153 (see below).

The Mayor may recover the reasonable expenses of exercising this power (section 152(7)).

Directions by the Mayor

Section 153 enables the Mayor to give written binding instructions to a **8.17** London borough council or the Common Council of the City of London on the manner in which it is to perform its duties in respect of its LIP. Such directions may be general or specific. In particular, a direction under section 153 may dictate:

(a) the timetable for preparing or revising a LIP;

(b) the bodies or persons the council must consult about a LIP or revisions to a LIP;

(c) the timetable for implementing the proposals in a LIP;

(d) the date by which all the proposals in a LIP will be implemented;

(e) the action to be taken to implement the proposals in a LIP in accordance with that timetable or date;

(f) the steps to be taken to remove the effects of action which is incompatible with such proposals.

Replacement of Local Plans

To the extent that they do not relate to GLA roads or side roads, local **8.18** plans prepared by a London borough council or the Common Council of the City of London (under the Road Traffic Act 1991, s.54) continue in force until superseded by LIPs as if they were prepared as such plans (section 294(7)).

Chapter 9

TRANSPORT FOR LONDON

Overview

9.01 An important new statutory body, Transport for London (TfL) is created by the GLA Act (section 154). Whilst the Mayor and Authority will set policy and budgets for transport services, TfL will be the functional body that will actually deliver these. The White Paper, "A Mayor and Assembly for London: The Government's proposals for modernising the governance of London" Cm. 3897 (1998), described the role of TfL in this way (paragraphs 5.17 and 5.18):

> "TfL's role will be an executive one, implementing the Mayor's transport strategy and running or managing a wide range of transport functions and services on a day-to-day basis. It will also advise the Mayor on transport issues and be able to promote transport schemes across all modes. Responsibility for policy and all statutory duties will rest with the Mayor.
>
> On transport matters, TfL will manage the Mayor's relationship with the London boroughs, the Highways Agency, the rail industry, the Port of London Authority and other bodies with whom they will need to work closely."

TfL must exercise its functions in accordance with guidance or directions from the Mayor (section 154(3)(a) and section 155(1)). TfL's functions must also be used to facilitate the general transport duty (see above, section 141) and to secure or facilitate the implementation of the transport strategy (section 154(3)(b) and (c)—see above, section 142).

9.02 TfL will draw together functions relating to transport previously undertaken by a wide range of bodies, such as London Regional Transport, the Traffic Director for London, the Traffic Control Systems Unit and the Public Carriage Office. TfL will also assume responsibility for most of the work of the Highways Agency in London. It will be responsible for traffic management and maintenance for a network of important roads across London, to be known as GLA roads (Chapters XIII and XIV of Part IV, ss.259–294). TfL also has some new roles such as those in relation to railways (Chapter VI of Part IV of the GLA Act, ss.196–207).

This will enable TfL to run or manage a wide range of public transport services for London (section 173 and Schedule 11). TfL will have full responsibility for London Underground once the Public Private Partnership ("PPP") is implemented (sections 210–224).

The provisions relating to TfL will be fully in force from July 3, 2000. However, TfL itself is established from May 8, 2000 because section 154(1), creating TfL, and section 154(4), that brings Schedule 10 into effect, come into force from that date (S.I. 2000 No. 801).

The Status of Transport for London

Transport for London is not treated as a servant or agent of the Crown, **9.03** and no status, immunity or privilege of the Crown is extended to it. Its property is not treated as Crown property (Schedule 10, paragraph1(1) and (2)). Paragraph 31 of Schedule 11 also makes provision for TfL not to be regarded as a common carrier by rail or inland waterway and for it to be exempted from certain duties imposed by local enactments relating to railways.

Transport for London's Finances

Transport for London's budget will be set by, and received from, the **9.04** Mayor. A substantial part of the funds received from central government will be specifically earmarked for TfL and received as the GLA transport grant (Part III, especially section 101—see above,). TfL must administer its financial affairs in accordance with Chapter V of Part III of the GLA Act, ss.127-135 (see above).

TfL is treated as a local authority for the purposes of income, corporation, and capital gains taxes. This means that it is exempt from liability to pay those taxes (section 419).

Restriction on Exercise of Certain Powers Except through a Company

The Secretary of State may restrict the powers of TfL so that they may not **9.05** be exercised except through a company that is either a subsidiary of TfL or a company formed by TfL under section 156 (section 157—see below, under the subheading, "Transport for London's general powers"). Any such order must have the consent of the Treasury (section 157(1)) and be exercised by statutory instrument, and may be annulled by a resolution of either the House of Commons or the House of Lords (see section 420). This power of the Secretary of State is a consequence of the exemption that TfL, but not its subsidiaries, enjoys from liability for income tax. If TfL can be required to carry on certain activities only through a body that is liable to tax, an order under section 157 will ensure that the activities are accordingly taxable.

The Transport for London (Specified Activities) Order 2000 (S.I. 2000 No. 1548) prohibits TfL from carrying on a wide range of activities (specified in the Schedule to the Order) except through a company that is (a) limited by shares, (b) registered under the Companies Act 1985, and (c) either a subsidiary of TfL or a company which TfL formed, or joined with others in forming, by virtue of section 156(1) and which is not a subsidiary of TfL.

Financial Assistance by Transport for London to Others

9.06 Transport for London is authorised to make grants, loans or other payments to others for expenditure that TfL considers will be conducive to the provision of safe, integrated, efficient and economic transport facilities or services to, from or within Greater London (section 159—these aims correspond to those in the general transport duty, above, (section 141)). Financial assistance may be given with or without conditions (section 159(6)).

Abolition of transport grants to London authorities

9.07 The London borough councils and the Common Council of the City of London will no longer be on the list of authorities to which the Secretary of State must pay transport grants (section 159(8), amending section 88(2) of the Local Government and Finance Act 1988). Instead, TfL may provide financial assistance to such authorities in respect of expenditure incurred in discharging any function of a highway authority or traffic authority. TfL may have regard to previous financial assistance or authorisation to incur financial obligations given to an authority, and the use it made of that assistance or authorisation (section 159(4)).

Guarantees

9.08 A guarantee is a contract by which one person (the promisor) undertakes to answer to another (the promisee) for the debt or default of a third person (usually referred to as the "principal debtor"), whose primary liability to the promisor must exist or be contemplated at the time the guarantee is entered into.

Any guarantee provided by TfL must comply with the general law about guarantees as well as the requirements of section 160 set out below. To be valid, a guarantee must not only be a contract (in other words, an agreement, made between parties who intend to create legal relations and with the capacity to contract, supported by actual or implied consideration) but must also comply with the provisions of section 4 of the Statute of

Frauds (1677), as amended. It must either be in writing or there must be a memorandum of the guarantee signed by or on behalf of the promisor.

TfL may guarantee to discharge the financial obligations of (a) its subsidiaries, and (b) if the guarantee is to enable the person to carry out the agreement, (i) those it enters into agreements with under section 156(2) or (3) (for which, see below under the subheading, "Transport for London's general powers") (ii) any person (other than a subsidiary) with whom a subsidiary has entered into a transport subsidiary's agreement under section 169 (section 160(1)—see below).

TfL may also, but only for the purpose of discharging any of its functions, **9.09** guarantee the financial obligations of any person for the purposes of (a) an undertaking carried on by him, or (b) where the person is a body corporate, an undertaking carried on by a subsidiary of the body corporate (section 160(2)). The meaning of "undertaking" is not defined for the purposes of the GLA Act, but it is thought that the word is used to mean an enterprise in which a person has bound himself to engage.

TfL may also arrange for a third party (such as a bank) to provide the guarantee, and then indemnify the third party (section 160(4) and (5)).

The Influence of the Mayor

The Mayor's transport strategy (section 154) will set the policy for TfL. **9.10** TfL will be directly answerable to the Mayor, and will be required to exercise its functions in accordance with written guidance and directions given by the Mayor (section 154(3)(a)). The functions of the Mayor that are exercisable on behalf of the Authority may also be delegated to TfL (section 38).

Guidance and Directions by the Mayor

The Mayor's power to control the way in which TfL exercises its functions **9.11** is contained in section 155. The Mayor exercises control by issuing written guidance, or general or specific directions about the way in which TfL is to exercise its functions. In particular, the Mayor may control the way TfL performs its duties and conducts legal proceedings. The Mayor may, for example, issue guidance about the general approach to an issue such as where bus stopping places should be situated, may issue a direction on a specific question such as the position of a particular bus stop, or may direct TfL to refrain from litigation against a particular bus company. Both TfL's duties and powers can be controlled in this way.

TfL is required to exercise its functions in accordance with such guidance or directions (section 154(3)).

Notification

9.12 The Mayor's guidance or direction must be in writing and notified to the nominated officer of TfL. Section 75 enables the Authority to take advantage of the provisions of section 233 of the Local Government Act in relation to the service of notices. Assuming that the guidance or direction is a "notice" (see section 233(1) of the 1972 Act), the Mayor may notify the correct officer of TfL by using any of the methods set out in that section, such as: by delivering it to the officer personally, by leaving it at the officer's proper address or by sending it to the officer at that address (1972 Act, s.233(2)). TfL's proper address will be its registered or principal address (1972 Act, s.233(3)). As a result of these provisions, it is possible that even if the nominated officer has not in fact received notification, TfL will still be deemed to have been "notified" and bound to follow the guidance.

The Mayor's Power to Transfer Transport for London's Powers to Others

9.13 In order to enable a person to carry on activities for which provision is made by an agreement under section 156(2) or (3) (for which, see below under the subheading, "Transport for London's general powers"), the Mayor may by order transfer any statutory functions of TfL, or a subsidiary of TfL, to a person who has entered into such an agreement with TfL (section 158).

The Mayor can only exercise this power by order, which is of no effect until confirmed by an order of the Secretary of State. The Secretary of State's order must in turn be made by statutory instrument, and may be annulled by a resolution of either the House of Commons or the House of Lords (section 420). The opportunity to use this power does not arise in relation to any functions of TfL under the GLA Act or any statutory provision amended by it (section 158(5)).

Accountability and Scrutiny of Transport for London

9.14 TfL will be accountable to the Mayor, and through the Mayor to the electorate. For example, the Mayor could be required to answer questions about, and to report on, the actions of TfL (sections 45–48—see above).

TfL will be one of the bodies that must be actively monitored by a designated officer (a "monitorily officer") for apparent breaches of law or codes of practice or for maladministration (section 73—see above).

TfL's advice to the Mayor is generally protected from being disclosed in the Mayor's periodic report to the Assembly and from the general power of the Assembly to require information (sections 45 and 61—see above).

Annual Reports

TfL must submit a report on the exercise and performance of its functions **9.15** to the GLA as soon as possible after March 31 in each year (section 161(1) and section 424).

The report must deal with TfL's contribution towards implementing the transport strategy, the activities of its subsidiaries, so far as relevant to the performance of its functions in that year, financial assistance given under section 159, and guarantees, third party arrangements and indemnities given under section 160 (for which, see above under the subheading "Financial assistance by Transport for London to others". The report must include in relation to these topics any information that the Mayor has specified (section 161(3)).

TfL must also publish the report, although the time for doing this is not prescribed (section 161(4)). The Mayor must keep the report available for six years after publication (section 161(6) and (7)).

The Structure and Membership of Transport for London

Schedule 10 makes detailed provision about the structure of TfL. The basic **9.16** structure is of a board of between eight and 15 members, all appointed by the Mayor (Schedule 10, paragraph 2(1) and (2)).

The Mayor, or a person appointed by the Mayor, will be chairman of TfL and the Mayor must appoint a deputy (Schedule 10, paragraph 3).

When making appointments, the Mayor must consider the desirability of ensuring that the members of TfL have between them relevant experience and that the interests of women and persons who require transport accessible to persons with mobility problems are represented (Schedule 10, paragraph 2(3)). The areas of relevant experience are: transport (in particular the impact of transport on business and the environment), finance and commerce, national and local government, the management of organisations, and the organisation of trade unions, or matters relating to workers generally.

Most categories of elected politicians (an Assembly member, a Member of the House of Commons, European Parliament, National Assembly for Wales, Scottish Parliament, New Northern Ireland Assembly, or a member of a principal council) and all Members of the House of Lords are prohibited from being appointed to TfL (Schedule 10, paragraph 2(4)). Political influence will instead come from the Mayor.

Proceedings, Committees and Delegation

TfL may regulate its own procedure, subject to the restrictions in Schedule **9.17** 10 (Schedule 10, paragraph 5).

Vacancies or defects in appointments (Schedule 10, paragraph 5) do not affect the validity of TfL's proceedings.

Subject to any statutory provisions to the contrary, TfL may delegate its functions to committees, sub-committees, its wholly owned subsidiaries, a single member or officer of TfL and one or more members and/or officers. TfL may impose conditions on the delegated exercise of its functions by such persons. If TfL exercises the power to delegate any of its functions, TfL is not prevented from continuing to exercise a delegated function (Schedule 10, paragraph 6). A committee or sub-committee of TfL may include members who are not members of TfL, although such persons will have no voting rights (Schedule 10, paragraph 6). Provision is also made for committees and sub-committees to further delegate functions (Schedule 10, paragraph 8).

TfL will be treated as a local authority for the purposes of the provisions of the Local Government Act 1972 that relate to the appointment of joint committees with other local authorities and the discharge of functions through such committees. This does not disqualify TfL's representatives from voting if they are not members of TfL itself (Schedule 10, paragraph 9).

9.18 Written records must be made of all meetings of TfL and its committees and sub-committees. Minutes signed by a person purporting to be chairman of such proceedings are evidence of the proceedings to which they relate and the proceedings are, unless the contrary is shown, assumed to be validly convened and constituted (Schedule 10, paragraph 10).

Any authorised member, officer or member of staff of TfL may authenticate with their signature the seal of TfL. Similarly, such an authorised person may sign on behalf of TfL any document that TfL is authorised or required by any statute to serve, make or issue. A document purporting to be made or issued by or on behalf of TfL and under TfL's seal, or signed or executed by a person authorised by TfL for the purpose, must be received in evidence and treated as so made or issued unless the contrary is shown. An authenticating signature includes a facsimile of such a signature (Schedule 10, paragraphs 11 and 12).

Disclosure of Members' Interests

9.19 A member of TfL must disclose all interests he may have in any matter arising for consideration at a meeting of TfL, and must take no part in any deliberation or decision on the matter. The minutes must record the disclosure. These restrictions apply to indirect as well as direct interests, and non-pecuniary as well as pecuniary interests. A member need not attend a meeting personally to make such disclosure if he takes reasonable steps to ensure a notice read and considered at the meeting makes disclosure. If the Mayor considers that these restrictions would disable so great a proportion of the members of TfL as a whole that its business would be impaired, he may remove them subject to such conditions as he thinks appropriate. If the Mayor exercises this power, he must notify TfL of that fact and of his reasons, and TfL's minutes must record the removal of the disability and the reasons (Schedule 10, paragraph 13).

The Director of Public Prosecutions may prosecute a person who fails to comply with these restrictions. The offence is punishable on summary conviction by a fine up to level 4 on the standard scale (currently £2,500 under the Criminal Justice Act 1982, section 37 (as amended))—Schedule 10, paragraph 13).

TfL may also generally exclude a member from meetings of TfL while any contract, proposed contract or other matter in which he has an interest is under consideration. A person who contravenes such an exclusion does not commit an offence (Schedule 10, paragraph 13).

Other statutory provisions relating to disclosure of members' interests are applied to TfL, with appropriate modifications, in other words those contained in sections 95, 96 and 97(4) and (5) of the Local Government Act 1972 and section 19 of the Local Government and Housing Act 1989 (Schedule 10, paragraph 13).

Staffing of Transport for London

TfL may appoint staff to assist in carrying out its functions (Schedule 10, **9.20** paragraph 4). The restrictions in sections 1 to 3 of the Local Government and Housing Act 1989 (disqualification and political restriction) apply to the staff of TfL as if it were a local authority: section 68. Staff are not treated as civil servants (Schedule 10, paragraph 1(2)).

Transport for London's General Powers

Section 156 gives TfL general powers similar to those of London Regional **9.21** Transport under the London Regional Transport Act 1984. However, whereas LRT's powers were only exercisable in relation to public passenger transport, TfL will be able to exercise its powers in respect of all its functions, which relate to all modes of transport in London. TfL has a general power to do such things and enter into such transactions as are calculated to facilitate, or are conducive or incidental to, the discharge of any of its functions (Schedule 10 paragraph 1(3)).

TfL can form, promote or assist companies, either by itself or with others, in order to carry out its transport functions (section 156(1)). TfL can transfer its property, rights and liabilities to such a company (section 156(5)).

Section 156(2) Agreements

TfL will be able to enter into agreements with others in order to carry out **9.22** activities which TfL has power to carry on, whether or not the other person acts as TfL's agent (section 156(2)). TfL can transfer its property, rights and liabilities to such a person (section 156(5)).

Section 156(3) Agreements

9.23 In certain circumstances, TfL can arrange for others to carry out activities, including those which it does not have power to carry on itself (section 156(3)). It can do so by making an agreement with another person ("the contractor") which includes provision for the contractor to (a) carry on activities which TfL has power to carry on, or for activities TfL has power to carry on together with others which it does not have power to carry on, or (b) provide to TfL services ancillary to the provision of public passenger transport services, or (c) use land or property owned by TfL, or transferred to the contractor by TfL, for the purposes of the agreement. TfL can transfer its property, rights and liabilities to such a contractor (section 156(5)).

9.23A If TfL exercises its powers to enter agreements under section 156(2) or (3), it may enter and carry out further agreements to fulfil conditions which must be fulfilled before the agreement can take effect or to satisfy requirements imposed by or under the agreement (section 156(4)).

TfL may provide to its subsidiaries, or persons with whom it has made agreements under section 156(2) or (3) assistance by making available services, amenities, facilities, works, land and property (section 156(6)).

TfL has a general power to do all things necessary or expedient for the discharge of its functions and to fulfil contracts entered into by its predecessor bodies before they were abolished (Schedule 11, paragraphs 32 and 33).

Transport for London's Specific Powers

Transport for London's Powers to Make Byelaws

9.24 TfL may make byelaws (section 166). This discretionary power is in similar terms to section 76, which gives the Authority power to make byelaws (see above).

TfL may also make bye-laws in relation to railways (Schedule 11, paragraph 26) and waterside landing places (Schedule 11, paragraph 27).

Transport for London's Power to Promote and Oppose Local Bills

9.25 TfL may promote and oppose local Bills (section 167). This power may only be exercised with the consent of the Authority (subsections (2) and (6)). Compare the Authority's powers to promote and oppose local and private Bills (see above, section 77).

Schedule 13 makes provision for the way in which TfL may promote a local Bill. TfL must consult the Mayor, Assembly, the London borough councils and the Common Council of the City of London about its draft Bill

(Schedule 13, paragraph 2) and then publicise the Bill for a reasonable period after the draft Bill has been sent to those consultees (Schedule 13, paragraph 2). The draft may then be revised to take account of representations received during the consultation period and other material considerations (Schedule 13, paragraph 4). The Bill is then deposited in Parliament and publicised for a further 14 days (Schedule 13, paragraphs 4 and 6).

If the Bill will affect the statutory functions of any London borough council or the Common Council at least 90 per cent of the affected authorities must consent to the Bill (Schedule 13, paragraph 5).

Transport for London's Power to Apply for and Object to Certain Transport Orders

TfL may, with the written consent of the Mayor, apply for or object to **9.26** certain transport orders (section 168, amending section 20 of the Transport and Works Act 1992).

By virtue of section 20 of the Transport and Works Act 1992, a body which has power to promote or oppose Bills in Parliament also has power to apply for and object to orders under sections 1 and 3 of the 1992 Act. TfL is now added to the bodies who may exercise such powers by virtue of section 167. Orders under sections 1 and 3 of the 1992 Act are made by the Secretary of State and relate to, or to matters ancillary to the construction or operation of railway, tramway, trolley vehicle and certain other guided transport systems, and the construction or operation of inland waterways and certain works interfering with navigation rights.

Miscellaneous Powers and Duties of Transport for London

Schedule 11 makes detailed provision in relation to the powers of TfL.   **9.27**

TfL may carry passengers by any form of land or water transport (including hovercraft) within, to or from Greater London. It may also carry passengers by such transport methods between places outside Greater London in certain circumstances, such as to avoid interruption of some services. TfL will be able to arrange for others to provide air transport between places in Greater London or between Greater London and places outside. TfL may arrange for others to make passenger vehicles available for hire in or between places in Greater London or between such places and places outside Greater London (Schedule 11, paragraphs 1–2).

Although TfL has power to carry luggage and other goods, and provide storage for goods (Schedule 11, paragraphs 1(3) and 3), the government has made it clear that this power should be interpreted narrowly. During the passage of the bill through the House of Lords, the Under-Secretary of State for the Department of the Environment, Transport and the Regions, Lord Whitty, explained that the Schedule was "not creating a new freight company" and that "the reference to luggage and other goods merely relates to goods similar to luggage." *Hansard* H.L. Vol. 603, col. 469.

9.28   TfL can provide incidental amenities and facilities for other parties with whom it has entered into agreements, for the other party to use those facilities to carry out transport services. It may provide, or arrange for others to provide, amenities and facilities which TfL considers would benefit people using other transport facilities and services, whether or not those other facilities or services are provided by TfL. TfL may also provide car parks and parking for public service vehicles (Schedule 11, paragraphs 4–6).

TfL may charge for its services and facilities, and has the discretion to waive such charges (Schedule 11, paragraph 7). Likewise, TfL may charge for technical assistance and advice that it provides to others (Schedule 11, paragraph 9).

TfL has power to manufacture and repair supplementary machinery (such as spare parts and components) that is required to operate its existing vehicles or those of its subsidiaries. Its power to repair vehicles or other equipment is much wider and extends even to vehicles and equipment that are not owned by TfL or its subsidiaries. Fir the purpose of repairs to vehicles and equipment that do not belong to TfL, it may supply any necessary parts and components (Schedule 11, paragraph 8).

9.29   TfL and other transport operators may enter into reciprocal arrangements with any other person for ancillary services. Such services might include the sale of tickets (Schedule 11, paragraph 10).

TfL has power to exploit certain commercial opportunities such as hiring out vehicles, selling or leasing assets the Mayor does not require for the implementation of the transport strategy, supplying spare parts for passenger vehicles it sells, investing money and using its resources so far as not immediately required for discharging its functions, and spending reasonable sums to exploit commercial opportunities (Schedule 11, paragraph 11–13).

TfL may provide facilities for transferring freight between railways, waterways and other modes of transport (Schedule 11, paragraph 14).

TfL has power to acquire, develop, sell and lease land (Schedule 11, paragraphs 15–21).

The Secretary of State may authorise TfL to acquire land compulsorily: the consent of the Mayor is required. (Schedule 11, paragraph 19).

TfL has power to undertake research and development in relation to its transport functions, and arrange for others to do so (Schedule 11 paragraph 22).

TfL may provide for the welfare and efficiency of employees and the efficiency of its equipment (Schedule 11, paragraph 23).

9.30   TfL has power to acquire an undertaking if the assets to be acquired are wholly or mainly required for discharging any of its functions. The meaning of "undertaking" is not defined for the purposes of the GLA Act, but it is thought that the word is used to mean an enterprise in which a person has bound himself to engage. TfL may subscribe for or acquire securities of a body corporate for the purpose of discharging its functions (Schedule 11, paragraphs 24–5).

TfL may provide a museum (Schedule 11, paragraph 28).

TfL must act as a commercial entity (Schedule 11, paragraph 29).

TfL has power to make investments by lending money to acquire securities and to inherit loans and guarantees made by LRT and any securities acquired by LRT (Schedule 11, paragraph 30).

Schedule 11, paragraph 31 states that TfL and its subsidiaries are not to be regarded as common carriers by rail or inland waterway. It also provides that certain local enactments in relation to railways have a restricted application to TfL.

Information about Public Passenger Transport Services

TfL is required to provide information about public passenger transport **9.31** services required by members of the public in deciding what use to make of services to, from and within Greater London (section 162). This information must be made available to both the general public and any other person TfL thinks fit (for example, a private provider of travel information). Although this duty is expressed in mandatory terms ("shall" is used), TfL has a free hand in deciding what information to make available (it must provide "such information as it thinks fit" and "in such manner as [it] thinks fit"), subject to general public law principles.

TfL may make "such charges as it thinks fit" for providing information under this section, but no charge may be made for information that relates to services provided exclusively by TfL or its subsidiaries or other persons under a transport subsidiary's agreement (for which, see below) or agreements entered into under section 156(2) or (3) (for which, see above under the subheading, "The general powers of Transport for London") (subsection (3)).

TfL also has a duty to provide general information to councils and the London Transport Passenger Users' Committee (see below, section 178).

TfL's Powers to Dispose of Railway or Tramway Lines or Stations

TfL's (and the Authority's) power to dispose of railway or tramway land is **9.32** restricted by section 163. The restriction applies to land that is or has been within the last five years operational land (section 164(1) and (3)).

Operational land is land which is used, or in which an interest is held, for the purpose of carrying on any railway or tramway undertaking of TfL or one of its subsidiaries. Land which has been used, or an interest held, by London Regional Transport or a subsidiary of LRT for the same purpose is treated as if the railway or tramway undertaking was at the time that of TfL or one of its subsidiaries, and is accordingly operational land. Land is not treated as operational land if, in respect of its general nature and situation, it is more comparable with land in general than with land used, or in which interests are held, for the purpose of carrying on a railway or tramway undertaking (section 163(8)).

The consent of the Secretary of State is required before TfL can dispose of operational land either by outright sale or the grant of a lease with a term longer than 50 years. The Secretary of State's consent must be given in a statutory instrument, and may be annulled by a resolution of either the House of Commons or the House of Lords (section 420).

There is also provision to ensure operational land is not disposed of by a subsidiary of TfL. The Secretary of State's consent is required for any transaction or series of transactions that will result in a company in which operational land is vested ceasing to be a subsidiary of TfL (section 163(2) and section 164—for which, see below). An agreement that is made in contravention of these provisions would be void.

Control over Subsidiaries of Transport for London

9.33 The Authority and TfL are required to ensure that subsidiaries of TfL do not do anything that TfL has no power to do (section 164). The activities of any company are usually set out in the memorandum and articles of association that establish the company. In the case of a company established by TfL, the powers and restrictions set out in the GLA Act will override anything which contradicts them in these legal documents.

These provisions may operate, for example, to ensure that a subsidiary of TfL does not dispose of operational land in contravention of section 163 (for which, see above). Whilst the company remains TfL's subsidiary, it is subject to the same prohibitions on disposing of operational land as TfL. The consent of the Secretary of State is required before the company may cease to be TfL's subsidiary (section 163(2)).

The way in which TfL's subsidiaries can raise money is also restricted (section 164). Selling stock or shares increases the risk that TfL could lose control of the subsidiary, and the consent of the Mayor is therefore required before such a sale can take place.

Transfer of Property, Rights and Liabilities

9.34 TfL may make detailed arrangements for transferring the legal ownership of its property, rights and liabilities between itself and its subsidiaries (section 165). The Mayor's approval is required, however.

This simplified procedure for transfer will avoid the cost and time involved in the normal process of conveyancing.

Schedule 12 makes detailed provision for the operation of transfer schemes under sections 165 and 217). It sets out:

(a) the property, rights and liabilities that may be transferred (paragraph 2);
(b) how apportionment or division of property, rights and liabilities may take effect (paragraph 3);
(c) how property, rights and liabilities may be defined (paragraph 4);
(d) what provision may be made for creating rights, liabilities and obligations (paragraph 5);
(e) the supplementary provisions that may be made (paragraph 6);
(f) how statutory functions may be transferred (paragraph 7);
(g) the date for the transfer of the property, rights and liabilities (paragraph 8);
(h) legal continuity between the transferor and the transferee (paragraph 9), including continuity in the employment context (paragraph 10);
(i) the way in which information about the scheme must be provided to TfL (paragraph 11); and
(j) how the scheme may be modified (paragraph 12).

Transport Subsidiary's Agreements

A transport subsidiary's agreement is defined in section 169. It as an **9.35** agreement:

"(1) . . . with a person ("the contractor")—

(a) which is entered into by, or transferred to, a subsidiary of Transport for London, and
(b) which falls within subsection (2) or (3) below.

(2) An agreement falls within this subsection if it includes provision for the carrying on by the contractor, whether as agent for the subsidiary or otherwise, of any activities which Transport for London has power to carry on; and such an agreement may include provision with respect to the provision or financing of any public passenger transport services.

(3) An agreement falls within this subsection if it includes provision for the carrying on by the contractor of any activities which Transport for London does not have power to carry on and also provision for one or more of the following, namely—

(a) the carrying on by the contractor of such activities as are mentioned in subsection (2) above;
(b) the provision by the contractor to the subsidiary of services ancillary to the provision of public passenger transport services; and
(c) the use by the contractor of land or other property owned by Transport for London, or a subsidiary of Transport for London, or

transferred to the contractor by Transport for London or a
subsidiary of Transport for London, for the purposes of the
agreement."

9.36   The definition applies to a wide variety of agreements between a
contractor and a subsidiary of TfL. Such agreements may be entered into
in the same circumstances as agreements made between TfL itself and
other parties under section 156, but with appropriate modifications to take
account of the fact that a subsidiary of TfL is making the agreement (see
above, under the subheading, "General powers of Transport for London").

Contractors to a transport subsidiary's agreement may benefit from
guarantees from TfL (see above, section 160), and their activities may be
the subject of representations to the London Transport Users' Committee
(see below, and section 248).

Chapter 10

LONDON REGIONAL TRANSPORT/ TRANSPORT USERS' COMMITTEE

Introduction

London Regional Transport (LRT), formerly the London Transport Execu- **10.01** tive (LTE), is a staturory body created the London Regional Transport Act 1984. Its responsibility is to provide or secure the provision of public passenger transport services for Greater London, having regard to the transport needs for the time being of Greater London and efficiency, economy and safety of operation. LRT works with Railtrack, British Rail, Docklands Light Railway and the private bus companies to plan and co-ordinate London's public transport and to provide integrated ticketing and information for Underground, bus and rail services.

The Act provides for the abolition of LRT, the repeal of the 1984 Act and the transfer of its property, rights and liabilities to Transport for London (TfL) so that it can continue to provide the services LRT currently provide. Further, any functions of the LTE exercised by the LRT by virtue of section 67(1), London Regional Transport Act 1984 are also transferred to TfL (section 301).

Transitional Period

Under section 297 of the GLA Act the Secretary of State is required to **10.02** prepare programmes for transferring to TfL the property, rights and liabilities of LRT, and a transfer programme may provide for different property, rights or liabilities to be transferred on different days. Until a programme has been implemented it can be varied or replaced by another programme. Section 298 of the GLA Act makes provision for the exercise of various functions during the transitional period (starting when the section comes into force and ending when LRT ceases to provide or secure public passenger transport services). Before this section comes into effect LRT are required, and are taken to have had the power, to do anything appropriate for the five transitional purposes, namely:

- facilitating and securing and carrying into effect the Private Public Partnership (PPP) agreements under Part IV, Ch. VII (GLA Act, s.298(1)(a));
- facilitating the transfer of property, rights and liabilities of LRT to TfL (GLA Act, s.298(1)(b));
- facilitating the transfer of functions, property, rights and liabilities to TfL from any other body or person from whom they are or may be so transferred under the Act (GLA Act, s.298(1)(c));
- facilitating the exercise by TfL of any functions so transferred (GLA Act, s.298(1)(d)); or
- securing the public passenger transport services continue to be provided without disruption (GLA Act, s.298(1)(e)).

The Mayor, LRT and TfL are required to consult and co-operate with each other for any transitional purpose (GLA Act, s.298(3)). This will involve providing information to each other (GLA Act, s.298(5)) and entering into arrangements with each other to provide services and discharge their functions (GLA Act, s.298(6)). During the transitional period the Mayor must not prejudice the financial or other interests of LRT when giving directions to LRT (GLA Act, s.155) or determining its fare structure (GLA Act, s.174), and he must also have regard to the interests of TfL.

TfL is also required, if given the power to enter into concessionary fare arrangements on behalf of LRT (GLA Act, ss.240 to 243 and Sched.16), not act in a way which it considers will not prejudice the financial or other interests of LRT (GLA Act, s.299).

Section 300 of the GLA Act provides for continuity between the repealed or revoked functions of LRT and TfL. Anything done by LRT is to be treated as if it has been done by TfL, and TfL may continue it (GLA Act, s.300(2) and (3)). TfL is automatically substituted for LRT in instruments (*e.g.* a deed, contract or charter), contracts and legal proceedings relating to the abolished functions of LRT (section 300(4)). Section 301(2) of the GLA Act amends section 144 of the Transport Act 1968 so that LRT's duty to preserve certain historical records and relics is transferred to TfL. When the Secretary of State is satisfied that all property, rights and liabilities of LRT have been transferred to TfL, he may by order dissolve LRT (GLA Act, s.302).

Extension of LRT Powers

10.03 Chapter III, Part IV of the GLA Act makes three amendments to the London Regional Transport Act 1984. First, the amendment to section 9 of the London Regional Transport Act 1984 relates to LRT's powers of disposal (GLA Act, s.170). This amendment clarifies LRT's power to dispose of the securities of subsidiaries. Section 68 of the 1984 Act defines securities, in relation to any body corporate, as shares, stock, debentures, debenture stock and any other security of a like nature of a body corporate. "Disposal" is now defined in the 1984 Act as disposal by any means other than appropriation or mortgage (London Regional Transport Act 1984, s.9(8) is inserted by the GLA Act, s.170(3)). Both once-and-for-all sales, and disposals under PPP agreements (for which, see section 210) will therefore be included. The disposal may be by way of lease, but this does not include an option to take a lease or mortgage. Such an option will be *ultra vires*: see, for example, *Stretch v. West Dorset D.C.* (1999) 2 L.G.L.R., CA. Where the authority seeks to discharge one or more of their principle functions the Secretary of State can, after consultation (GLA Act, s.32), direct TfL to exercise its powers of disposal under section 9 of the London Regional Transport Act 1984 (London Regional Transport Act 1984, s.10).

It is anticipated that LRT will use the powers in this section as the **10.04** means of transferring to private sector PPP companies (for which, see section 210) the assets, contracts, etc., that they will need in order to carry out their activities.

Secondly, section 17 of the London Regional Transport Act 1984 modifies LRT's power to give financial assistance to subsidiaries, contractors and others. The power is widened so that the power to indemnify others who provide guarantees is added to the existing powers to give money, lend money or give a guarantee (London Regional Transport Act 1984, s.17(2) and (3)).

Finally, the amendment to section 27 of the London Regional Transport Act 1984 modifies the provisions relating to schemes for the transfer of property, right and liabilities under sections 4, 5 and 9(6) of that Act (GLA Act, s.172).

London Transport Users' Committee

The London Regional Passengers Committee (LRPC) as established under **10.05** the London Regional Transport Act 1984 is abolished by the provisions of Chapter X of the GLA Act and replaced with a new body called the London Transport Users' Committee (LTUC). Schedule 19 of the Act, which amends various provisions, for example the Transport Act 1985, so that they will refer to LTUC rather than its predecessor, the London Regional Passengers' Committee (GLA Act, s.252(2)). This body has a slightly wider remit than its predecessor in that it will be able to assist with any representation about transport in London, not just services and facilities provided by LRT, their subsidiaries, certain of LRT's contractors and operators of railways (*cf.* London Regional Transport Act 1984, s.40). LTUC will have power to assist with representations (which will usually be complaints) about TfL and the transport functions of the GLA (GLA Act, s.248).

The Assembly must appoint the chairman and members of LTUC so that the interests of transport users are represented (GLA Act, s.247(3)). Section 247 of the GLA Act introduces Schedule 18 which makes detailed provision for remuneration for the chairman, members and officers of LTUC (paragraphs 1 to 6) and their pensions (paragraph 7), the keeping of accounts (paragraph 8), office accommodation (paragraph 9), the regulation of its procedure (paragraphs 10–14), the right of the public to be admitted to its meetings (paragraph 15), and the procedure for investigating complaints against LTUC (paragraph 16).

10.06 LTUC is required to exercise its functions according to written guidance and directions from the Assembly (GLA Act, s.251). Section 250 of the GLA Act ensures that LTUC's proceedings and recommendations are transmitted to the Assembly, the Mayor and TfL, and that those bodies in turn inform LTUC of action that will be taken in response. Kate Hoey, the Parliamentary Under-Secretary of State for the Home Department, stated that there was no need to amend this provision to ensure that LTUC would be given reasons for decisions of the Assembly, Mayor or TfL. She explained that:

"the assembly, as well as having a scrutiny role, will be a public body and its decisions will therefore be public. The reasons will be public if it decides on something proposed by the London Transport Users' Committee. It is common sense and good practice throughout central and local government that, where a decision is given, the reasons for the decision are also given." *Official Report Standing Committee A*, March 2, 1999, col. 901.

LTUC's Mandatory Duties

10.07 Section 248 of the GLA Act requires LTUC to represent the concerns of transport users in London. LTUC must consider and make recommendations (for which, see in particular the GLA Act, s.249) on representations and referrals made to it relating to any of the transport functions of the GLA. Such representations will often be complaints. Cyclists and pedestrians are to be specifically considered when LTUC makes recommendations in response to representations concerning highways (GLA Act, s.248(4)). LTUC's remit will therefore be as wide as TfL's. The only exceptions to LTUC's duty to consider representations arise in relation to freight (GLA Act, s.248(1)(b)), or if LTUC considers that the representations are frivolous (GLA Act, s.248(3)(a)).

If LTUC is not the appropriate body to deal with a particular matter, it must refer the matter to a appropriate person (GLA Act, s.248(5)) and tell the complainant that it has done so. The use of the word "inform" (contrast the word "notify" in the GLA Act, s.248(6)) suggests that the complainant need not be informed of the referral in writing.

LTUC must refer to TfL representations relating to hackney carriages and private hire vehicles that raise issues about offences, illegality or breaches of licence conditions (section 248(2)(d) and (e) and (6)). LTUC must also notify the complainant in writing that it has done so (section 248(6)).

LTUC's Discretionary Powers

10.08 LTUC has a discretion to consider other matters affecting the Authority's or TfL's transport functions which come to its attention and seem worthy of attention (GLA Act, s.248(3)(c)). LTUC may also make voluntary arrangements, subject to the approval of the Assembly, under which LTUC will consider matters relating to transport in Greater London (GLA Act, s.249).

Rail Users' Consultative Committee

10.09 Section 252 of the GLA Act substitutes the London Transport Users' Committee in place of the London Regional Passengers' Committee as the Rail Users' Consultative Committee for Greater London. Rail Users' Consultative Committees are statutory committees with duties to investigate and make representations about (to service providers and, in certain circumstances, the Rail Regulator) matters relating to railway passenger services and station services upon representations being made by a user or potential user of the service in question (see in particular the Railways Act 1993, ss.77–79).

Chapter 11

PUBLIC PASSENGER TRANSPORT

Introduction

11.01 Although TfL is not under a general duty to provide for or secure the provision of public passenger transport services in Greater London, it is very unlikely that it will not be required to provide or secure such services when its specific statutory duties are considered. It is hard to imagine how TfL could implement the Mayor's transport strategy (see the GLA Act, s.142) or facilitate the Authority's discharge of the general transport duty (see the GLA Act, ss. 141 and 154) without providing or securing such services. In addition, TfL is under a specific duty to provide or secure the provision of certain transport, for example, the London bus network (see the GLA Act, s.181).

Provision of Public Passenger Transport

11.02 The provision of public passenger transport services can be secured either by TfL, any of its subsidiaries or any party who has entered into an agreement with TfL under section 156(2) or (3)(a) of the GLA Act or a transport subsidiary's agreement (as defined by section 169, GLA Act). Any such agreement may provide for combined services, the quoting of rates, the pooling of receipts and expenses for the through carriage of passengers or goods to be provided by TfL. The agreement may also provide for the securing of efficiency, economy and safety of operation in providing the services, the route for those services, their frequency and the making of payments by TfL (GLA Act, s.173,).

The Mayor is required to issue guidance and directions to TfL to control the general level and structure of fares and services (GLA Act, s.174,). The Mayor should control only the general scheme: TfL and the operators of the services should determine the detail.

TfL is required each year to provide information of its current plans regarding the general level of transport services and facilities to be provided; the general structure of such services; the general level and structure of the fares, and the general level of the fares to be made for such facilities (GLA Act, s.178(1)). TfL must provide this information to the London borough councils, the Common Council, any Greater London whose area appears to be significantly affected by TfL's plans, together with the London Transport User's Committee (GLA Act, s.178(2)). There is no provision for these bodies, having been given the information, to make representations to TfL, nor provision requiring TfL to consider any representations that are made. It is likely, however, that TfL will take into account any such representations as failure to do so may expose it to judicial review proceedings.

It is not clear whether this duty to inform the London boroughs, etc. **11.03** arises just once in each year (as implied by the use of the words "in each year"), or whether it is a recurring duty that arises whenever TfL revises its "current plans" (GLA Act, s.178(1)). As section 162 of the GLA Act provides for a continuing duty to make available information relating to public passenger transport services and how members of the public may use such services, it is unlikely that section 178 will be interpreted to restrict this general duty to only require this information to be provided to the London boroughs, etc. once a year or only when its plans regarding the services, facilities and structure and level of fares are amended.

TfL is also under a duty to publish, as it thinks fit, the general structure of the fares to be charged for the services to be provided by TfL, its subsidiary or any other person under an agreement with TfL (GLA Act, s.178(3)).

Duty to Co-operate

In discharging their respective functions (see the GLA Act, section 154(3), **11.04** for the functions of TfL, and the Railways Act 1993, ss. 23 to 31, 37 and 38, for the functions of the Franchising Director (GLA Act, s.175(3))) TfL and the Franchising Director are under a duty to co-operate with each other for the purpose of co-ordinating the passenger transport services for persons travelling to, from and within Greater London, and securing or facilitating TfL's discharge of its functions under section 154(3) of the GLA Act. This duty extends to providing one another such information as to their respective services as may reasonably be required to discharge their respective duties (GLA Act, s.175(1)). The reason for the imposition of this duty is to ensure that, as far as possible, the two services will interact in a way that fulfils the respective statutory obligations of each party. To that end TfL and the Franchising Director may enter into agreements with each other for that purpose (GLA Act, s.175(2)).

Where a public passenger transport service is provided by a person other **11.05** than a subsidiary of TfL, that person and TfL are under a duty to co-operate with each other in discharging their respective duties for the purpose of co-ordinating passenger transport services; securing or facilitating the general transport duty of the authority, and the implementation of the transport strategy (GLA Act, s.176). The duty of co-operation imposes a requirement to exchange information to further the specified purposes. If the statutory duty conflicts with a company's private law duties (such as to act in the interests of its owners or in accordance with its articles of association), the statutory duty will prevail.

Local authorities in Greater London are able to enter into agreements with TfL, the Franchising Director or any person holding a passenger licence, network licence or station licence in order to secure the provision of public passenger transport services (GLA Act, s.177). However such agreements can only be entered into as a last resort since the power does not arise unless the public passenger transport services and facilities would not be available unless such an agreement is made (GLA Act, s.177(1)).

Forms of Transport Services

11.06 Public passenger transport in Greater London will inevitably be secured by TfL as it is the new executive body through which the GLA's general transport duty is discharged (GLA Act, s.141) and the Mayor's transport strategy is implemented (GLA Act, s.154(3)). The public passenger transport services is provided through the provision or control of the following services:

- bus services (Chapter V);
- railways (Chapter VI);
- hackney carriages and private hire vehicles (Chapter XI);
- water transport (Chapter XII).

Where a person travels without a valid ticket on any bus or train service operated by TfL, any of its subsidiaries or any other person under agreement with TfL, he will be liable to pay a penalty fare (see below, paragraph 11.53). Further, as was previously the case, local authorities may make voluntary arrangements for travel concessions for their eligible residents travelling on TfL buses or trains. In the absence of agreement, TfL will be required to implement a "reserve free travel scheme" the cost of providing which it will be able to charge to the local authorities concerned (see below, paragraph 11.48).

Bus Services in Greater London

11.07 Unlike bus services in the rest of Great Britain, bus services in Greater London were not deregulated under the Transport Act 1985. London has retained a regulated regime operated by London Regional Transport (LRT) under Part II of the 1985 Act, and most services are secured by private bus companies under contract to LRT through its powers under the London Regional Transport Act 1984. There is also a small number of bus services that are licensed by the Traffic Commissioner through his powers in the Transport Act 1985. The Traffic Commissioners in Great Britain were established by sections 3 and 4 of and Schedule 2 to the Public Passenger Vehicles Act 1981. There are 11 areas, and the Traffic Commissioner for the traffic area in which Greater London is situated is referred to in the GLA Act as the traffic commissioner for the Metropolitan Traffic area. Each commissioner is responsible for the issuing of licences under the 1981 Act, s.4 and certain functions in relation to goods and passenger carrying vehicles (see the Road Traffic Act 1988, s.111).

This dual system, which will continue to apply following the transfer of LRT's property, rights and liabilities to TfL (see Chapter 10), will be adapted by Chapter V, Part IV under TfL. TfL, its subsidiaries and their contractors will provide such bus services in Greater London as are required for safe, integrated, efficient and economical transport services (sections 180–184). Other bus services may be provided in Greater London by any person who holds a London service permit (sections 185–190).

The London Bus Network

Chapter V, Part IV of the Act adapts the regulation of bus services in **11.08** Greater London and determines the way in which most of them will be regulated. TfL is required to determine which London local services are required to provide a safe, integrated, efficient and economic transport service in Greater London (section 181(1)—*cf.* section 141 at paragraph 8.01). No London local service can be provided except in accordance with Chapter V, and any operator providing such a service in contravention of this chapter is liable on summary conviction to a fine not exceeding level 3 on the standard scale (£1,000).

A London local service is defined in section 179 as a local service with one or more stops in Greater London. Such services will be collectively known as the "London bus network". Section 179 imports the definition of "local service" from section 2 of the Transport Act 1984, namely, any service using one or more public service vehicles for the carriage of passengers by road at separate fares. The definition of a public service vehicle (PSV) is found in section 1(1) of the Public Passenger Vehicles Act 1981, although this definition must be read subject to section 1(2)-(6) of and Schedule 1 to that Act:

> "a motor vehicle (other than a tramcar) which—(a) being a vehicle adapted to carry more than eight passengers, is used for carrying passengers for hire or reward; or, (b) being a vehicle not so adapted, is used for carrying passengers for hire or reward at separate fares in the course of a business of carrying passengers".

A local service with a stopping place inside Greater London, including **11.09** the Greater London section of a service that also runs partly outside that area, will be a London local service. However, where the service in Greater London is provided pursuant to an agreement for the temporary interruption of railway services it is not a London local service (section 179(3)).

TfL is required so far as reasonably practicable to provide or secure the provision of the London bus network. Only TfL, its subsidiaries or a person acting under a London local service agreement may operate a London local service that is part of the London bus network A London local service agreement is defined as either an agreement with TfL to provide a London local service or a transport subsidiary's agreement (as defined by section 169). Where part of the service runs outside Greater London the London local service agreement is subject to any restrictions imposed by a traffic commissioner (as defined by section 195) for that part of the service (section 182(3)). It should be noted that a person providing such a service under a London local service agreement is not required to be a party to the agreement (section 181(4)).

11.10 Following TfL's determination of the London local services needed for Greater London, it is under a duty to keep them under review (GLA Act, s.181(2)). TfL is vested with the power to revise the London local services and where a new or revised London local service that alters the London bus network is proposed, TfL is under a duty to consult before implementing such changes (GLA Act, s.183(2)). Where TfL propose to provide a new or revise an existing London local service it must consult with the commissioner(s) of police affected by the proposed change (*i.e.* the Commissioner of Police of the Metropolis, or the Commissioner of Police of the City of London (GLA Act, s.183(6))); the London authorities (which is a London borough council or the Common Council (GLA Act, s.183(7))) affected; the London Transport Users' Committee, and any other person whom TfL considers appropriate to consult (GLA Act, s.183(2)). The matters on which TfL are obliged to consult are: the route; the terminal points; the points at which passengers may or may not be taken up or set down, and the place used for turning at a terminal point (GLA Act, s.183(3)). Those London authorities that must be consulted by TfL about any addition to or variation of the network service are those in whose areas any part of the route is situated, or where the pick up and set down points, the terminal points and/or the turning places at terminal points are located their areas (GLA Act, s.183(4)). This duty to consult extends beyond Greater London to those authorities through whose boroughs the route passes (GLA Act, s.183(5)).

The same duty to consult arises where TfL or any of its subsidiaries propose to discontinue or not renew a London local service (GLA Act, s.184).

Bus Services outside London Bus Network

11.11 Where a provider of a London local service, which does not form part of the London bus network, operates outside the London bus network it must obtain a permit from TfL (GLA Act, s.185(1)). This permit is known as "a London service permit". By definition, a service that requires such a permit is one that has not been determined by TfL as "required for the purpose of providing safe, integrated, efficient and economic transport services in Greater London" (GLA Act, s.181).

The decision whether to grant a permit
11.12 The Mayor is under a duty to prepare and adopt a document (known as "the guidance document") that sets out the criteria by which

applications for London service permits will be considered by TfL (GLA Act, s.185(2)). The Mayor must keep this guidance document under review and may revise it at any time (GLA Act, s.185(3)). TfL will be required to consider the guidance document (if revised, as revised (section 185(4)) (for the preparation of which, see paragraph 11.20) when deciding whether to issue a London service permit (GLA Act, s.186(3)). Although there appears to be no express provision that will ensure that the guidance document is conveyed to TfL so that TfL can consider it, section 192 of the GLA Act contains provisions for ensuring the guidance document is accessible.

An application for a permit shall be made in the manner prescribed by TfL and accompanied by such information as required (GLA Act, s.186(1)). TfL may charge a fee for processing and/or granting the permit (GLA Act, s.186(2)). TfL is required to consult the local authorities affected, the commissioner(s) of police affected, the London Transport Users' Committee and any other person considered appropriate when deciding whether to grant a permit (GLA Act, s.186(4)). Although TfL is not explicitly required by the Act to consider any responses which may be made to the consultation, section 186(3) requires TfL to have regard to "any" material consideration, which may include any consultee's response. All material considerations must be taken into account and if TfL inadvertently omits to consider any relevant matter, a decision to grant, refuse or attach conditions to a permit may be susceptible to challenge by appeal under section 189 of the GLA Act.

11.13 Where TfL grants a permit it is required to notify the details of the services permitted to the London authorities affected, *i.e.* an authority in whose area part of the service route is permitted to pass; the police commissioner(s) affected; and the London Transport Users Committee (GLA Act, s.186(5)).

TfL may grant a permit subject to such conditions as it thinks fit. The conditions that may be attached include conditions for securing suitable routes, specifying the pick up and set down points for passengers and safety and convenience for the public, including those who have mobility problems (GLA Act, s.187(2)). TfL cannot impose a condition as to fares (GLA Act, s.187(3)). Where TfL has imposed a condition it may subsequently vary the permit by altering, removing conditions or imposing new conditions (GLA Act, s.187(4)). TfL is required to notify a permit holder of the reasons for any variation to the conditions attached to a permit (GLA Act, s.189(3)).

11.14 Failure to comply with a condition attached to a permit is a criminal offence (GLA Act, s.187(3)) (see below, paragraph 11.17), but where compliance with the condition would be unduly onerous, due to circumstance unforeseen at the time when the condition was attached, and there would be no adverse effect on public safety or convenience if the condition was temporarily dispensed with, TfL has the power to temporarily dispense with the condition (section 187(5)). TfL also has the power to revoke or suspend a London service permit for frequent, intentional or serious breaches of a condition attached to it (GLA Act, s.188).

A person may have a legitimate expectation of being treated in a certain way by a licensing authority even if there is no private law right to receive such treatment. That person may be entitled to apply for judicial review of a decision which breaches that legitimate expectation. In relation to licences, a licence holder may receive greater procedural protection. He may even have a legitimate expectation that the licence will be renewed in circumstances where a person making their first application for a licence may not be able to rely on any presumption that licence would be granted: see the classification of such cases used by Sir Robert Megarry V.-C. in *McInnes v. Onslow-Fane* [1978] 1 W.L.R. 1520 at 1528.

Appeal to Mayor

11.15 Section 189 of the GLA Act makes provision for an appeal to the Mayor against an adverse decision regarding a permit. When an appeal is made the Mayor must refer the appeal to an independent appeals panel appointed by him (GLA Act, s.189(6)). The appeal will be conducted on the documentary evidence unless the appellant requests otherwise (GLA Act, s.189(10)), and the panel appointed by the Mayor will prepare a report including any appropriate recommendation (GLA Act, s.189(11)). The Mayor will then issue such guidance or direction to TfL as appropriate, having regard to the panel report (GLA Act, s.189(13)).

Any appeal under this section must be "made" before the end of the period of 28 days beginning with the "date of issue" of the notice of the decision (GLA Act, s.189(5)). The time limit for bringing an appeal must be observed, otherwise the appeal may be invalid. Unless a statute expressly provides for it, the appeal panel probably lacks the power to extend the time for appealing (see *Kerridge v. Lamdin* [1950] 2 All E.R. 1110, CA at 1114). The words "beginning with" indicate that the date of issue must be included in the calculation of the 28 days (*Hare v. Gocher* [1962] 2 Q.B. 641, DC; *Trow v. Ind Coope (West Midlands) Ltd* [1967] 2 Q.B. 899, CA).

11.16 In the event that TfL do not comply with their duty to issue a notice under section 189(1) stating the reasons for the adverse decision, it may be possible to seek redress by applying for judicial review of the decision. Similarly, a challenge to the Mayor's directions to TfL about an appeal panel (section 189(6)) might be challenged by way of judicial review.

If granted, a London service permit shall not last longer than five years. Provided an application for renewal is submitted prior to the expiry of the current permit it shall continue in force until the application is finally determined (including any appeal). However, if conditions attached to the permit are breached, TfL may use its powers under section 188 to revoke the permit and override any extension given by this section (GLA Act, s.188(2))

Validity of Agreements and Permits

11.17 Those operators, save for TfL, who provide a London local service, whether under an agreement or permit, must comply with the public service vehicle licensing regime (GLA Act, s.193). The service operator must hold a PSV operators' licence (for which see section 12 of the Public Service Vehicles Act 1981), a community bus permit or be exempt from the requirements to hold either. Failure to hold such a licence or permit, unless the operator is exempt, nullifies the London local service agreement or permit and is a criminal offence. A PSV operator's licence is granted by a traffic commissioner and permits the use of a PSV vehicle on a road as a stage, express or contract carriage (see Part II of the Public Passenger Vehicles Act 1981, especially section 12).

Sections 57, 58(2) and 84 of the Public Passenger Vehicles Act 1981 applies to London service permits, which means that in certain circumstances, for example that if a holder of a London service permit dies or becomes bankrupt, the permit is terminated (GLA Act, s.194). TfL nevertheless has power to defer such termination under these statutory provisions if this is appropriate, *e.g.* section 57(4) of the Public Passenger Vehicles Act 1981 in the context of the GLA Act reads that TfL may direct that the termination of the permit be deferred while some other person carries on the business authorised by the permit for such time and under such conditions as imposed by TfL.

Offences

As mentioned above, TfL is under a duty so far as is reasonably practicable to provide or secure the London bus network. It is an offence to operate a London local service without a London local service agreement, a transport subsidiary's agreement or a London service permit (GLA Act, s.180(2)). It is also an offence to contravene any condition attached to a London service permit (GLA Act, s.187(6)). **11.18**

Natural justice requires that any person accused of an offence must be told in detail what they are alleged to have done wrong: the summons will have to give full particulars of the way in which the offence is said to have arisen. This is because of the wide range of facts that can give rise to an offence under this section.

There is a "due diligence" defence for the offence of operating without agreement or permit (GLA Act, s.180(3)). However, that defence may not be available if matters that could have been raised on appeal under section 189 were not pursued: see, for example, *A Lambert Flat Management Ltd v. Lomas* [1981] 1 W.L.R. 898, DC, but contrast *Butuyuyu v. Hammersmith and Fulham L.B.C.* (1997) 29 H.L.R. 584, DC. See further Carter, Pengelly and Saunders, *Local Authority Notices* (Sweet & Maxwell, London, 1999) pages 85–86.

The maximum punishment for this offence is a fine of level 3 on the standard scale. Level 3 is currently set under the Criminal Justice Act 1982, section 37 (as amended) at £1,000. Clearly, such a fine will be only a small deterrent for an offender who could make a substantial profit from contravening the rules about operating London local services. **11.19**

In the case of a contravention of a condition attached to a permit or a breach of an agreement, perhaps a more potent deterrent will be the risk of losing a PSV operators' licence (for which, see section 82(1) of the Public

Passenger Vehicles Act 1981), a London service permit (see the GLA Act, s.185) or the benefit of an agreement with TfL to provide a London local service (GLA Act, s.182). Clearly, a permit holder who has not been notified of variations to their permit is more likely to be able to establish this defence.

Guidance Document

11.20 The Mayor is required to prepare and adopt a document containing the criteria by which applications for a London service permit are to be considered by TfL. This document is known as the guidance document (GLA Act, s.185(2)). When preparing the guidance document (or revising it in a way that will affect all of Greater London), the Mayor is required to consult each London authority; each local authority he considers would be affected by the guidance document; the commissioners of police in London; the traffic commissioners in London; the London Transport Users' Committee, and any other person the Mayor considers it appropriate to consult.

This duty to consult does not arise if a revision will not affect the entire area of Greater London. This is so even if a revision might, for example, affect all of Greater London except the City of London. Instead, a newspaper notice must be published in the areas the Mayor considers will be affected.

11.21 The Mayor is required to publish the guidance document no later than 180 days after the transport strategy is published (GLA Act, s.192(4)). That period gives time to those who wish to apply for a London service permit to consider how their applications can conform to the transport strategy. Applications conforming with the guidance document can be submitted once the guidance document is published.

The Mayor must keep the guidance document available for six years. This period corresponds to the period for which other documents such as the Mayor's annual report (GLA Act, s.46) must be retained.

Once adopted, the Mayor must keep his guidance document under review and may revise it at any time (GLA Act, s.185(3)). If the guidance document is revised, the Mayor must adopt the revised version, and keep a copy of it available at the principal offices of the Authority and/or such other places as he considers appropriate. A copy must also be sent to the Common Council and each London borough council and supplied for a reasonable fee to those who request it.

Railways

11.22 After a period of nationalisation that lasted from 1947 to 1993, private sector involvement was reintroduced to the United Kingdom's railways by the Railways Act 1993. Under the 1993 Act passenger services were gradually transferred to the private sector by a series of franchise arrangements, and freight and parcel services were sold outright. Track operations were dealt with separately by the creation of Railtrack. Passenger rail services operate under franchise agreements between the Director of Passenger Rail Franchising (the "Franchising Director") and train operating companies. There are 16 different train operating companies operating over infrastructure owned by Railtrack. London's train companies serve not only the Travelcard zones and the commuter belt but a wide area beyond. As stated above, passenger rail franchises are controlled by the Franchising Director who is an independent person appointed by the Secretary of State to be responsible for arranging and managing the provision of rail passenger services in Great Britain. The role of the Franchising Director is created by statute (Railways Act 1993, s.1). The duties of the Franchising Director are defined in section 5 of that Act.

The Franchising Director has a duty to determine which services for the **11.23** carriage of passengers by railway are eligible to be operated under franchises, and to designate those services accordingly (Railways Act 1993, s.23(1)). There is then a process by which potential franchise operators tender for the opportunity to provide the service (Railways Act 1993, s.26). The Franchising Director then enters into agreements (franchise agreements) with the successful tenders, known as franchise operators, for the provision of the services by them. Franchised services are the services for the carriage of passengers by railway which are to be provided under a franchise agreement (Railways Act 1993, s.23(3)).

Railways in Greater London

Chapter VI, Part IV of the GLA Act deals with railways. The GLA and TfL **11.24** are not permitted to run franchised railway services on the national rail network (GLA Act, s.202). The prohibition extends to a body corporate (for which, see the Railways Act 1993, s.151(1)) whose members are appointed by the GLA or TfL or by a body corporate whose members are so appointed. This prohibition already affects local authorities and other public bodies in Great Britain (Railways Act 1993, s.25(1)).

The GLA or the Mayor acting on behalf of the Authority can issue instructions or written guidance to the Franchising Director about the management of passenger rail services for London (GLA Act, s.196(1)). By virtue of section 196(7), instructions or guidance may be given in respect of (i) the provision of services for the carriage of passengers by railway in Great Britain; or (ii) the operation of additional railway assets under or by virtue of any franchise agreement or any provisions of sections 30 and 37 to 49 of the Railways Act 1993 (Railways Act 1993, s.5(1)(a)).

There is a corresponding duty on the Franchising Director to seek to implement the Authority's instructions or guidance (section 196(3)). The only exceptions to that duty arise when the Authority's guidance:

- conflicts with guidance from the Secretary of State;
- will have an adverse impact on passenger services outside London; or

- will require the Franchising Director to make certain additional payments from his own budget (GLA Act, s.196(5)(c)).

11.25   The Franchising Director must give written notice to the Authority of his reasons if he decides not to implement the Authority's guidance (GLA Act, s.196(6)).

The Franchising Director is under a duty to consult the Mayor about the general level of provision for railway passenger services and the fares for such services. This should assist the Mayor in fulfilling his general transport duty (for which, see the GLA Act, s.141) and developing and revising the transport strategy (for which, see the GLA Act, s.142).

Any franchising agreements completed prior to the GLA Act coming into effect, will be amended so that the GLA is included in the definition of a local authority in such agreements (GLA Act, s.205). This will put the GLA on the same footing as local authorities outside Greater London to make arrangements such as concessionary travel schemes.

Licences, Access Contracts and Franchising

11.26 Under section 6 of the Railways Act 1993 the Secretary of State, after consultation with the Rail Regulator (see below, paragraph 11.29), or the Rail Regulator with the consent of or authority given by the Secretary of State may grant any person a passenger licence to operate such railway assets as may specified in the licence. A railway asset is any train used on a network for the purposes of carrying passengers or goods by railway; any network; any station; or any light maintenance depot. It is an offence to operate a railway asset without a passenger licence, but by virtue of the Railways (London Regional Transport) (Exemptions) Order 1994 (S.I. 1994 No. 573), every LRT company (*i.e.* LRT and their subsidiaries) is exempted from the licensing provisions. Section 198(2) of the GLA Act extends that exemption to TfL, their subsidiaries and PPP companies so far as carrying out qualifying activities, namely, light maintenance services, network services or station services carried out by the PPP company in fulfilment of obligations imposed under a PPP agreement (GLA Act, s.198(3)).

11.27   Futher, the Secretary of State can grant exemptions under section 7(1) of the Railways Act 1993 in respect of regular scheduled passenger services operated by LRT, TfL or the subsidiaries of either body. Section 6 of the 1993 Act requires every operator of a railway asset to be authorised by an operating licence. Section 7(1) of the 1993 Act permits the Secretary of State, after consulting the Rail Regulator (see below, paragraph 11.29), to grant exemptions from this requirement. Such exemptions may be specific to a particular person (such as TfL) or block exemptions granted to a class of persons (such as TfL's subsidiaries). As sections 17 and 18 of the 1993 Act enable the Rail Regulator to require owners of railway facilities to enter into contracts to permit others to use their facilities, and section 20 of the 1993 Act permits the Secretary of State to grant exemptions from such requirements, TfL will be able to fully integrate with the national network by agreement if such integration is not covered fully by the provisions of the GLA Act.

There are limited circumstances in which TfL may enter into or perform agreements with respect to the provision, retention or financing of public passenger transport services which involves the holding of a passenger licence (as defined by the Railways Act 1993, s.83(1)). The general position is that TfL may not enter into or carry out any agreement where the agreement involves the holding of a passenger licence, save where it is an exempt agreement (GLA Act, s.201(3)). If TfL is required to hold a passenger licence or the agreement is not exempt then it cannot provide, retain or finance those public passenger transport services.

Access Contracts

In the context of Chapter VI, an access contract is either (a) a contract **11.28** under which a person obtains (whether for himself or an associate) permission from a facility owner to use the facility owner's railway facility, or (b) a contract conferring an option for such a contract (1993 Act, s.17). A facility owner is a person who has an estate or interest in, or right over a railway facility, and whose permission to use that railway facility is needed by another before that other may use it. Railway facilities include track, stations and light maintenance depots (see the 1993 Act, s.83).

A facility owner must not enter into an access contract unless (1) he does so pursuant to directions from the Rail Regulator, (2) the Regulator has approved the terms of the access contract, or (3) an exemption applies (1993 Act, ss.17 and 18). Section 18 of the Railways Act 1993 gives the Rail Regulator powers to approve access contracts and issue directions about the terms that should be included in such contracts. On the other hand, the Secretary of State can by order, after consultation with the Rail Regulator, grant exemptions from the provisions that relate to directions requiring facility owners to enter into contracts for the use of their railway facilities and from the provisions that relate to access contracts requiring the approval of the Regulator. Section 200 of the GLA Act enables TfL and LRT to benefit from facility exemptions which may also provide for TfL and LRT to be exempt from directions from the Rail Regulator to enter into access contracts. Conditions may be imposed on such exemptions (Railways Act 1993, s.20). Such exemptions may allow TfL and LRT to enter into access agreements to use railway track, stations and light maintenance depots to meet any need relating to transport in or around, or to or from, Greater London.

Rail Regulator

The Rail Regulator is the independent person appointed by the Secretary **11.29** of State to be responsible for exercising functions in relation to Great Britain's railways, including protecting the interests of users of railway services, promoting the use of the railway network, and promoting efficiency and economy and competition (see Railways Act 1993, s.4). The role of the Rail Regulator is created by section 1 of the Railways Act 1993. The duties of the Rail Regulator are defined in section 4 of that Act.

By referring to the Rail Regulator's power to approve access contracts section 200 of the GLA Act expressly acknowledges the power of the Rail Regulator to exert a considerable amount of control over the way in which LRT and TfL exercise their functions in relation to such a contract (see, in particular, the Railways Act 1993, s.18). In order to minimise conflicts between, on the one hand, the Mayor, TfL and LRT and, on the other hand, the Rail Regulator, the Rail Regulator, when exercising his functions under Part I of the Railways Act 1993, is required to have regard to the ability of the Mayor, TfL and LRT to carry out their respective functions conferred by any enactment (GLA Act, s.200(4)).

Closures

11.30 Where the Franchising Director is required by any provision of sections 37–42 of the Railways Act 1993 to publish any notice proposing that a railway should be closed, for example, when he is of the opinion that the proposed closure of a particular line or station should take effect, he must publish a notice in a local newspaper to that effect and serve on the Rail Regulator a copy of that notice, together with a statement of reasons why the particular service is to close, and his statement of recommendations with respect to any conditions to be attached to any consent to the closure (Railways Act 1993, s.43(1)). The GLA Act amends section 43 of the Railways Act 1993 by providing that the same notice, etc. must be served on the Mayor, in addition to the Rail Regulator and any Rail Users' Consultative Committee whose area is affected by the proposal (for which, see the Railways Act 1993, s.2), if the whole or part of the area affected by the closure is in Greater London (GLA Act, s.203).

Objections to the closure must be lodged with the Rail Regulator. Such objections must be lodged within the period specified in the notice, which period must not be less than six weeks after the date the notice was last published in a local newspaper in accordance with section 37(6)(e) of the Railways Act 1993 or the corresponding provisions in sections 38–42 of the Railways Act 1993.

11.31 In most cases, the Rail Regulator or, on a reference by the Rail Regulator, the Secretary of State, takes into account any objections and decides whether the railway may be closed: see sections 43 and 44 of the Railways Act 1993. The procedure for closing railway passenger services that fall within the definition of "qualifying London services" is set out in the amendment to Schedule 5 of the Railways Act 1993 (GLA Act, s.204). The effect of the amended procedure is that the Mayor, as opposed to the Secretary of State, decides on the closure of railway passenger services that are provided by TfL or a subsidiary, or such services that are provided wholly within Greater London and are services the Secretary of State has by order made be services to which paragraph 5A (as inserted by the GLA Act, s.204(3)) apply. Where the closure relates to a service that wholly or partly outside Greater London there is the right of appeal to the Secretary of State (Railways Act 1993, Sched. 5, para. 5A(3), as inserted by the GLA Act, s.204(3)).

When section 204 was introduced into the Bill at Committee stage in the House of Lords, the Under-Secretary of State for the Department of the Environment. Transport and the Regions, Lord Whitty, explained:

"The purpose of this amendment is to carry forward the existing procedure for discontinuance of Underground and DLR services and those to be operated under the Croydon Tramlink."

He added: **11.32**

"The only significant change which the amendment makes to the current procedures is that it will be the mayor who takes decisions on closures rather than the Secretary of State with the proviso that for TfL services wholly or partly outside London those aggrieved by a mayoral decision will have a right of appeal to the Secretary of State." *Hansard* H.L. Vol. 603, col. 557.

A person aggrieved by a decision of the Mayor to consent to the closure of a railway wholly or partly outside London can refer the matter to the Secretary of State. The referral is made by notifying the Secretary of State (Railways Act 1993, Sched.1, para.5A(3)). This must be done within four weeks of the Mayor's decision. The referral must include a statement of reasons why the person is aggrieved by the Mayor's decision.

The Secretary of State can confirm the Mayor's decision, modify any conditions attached to the Mayor's decision or give an entirely different decision.

Contracting Out

Section 207 of the GLA Act ensures that TfL and its subsidiaries will retain **11.33** certain station and train operating functions. TfL must not, without the consent of the Secretary of State, agree with an outside contractor to provide or secure for it the provision of a reserved service (GLA Act, s.207(2)). The reserved services are the performance, for the purpose of any TfL passenger rail service, of any station-operating function or any train-operating function (GLA Act, s.207(1)). These are defined in sections 207(7) of the GLA Act as follows:

(a) "station-operating service" are:

- the sale or collection of tickets at stations;
- the inspection of tickets or imposing penalty fares;
- the making or oral announcements at the station;
- the provision of information to members of the public;
- any duties of staff employed on platforms at stations or in any place where the whole or part of a station is controlled;
- any other function that involves the management or operation of a station.

(b) "train-operating services" are:

- the driving of passengers trains;
- any duties as guards on trains;
- the sale, collection or inspection of tickets, or the imposing of penalty fares on passenger trains;
- the operation of signals;
- controlling the movement of passenger trains otherwise than in the depot
- any other function involved in the operation of passenger trains otherwise than in the depot.

11.34   The Secretary of State's consent is required before TfL or its subsidiaries can agree to any one else performing or securing the performance of the reserved functions (GLA Act, s.207(5)). The Secretary of State's consent must be given by way of provisions in a statutory instrument, and is subject to the negative resolution procedure by either the House of Commons or the House of Lords (see the GLA Act, s.420).

Lord Whitty, the Under-Secretary of State for the Department of the Environment. Transport and the Regions, explained that:

> "The purpose of the new clause is to ensure that the Underground trains and stations continue to be operated by a publicly owned, publicly accountable London underground. . . . The new clause places restrictions on TfL's ability to franchise or contract out London Underground's services which impinge directly on the travelling public." *Hansard* H.L. Vol. 603, col. 559.

Docklands Light Railway and Croydon Tramlink

11.35 Section 208 of the GLA Act transfers to the Mayor the power of the Secretary of State to transfer functions of Docklands Light Railway Limited to another person for the purpose of the construction and maintenance of the extension of the Docklands Light Railway to Lewisham. Section 209 of the GLA Act transfers to the Mayor and TfL certain powers and responsibilities in relation to the Croydon Tram Link, for example, where there is dispute over the giving of consent for the laying and maintenance of tramways, that difference shall be determined by the Mayor as opposed to the Secretary of State (Croydon Tramlink Act 1994, s.9(3), as amended by the GLA Act, s.209(2)). It also passes to the Mayor the power of the Secretary of State to transfer functions of the Croydon Tramlink to another person for the purpose of the construction and maintenance of the tramlink.

11.36   Lord Whitty the Under-Secretary of State for the Department of the Environment Transport and the Regions, explained that by section 209 of the GLA Act the Mayor and TfL will inherit some of the functions of the Secretary of State and the responsibilities of London Regional Transport in respect of the Croydon Tramlink. The Croydon Tramlink Act 1994 as amended by the GLA Act provides that the Mayor assumes the role of the Secretary of State in transferring functions to the Tramlink concessionaire (see the Croydon Tramlink Act 1994, s.50, as amended by the GLA Act, s.209(3)). The amendments to the Croydon Tramlink Act 1994 also transfer to the Mayor the role of the Secretary of State in determining any differences arising from proposals to alter the level of a street in relation to the tram, and they place a duty on the London Transport Users' Committee to consider representations in respect of the Tramlink. Additionally:

> "The amendments also provide for the continuation of the terms of agreements entered into by LRT dealing with the performance of LRT's statutory duties, notwithstanding that certain statutory duties of London Regional Transport are to be re-enacted and held by the mayor and Transport for London. The Tramlink is such an agreement." *Hansard* H.L. Vol. 606, col. 619.

Hackney Carriages and Private Hire Vehicles

London has its own system for licensing hackney carriages. The legislative **11.37** framework in the Metropolitan Police District and City of London is entirely separate from that which regulates taxis outside the area. The control of private hire vehicles, *i.e.* mini-cabs under the Private Hire Vehicles (London) Act 1998, on the other hand, is similar to that in operation elsewhere in England and Wales (Part II of the Local Government (Miscellaneous Provisions) Act 1976). The GLA Act transfers to TfL these functions currently exercised by the Secretary of State and the Commissioners of Police for the Metropolis. The Public Carriage Office, a civilian branch of the police commissioners that licenses taxis will transfer, in its entirety, to TfL.

Hackney Carriages

Hackney carriages have been regulated since the first half of the nine- **11.38** teenth century. Section 253 and Schedule 20 of the GLA Act transfer to TfL the functions relating to hackney carriages and their drivers which were previously held by the Secretary of State and the Police Commissioners.

In the Metropolitan Police District and the City of London, a hackney carriage means any carriage for the conveyance of passengers which plies for hire within the limits of the designated area (see, for example, the Metropolitan Public Carriage Act 1869, s.4).

Schedule 20

Under this Schedule TfL will take over regulatory functions formerly **11.39** performed by the registrar of metropolitan public carriages (paragraph 1).

The powers of the Police Commissioners, for example, the grant and regulation of hackney carriages and the powers of inspection, will also be transferred to TfL (paragraphs 1–5). TfL may, under a new power, charge fees to persons applying for a taxi driver's licence or a vehicle licence (paragraph 5). Lord Whitty, the Under-Secretary of State for the Department of the Environment Transport and the Regions, explained that such a provision was necessary because "The effect of the current charging system is that people have no incentive properly to prepare themselves or their vehicles before going forward for a test." *Hansard* H.L. Vol. 603, col. 632.

TfL can make London cab orders to regulate hackney carriages (see Metropolitan Public Carriage Act 1869, s.9), instead of the Secretary of State (paragraph 5(2) and (6)).

11.40　　TfL will licence vehicles (paragraph 5(3)) and drivers (paragraph 5(5)). Although the Police Commissioners will no longer licence taxis, applications for licenses may still be referred to the police. This will, for example, enable criminal records to be checked so that unsuitable applicants are refused licences (paragraph 5(5)). TfL will also be able to increase by order the "compellable distance" (the distance from the point of hire that the driver of a taxi is by law obliged to complete) and prohibit the display of certain signs, such as those reading "taxi", on private hire cars (paragraph 7).

TfL can also provide for taxis to carry passengers at separate fares without becoming public service vehicles, and consequently requiring licences under the separate regime for the regulation of buses (paragraph 8).

Finally TfL can prescribe certain periods for London taxi and driver-licensing appeals (paragraph 8).

Regulation of fares and charges

11.41　　TfL can fix the fares for cabs fitted with taximeters and the charges for entering railway stations (paragraph 6) and to regulate fares for non-obligatory journeys (paragraph 7). The Mayor may give written directions (section 421) to TfL as to the basis on which rates and fares must be calculated (paragraph 5(6)).

Transitional provisions

11.42　　Paragraphs 9 to 17 make transitional provision in relation to the transfer of functions to TfL from the Secretary of State and the Police Commissioners.

Private Hire Vehicles

11.43　Section 254 to and Schedule 21 of the GLA Act transfer to TfL functions in relation to the regulation of private hire vehicles (*i.e.* "mini-cabs") previously held by the Secretary of State. A private hire vehicle is defined in section 1(1) of the Private Hire Vehicles (London) Act 1998 as "a vehicle adapted to seat fewer than nine passengers which is made available with a driver to the public for hire for the purpose of carrying passengers, other than a licensed taxi or a public service vehicle".

The 1998 Act regulates private hire vehicles and their drivers and operators in London. For example, sections 2, 4–7, and 12 of the 1998 Act impose requirements for licences to use, drive or operate a private hire vehicle in London. There are criminal penalties for contravening those requirements. Appropriate identification discs and badges must be displayed in licensed vehicles and by licensed drivers, unless specially exempted (sections 10 and 14).

Schedule 21

11.44 Schedule 21 amends the Private Hire Vehicles (London) Act 1998, to take account of TfL's role as the licensing authority for minicabs subject to the public hire vehicle regime.

Alteration of metropolitan police district

11.45 Section 255 of the GLA Act makes changes to the licensing regime for taxis and minicabs, required because the area of the Metropolitan Police District (MPD) will be altered. The MPD area will be reduced in size and consist only of the 32 London boroughs, and certain 'fringe' areas will no longer be part of the MPD (GLA Act, s.323). The affected areas are Epsom and Ewell, Hertsmere and Spelthorne (all currently wholly within the MPD) and Broxbourne, Elmbridge, Epping Forest, Reigate and Banstead and Welwyn Hatfield (whose areas are currently partly within the MPD).

Once the MPD's boundaries are altered, each district councils removed from the MPD will licence taxis and minicabs for their areas as do other local authorities outside London (GLA Act, s.255(2) and (3)). Within the MPD, TfL will be the licensing authority.

Water Transport

11.46 When preparing or revising the transport strategy (GLA Act, s.142), the Mayor has a duty to promote and encourage the use of the River Thames for transport (GLA Act, s.41(5)(d)). In turn, TfL has a duty to exercise its functions so as to secure or facilitate the implementation of the Mayor's transport strategy (GLA Act, s.154). Section 256 of the GLA Act enables TfL to provide or secure the provision of such amenities and facilities as it consider would benefit persons using the waterways, which includes the River Thames, but before exercising such powers, it must secure any licence or consent that may be necessary, for example the consent of the Port of London Authority. It must be noted that TfL's bye-laws must not conflict with those of the Port of London Authority (GLA Act, Sched. 11, para. 27).

The duty to operate the Woolwich ferry transfers from the Secretary of State to TfL (GLA Act, s.257). The Woolwich ferry is a free river-crossing service used by motor vehicles, pedal cycles and foot passengers.

11.47   Finally, where any landing stage is transferred from the Port of London
Authority to LRT on or after March 31, 1999 but before section 258 of the
GLA Act comes into force, the rights and liabilities arising from the use of
the landing place by vessels also transfers to LRT. Any landing stage,
together with the rights and liabilities will subsequently transfer to TfL
(see Chapter 10).

When section 259 of the GLA Act was introduced at Report stage in the
House of Lords, the Under-Secretary of State for the Department of the
Environment Transport and the Regions, Lord Whitty, explained that it
transfers from the Port of London Authority "to London Transport and
thereafter to Transport for London, all the contractual and other liabilities
associated with piers." Lord Whitty responded to concerns about the
potential adverse impact of this section on operators of tourist services on
the Thames by saying that "there is no sinister purpose behind the clause".
Although he could not say specifically whether infrastructure that had been
separately provided (by operators of tourist services) would transfer when
ownership of property transfers, he expressed his confidence "that the
property and legal position will not change", *Hansard* H.L. Vol. 605,
col.1309.

Travel Concessions

11.48 Sections 50–54 of the London Regional Transport Act 1984 contain the
previous provisions for a concessionary travel scheme in London. The new
scheme contained in Chapter VIII, Part IV of the GLA Act largely re-
enacts the previous provisions and enables local authorities to make
voluntary arrangements whereby one or more local authorities arrange for
eligible persons to receive travel concessions (GLA Act, s.240(8)). Local
authorities will reimburse TfL the cost of granting the concessions. Travel
concession arrangements result in local authorities subsidising travel for
eligible residents. Eligible residents are defined as pensioners, blind
persons or persons who are unable to walk (GLA Act, s.240(5)). Such
arrangements can only be made in relation to journeys in Greater London
and the vicinity (GLA Act, s.240(3)).

Local authorities may either make travel concession arrangements with
TfL (section 240(1)) or the Director of Passenger Rail Franchising
(subsection (2)), or directly with the operators of certain bus, train,
underground, guided transport (*i.e.* transport by vehicles guided by means
external to the vehicle (Transport and Works Act 1992, section 67(1))),
tram, trolley vehicle and river services (section 240(2) and (6)). If the local
authorities do not make appropriate voluntary arrangements, a default
scheme will be imposed by TfL implementing a "reserve free travel
scheme" (which would only cover those services for which TfL is responsible). The detail of such a scheme is set out in Schedule 16 to the GLA Act
and TfL may charge local authorities for the cost of providing such a
scheme.

Pensionable Age

11.49 The definition of a person eligible to receive a travel concession by reason of his or her age (broadly, an elderly person), is by reference linked to the age at which that person would be eligible to receive a state pension (GLA Act, s.240(5)(a)). The pensionable age for women will be gradually equalised to that of men starting from the year 2010 until the pensionable age for both men and women is 65 years of age in the year 2020 (Pensions Act 1995, Sched. 4, para. 1). The women affected by these equalisation provisions are those born between April 6, 1950 and April 5, 1955.

Disability or Injury which . . . Seriously Impairs . . . Ability to Walk

11.50 The assessment of a person's ability to walk is, in the first instance, "a matter for local discretion" (Lord Whitty, the Under-Secretary of State for the Department of the Environment Transport and the Regions, *Hansard* H.L. Vol. 603, col. 592). Lord Whitty also indicated that the criteria used by local authorities in determining this issue would in certain circumstances be made public:

> "The present access to information rights in the Local Government (Access to information) Act 1985 mean that all papers put to a council are open to the public. Under our new proposals in the draft Local Government (Organisation and Standards) Bill, such papers will continue to be made available. In addition, if decisions are taken at an official level, those decisions, together with the reasons for them, must also be made public." *Hansard* H.L. Vol. 603, col. 592.

Section 240, sections 242–3 of, and Schedule 16 to, the GLA Act ensure that a basic travel concession scheme will always be in place for the eligible residents of London. Local authorities may enter into voluntary agreement as to their arrangements for travel concessions for the next following financial year (the period of 12 months ending with March 31 (GLA Act, s.424)) before the end of December 31 in the preceding year (GLA Act, s.240(1)). If they do not do so, or their arrangements fall short of the requirements set out in sections 242 and 243, the free travel scheme is imposed on them. TfL must then implement the free travel scheme (GLA Act, s.241(3)).

Schedule 16

11.51 The free travel scheme sets out the concessions to be granted to eligible London residents (GLA Act, s.241(4)) for fares otherwise payable for journeys on the London Transport Network (GLA Act, s.242(3)). In all cases, a travel concession permit must be produced in order for a fare to be waived under the scheme (GLA Act, Sched. 16, paras 1 and 2).

The free travel scheme makes different provision for the travel concessions to be granted to blind persons (the waiver of fares at all times, paragraph 1) and other eligible London residents (the waiver of fares only at certain times, paragraph 2).

TfL must notify the London authorities if the free travel scheme is to have effect in the next financial year (GLA Act, Sched. 16, para. 3). TfL will charge the local authorities for the cost of its provision (GLA Act, Sched. 16, paras 5 and 6). TfL's annual report (GLA Act, s.161) must contain a statement of the manner in which the charges fixed for operating the free travel scheme and each travel concession permit, and the aggregate amounts paid to TfL during that financial year (GLA Act, Sched. 16, para. 8).

Exercise of functions by joint committee

11.52   Section 244 of the GLA Act sets out the process by which the London borough councils and the Common Council of the City of London may arrange for their travel concession arrangements with TfL to be determined jointly through a joint committee. It operates on unanimous decisions, unless otherwise agreed unanimously by each local authority (GLA Act, s.244(6)), in which case the majority must not be less that two thirds of the member authorities (GLA Act, s.244(7)).

The joint committee system is not mandatory but, if it is used, it may avoid the inherent risk that the 32 London borough councils and the Common Council of the City of London will be unable to implement a suitable travel concession scheme because one or more authorities fail to agree before the December 31 deadline. As the joint committee must consist of one member from each London authority (GLA Act, s.244(4)), if one authority refuses to provide its member the committee will not be able to operate. All London authorities must enter into a arrangements for the discharge of their duty to provide travel concessions (GLA Act, s.244(1))

Penalty fares

11.53 A penalty fare is essentially a financial penalty set at a deterrent level (GLA Act, Sched.17, para.5) and imposed on a person who cannot show that he or she has obtained the appropriate ticket or authority before using a local service or a train services (GLA Act, Sched. 17, paras 2, 3 and 4). The imposition of a penalty fare is an alternative to prosecution for various offences associated with fare evasion (GLA Act, Sched. 17, para. 8). A local service is not defined, but by virtue of section 179 of the GLA Act section 2 of the Transport Act 1985 applies, which provides that a local service is a service using one or more public service vehicles for the carriage of passengers by road at separate fares.

Section 254 and Schedule 17 to the GLA Act provide for a penalty fare regime on TfL bus and train services. Schedule 17 largely re-enacts the penalty fares scheme created by the London Regional Transport (Penalty Fares) Act 1992 which is repealed by this Act. It is similar, but not identical, to that Act which covers the underground and the Docklands light railway. Further rail and tram services may be included in the regime by order of the Mayor (GLA Act, Sched. 17, para. 9).

In essence, a person travelling on a TfL bus or train service will be liable **11.54** to pay a penalty fare. The Mayor will be able to change the level of the penalty fare, following consultation with the Secretary of State (GLA Act, Sched. 17, para. 5). Lord Whitty explained that the Mayor will be required to consult the Secretary of State "so that there can be consistency about penalty fares on all relevant modes of transport. That is particularly the case where a number of stations are served by both London Transport and the operating companies. At those stations there could be some confusion were the two forms of penalty charge to be completely out of line with each other." Nevertheless, "At the end of the day, the decision lies with the mayor." *Hansard* H.L. Vol. 603, col. 596.

A person who does not immediately pay the penalty fare in cash must, if required to do so, supply his or her name and address. Failure to do so is a criminal offence punishable in the magistrates' court by a fine not exceeding level 2 on the standard scale (GLA Act, Sched. 17, para. 7). Level 2 is currently set under section 37 of the Criminal Justice Act 1982 (as amended) at £500. Notices warning about penalty fares must be displayed so as to be visible to passengers and, on trains, prospective passengers (GLA Act, Sched. 17, para. 7).

Chapter 12

PUBLIC-PRIVATE PARTNERSHIP AGREEMENTS

12.01 LRT had powers under the London Regional Transport Act 1996 to enter into agreements under the previous government's Private Finance Initiative (PFI). Those powers are modified, extended and conferred on TfL and its subsidiaries by Chapter VII of Part IV.

All the provisions relating to Public Private Partnership (PPP) agreements came into force on January 12, 2000 except for section 217 (schemes for the transfer of key system assets) and sections 220 to 224 (insolvency and PPP administration orders): S.I. 1999 No. 3434. At the time of writing, no date had been set for bringing these other provisions into force.

Public Private Partnership Agreements and the London Underground Railway

12.02 The GLA Act itself does not explicitly restrict PPP agreements to those involving the London underground railway: section 210(3) refers only to "a railway or proposed railway" and section 210(4) refers to a railway belonging to or provided, constructed, renewed or improved for Transport for London (TfL), London Regional Transport (LRT), or a subsidiary of theirs. However, the new regime relating to PPP agreements is intended to provide funding for the London Underground. When he introduced the Bill to the House of Lords for its second reading, Lord Whitty, the Under-Secretary of State for the Department of the Environment Transport and the Regions, referred to the PPP provisions in this way:

> "The Government intend that London Underground be restructured into three infrastructure divisions based on groupings of lines and one public sector operating division. . . . The operating division will remain in the public sector. We committed ourselves in our manifesto to a public private partnership for the Underground. The involvement of the private sector in modernisation and maintenance of the Tube's infrastructure will bring increased levels of investment and a better level of service for the travelling public; and it will avoid the mistakes of privatisation by

174

ensuring that the ownership of key assets remains in public hands."
Hansard H.L. Vol. 601, col. 444.

See also Chapter 15, paragraphs 15.01 and 15.02 below for the link
between PPP and the new transport charges and levies.

Defining PPP Agreements

In essence, a PPP agreement is one that involves a private person or body **12.03**
(a) providing, constructing, renewing or improving, and (b) maintaining, a
railway for LRT, TfL or their subsidiaries (section 210).
Five conditions must be fulfilled in respect of a PPP agreement:

1. at least one party to the contract must be TfL, LRT or a subsidiary
   of theirs (section 210(2));
2. the contract must involve (a) the provision, construction, renewal or
   improvement, and (b) the maintenance of a railway or proposed
   railway, and, if and to the extent the contract so provides, of
   stations, rolling stock or depots used in connection with the railway
   (section 210(3));
3. the railway or proposed railway must belong to or be provided,
   constructed, renewed or improved under the contract for TfL, LRT,
   or a subsidiary of theirs (section 210(4));
4. a person undertaking to carry out or secure any or all of the work
   mentioned in (2) above (a "PPP company"), who is a public sector
   operator (for which, see below) when the contract is made, must
   cease to be such six weeks after the contract is designated a PPP
   agreement (section 210(5)); and
5. the contract is designated (for which, see below), or is of a type
   designated as, a PPP agreement (section 210(6)).

Public sector operator
    The definition of a public sector operator has effect so that at least **12.04**
one party to a PPP agreement, the PPP company, will not be a public sector
operator (section 210(5)). Public sector operators include: Ministers of the
Crown, government departments, other emanations of the Crown, local
authorities, metropolitan passenger transport authorities, any corporate
bodies whose members are appointed by the above persons or bodies or by
a body corporate whose members are so appointed, a company of which the
majority of the issued shares or voting rights are held by such persons or
bodies, and a company the majority of whose board of directors can be
appointed or removed by such persons or bodies or in which the majority of
the voting rights are controlled by them (section 211).

The procedure for designating PPP agreements
    A PPP agreement must be in an approved form: such an agreement is **12.05**
referred to as a "designated agreement" (sections 210(6) and 212).
Individual agreements, or types of agreements, can be designated as PPP

agreements. Designation can take place either (a) at the same time as, or at any time within three months before, the PPP agreement is entered into or, (b) with the agreement of the PPP contractor and all other parties to the contract, after the PPP agreement is entered into.

Until London Underground Limited becomes a subsidiary of TfL, the Secretary of State will designate PPP agreements. After that date, the Mayor will undertake this task (sections 212(6) and 239).

Key System Assets and PPP Agreements

12.06 Key system assets are those assets that, due to their status as the assets needed to run the railway, will be given special protection under the provisions relating to PPP agreements in the GLA Act. This is similar to the protection given to franchise assets under section 27 of the Railways Act 1993.

Property, rights or liabilities are all potentially key system assets (section 213(1)). The only things that cannot be key system assets are rights or liabilities under contracts of employment (section 213(2)). This means that, for example, the obligation to pay wages to employees cannot be a key system asset.

Property, rights or liabilities become key system assets as soon as they have been so designated by London Regional Transport, TfL or a subsidiary of either body (sections 213(1) and 210(2)). Designation can take place in three ways: by original designation in a PPP agreement (section 213(1)(a)), by later designation under the terms of a PPP agreement (section 213(1)(b)), or by amendment to a PPP agreement (section 213(1)(b)). In each case, the agreement of the PPP company will be required.

Identifying key system assets

12.07   Key system assets will need to be easily identified. Identification of key system assets will be useful, for example, to anyone thinking of lending money to a PPP company on the security of their assets: such a person will need to know which assets can be relied on as good security and which will be protected (sections 216 and 218 and see below) by being designated as key system assets.

Details of all key system assets (save for one exception, for which see below) must be entered on a register kept by the "relevant authority" for inspection free of charge at all reasonable hours. Until London Underground Limited becomes a subsidiary of TfL, LRT is the "relevant authority". After that date, TfL is (section 239).

The only exception to the requirement to register key system assets arises if the relevant authority keeps other documents available for inspection free of charge at all reasonable hours which will allow a person inspecting them to identify the asset or description of assets and ascertain the date of designation (subsections (2), (3) and (4)).

Related Third Party Agreements

The relevant authority (for which, see above under the sub-heading, **12.08** "Identifying key system assets") has a discretion to enter into further agreements directly with third parties in connection with the PPP agreement. This power may be exercised whether or not a term of the PPP agreement relates to this other agreement (section 215(1)).

The relevant authority or a subsidiary of the relevant authority may also, if three conditions are fulfilled, agree with another person ("a PPP related third party") that property or rights will be designated as key system assets (section 215(2) and (3)):

1. a PPP agreement is or has been entered into;
2. the PPP company (for which, see above under the sub-heading, "Defining PPP agreements"), or the relevant authority or a subsidiary of either one of those parties enters into arrangements with the PPP related third party;
3. those arrangements are not a PPP agreement but do involve the provision of property or rights for use for the purposes of or in connection with the PPP agreement.

For the purpose of designation, the agreement between the relevant authority or subsidiary and the PPP related third party is treated as if it were a PPP agreement and the PPP related third party is treated as if it were the PPP company under such a PPP agreement.

These two powers will, for example, enable London Underground Limited to enter into direct contracts to acquire trains or other equipment from a manufacturer or a leasing company, and for the trains or equipment to be protected as key system assets.

Protection of Key System Assets

The assets needed to run a railway need to be immediately available to the **12.09** public sector at the end of a PPP contract so that train services are not disrupted by a lack of infrastructure.

Protection from dispersal

Key system assets are prevented from being dispersed, either inadver- **12.10** tently or deliberately, without the consent of the relevant authority (for which, see above under the sub-heading, "Identifying key system assets"). They cannot be transferred, and no interest in or right over them can be created or extinguished by a PPP company or a body which has been or is to be a PPP company: likewise, liabilities cannot be released, discharged or transferred to another person. Agreements to do any of these things are similarly prohibited (section 216(1) and (2)).

Any transaction that contravenes these protections for key system assets is void: section 216(3). No execution or other legal process can be commenced or continued, and no distress can be levied, against property or rights that are key system assets (section 216(4)). The use of the word "continued" indicates that, even if designation takes place after legal process has begun to recover the key system asset, it will be protected as soon as designation takes place.

Where a PPP agreement provides for any key system assets or shares in a PPP company to be transferred to London Regional Transport, TfL or a subsidiary of theirs, a PPP company or a PPP related third party, the relevant authority will be required to ensure that provision is also made in the agreement for specifying or determining the amounts to be paid for those assets or shares (section 216(5)).

Landlord and tenant law does not apply to a PPP lease

12.11   A PPP lease is any lease that constitutes a PPP agreement, is entered into in accordance with a PPP agreement, or is designated as a PPP lease (section 218(1)). A PPP lease is designated in the same way as a PPP agreement (for which, see above under the subheading, "The procedure for designating PPP agreements") (section 218(3)).

Landlord and tenant law is disapplied from PPP leases: no enactment or rule of law regulating the rights and obligations of landlords and tenants can prejudice the operation of an agreement between (a) LRT, TfL or a subsidiary of theirs, and (b) a PPP company as to the terms on which land which is the subject of a PPP lease is provided (section 218). For example, there will be no question that the protection for business tenants contained in the Landlord and Tenant Act 1954 can apply to a PPP lease. Instead, the PPP company and either LRT or TfL or a subsidiary of one of the two latter bodies will interpret their rights and duties solely in accordance with the PPP contract and lease.

12.12   The intention is to enable the public sector to recover all the real property it needs to continue train services at once when a PPP contract ends, without the risk of services being disrupted by the delays inherent in taking possession proceedings.

The suspension of the usual statutory and common law rules relating to landlord and tenant relationships is a serious matter. Therefore any instrument containing the lease must make it clear that it is a PPP lease. An instrument containing a PPP lease must contain or have endorsed upon it a certificate signed by or on behalf of the parties to the lease and stating that the instrument contains a PPP lease (section 218(2)).

Transferring key system assets

12.13   Transport for London may make detailed arrangements for the transfer of key system assets between TfL, its subsidiaries, PPP companies and PPP related third parties (section 217).

This procedure should avoid the cost and time involved in the normal process of conveyancing and transferring assets.

Schedule 12 of the GLA Act makes detailed provision for the operation of transfer schemes under sections 165 and 217. It sets out:

1. the property, rights and liabilities that may be transferred (paragraph 2);
2. how apportionment or division of property, rights, liabilities and rights and obligations under a contract may take effect (paragraph 3);
3. how property, rights and liabilities may be defined (paragraph 4), and what provision may be made for creating rights, liabilities and obligations (paragraph 5);
4. a power to make supplementary, incidental, consequential and transitional provisions (paragraph 6);
5. how statutory functions may be transferred (paragraph 7);
6. the date for the transfer of the property, rights and liabilities (paragraph 8);
7. legal continuity between the transferor and the transferee (paragraph 9); including continuity in the employment context (paragraph 10);
8. the way in which information about the scheme must be provided to TfL (paragraph 11); and
9. how the scheme may be modified by agreement (paragraph 12).

Modification of the Land Registration System in Relation to PPP Leases

12.14 The system for registering land is modified so that the usual requirement to register title to a lease over 21 years with the land registry does not apply to a PPP lease (section 219). Instead, a PPP lease is automatically an overriding interest, with the result that the land is deemed to be subject to it even though it is not mentioned on the register (see the Land Registration Act 1925, ss. 3 and 70).

The intention is to save the time and money involved in registering leases, for example in preparing plans and obtaining copies of deeds. In any event, registration of a PPP lease would serve little purpose because of the very restricted opportunities to transfer or otherwise deal with the land (see above under the subheading, "Protection of key system assets").

Statutory Undertaker Status

12.15 Statutory undertaker status will be extended to a PPP company when it is exercising statutory functions relating to a railway and carrying out the subject matter of a PPP agreement (section 238). This will effectively give the PPP company similar statutory undertaker status to that enjoyed by London Underground Limited.

Insolvency and PPP Administration Orders

Winding up of Companies

12.16 A registered company may only be extinguished by being wound up, dissolved or struck off the register. A company may be wound up voluntarily or, on application duly made, by the court.

Part IV, sections 73–219 of, and Schedule 4 to, the Insolvency Act 1986 provide the mechanism for winding up a company. Essentially, the process of winding up is one whereby a company's affairs are arranged, in accordance with strict rules, upon its dissolution.

A special regime will be used to deal with a PPP company that is in major financial difficulty or one that it is just and equitable to wind up (section 221).

Restriction on Winding up a PPP Company

12.17 The normal powers of the court to wind up a company are restricted in the case of a PPP company (section 221(5), applying a modified form of section 10 of the Insolvency Act 1986). During the period beginning with the presentation of a petition for making a PPP administration order and ending with the making of the PPP administration order or the dismissal of the petition, restrictions are placed on making winding-up orders or passing resolutions for winding-up orders, and on certain actions that might result in property of the company being dispersed.

Modification of the Usual Administration Order Regime in Relation to a PPP company

12.18 A court having jurisdiction to wind up the company (see below) may make a PPP administration order (section 220). A PPP administration order is a modified form of an administration order under the Insolvency Act 1986.

The High Court has jurisdiction to wind up any company registered in England and Wales. Certain county courts have concurrent jurisdiction over companies with paid up (or credited as paid up) share capital of less than £120,000 (Insolvency Act 1986, s. 117). It is thought that most if not all PPP companies will be of such a size that only the High Court can deal with their insolvency.

The definition of "company" that is used in sections 220–224 of, and Schedules 14 and 15 to, the GLA Act is linked to the definitions of "company" in the Companies Act 1985 and "unregistered company" in the Insolvency Act 1986 (section 224).

No administration order (made under Part II of the Insolvency Act 1986: see in particular sections 8, 9–12 and 18 of that Act) can be made in relation to a PPP company unless the Mayor has had 14 days' notice (section 223). An "ordinary" administration order would not necessarily protect the interests of the persons who rely on the PPP company's undertaking in the same way that a PPP administration order would (see below).

The Mayor has the opportunity to ask the court to exercise its discretion **12.19** to make a PPP administration order rather than make the administration order, under which the court appoints a person to manage the affairs, business and property of the company. That person is known as the "special PPP administrator" (section 221(1) and paragraph 21 of Schedule 14).

The general framework for administration orders under the 1986 Act is modified to take account of the special status of PPP agreements, the roles of the special PPP administrator and the Mayor in monitoring PPP administration orders, and the need to continue the undertaking and protect key system assets.

A PPP administration order will enable the undertaking to continue without interruption (section 221(2)), whilst protecting the interests of the members and creditors of the company (section 221(1)(b)). The order will result in the transfer of the undertaking to another person so that the relevant activities can be continued, and it will also provide for the undertaking to be carried on until that transfer is effected.

The regime is similar to that for railway administration orders under sections 59–65 of, and Schedule 6 to, the Railways Act 1993.

The Mayor is kept informed about the progress of the PPP administration order and may apply for the order to be discharged (GLA Act, Sched. 14, paras 7–9). If the special PPP administrator has exercised or is exercising, or proposing to exercise his powers in relation to the company in a manner which will not best ensure the achievement of the purposes of the order, the Mayor may seek an order of the court to control the way in which the PPP administration order is carried out (Schedule 14, paragraph 10).

Foreign Companies

Section 224 of the GLA Act sets out how the administration order **12.20** provisions of the Act apply to foreign companies. They are affected only insofar as they operate within the jurisdiction.

Part II of Schedule 14 of the GLA Act makes special provision for foreign companies that are subject to PPP administration orders.

Transfer of Relevant Activities in Relation to PPP Administration Orders

Schedule 15 of the GLA Act provides a comprehensive code for the transfer **12.21** of property, rights and liabilities from a PPP company that is subject to a PPP administration order (the "existing appointee": Schedule 15, paragraph 1(1)(a)) to a new undertaker ("the new appointee": Schedule 15, paragraph 1(1)(b)) on and after a date appointed by the court having jurisdiction to wind up the company.

The new appointee, and any other company in relation to matters affecting them, may give their consent to a scheme made by the existing appointee for transferring property, rights and liabilities. The scheme may not proceed without such consent, and it is of no effect unless approved by the Mayor. The Mayor may modify the scheme before approving it, with the consent of the interested appointees. Modifications after the scheme is approved must also be with consent of the appointees and may be made by order of the Mayor. While the PPP administration order is in force, the existing appointee can only make or consent to alterations to the scheme through the special PPP administrator (Schedule 15, paragraph 2).

12.22 The scheme comes into force on a day appointed by the court, which day must be before the PPP administration order takes effect (Schedule 15, paragraphs 1(2) and 3).

All property, rights and liabilities are capable of being transferred, even those outside the United Kingdom or that are not capable of being transferred except under Schedule 15, paragraph 3. For rights that cannot normally be transferred, see in particular the protection given to key system assets and PPP leases (sections 216 and 218 and see above under the subheading, "Protection of key system assets"). Schedule 15 even permits a scheme to create new interests in property and new rights and liabilities if this is done for the purpose of dividing property, rights or liabilities in connection with transfers in accordance with the scheme (Schedule 15, paragraph 3(2)).

Provision is also made for licences held by the existing appointee to be transferred to the new appointee (Schedule 15, paragraph 4), for a scheme to make supplemental, consequential and transitional provisions (Schedule 15, paragraph 5), for a scheme to impose duties on the existing appointee to ensure the effective transfer of property, rights or liabilities subject to foreign law and for the new appointee to bear the expenses of this (Schedule 15, paragraph 6), and for the transfer of functions under a PPP agreement from the existing appointee, and for concurrent exercise of such functions (Schedule 15, paragraph 7).

Procedure for Making a PPP Administration Order

12.23 The grounds that must exist before the court has discretion to make a PPP administration order in relation to a PPP company are set out in section 221. There are additional procedural requirements when the Mayor is not the person presenting the petition (see below).

Unable to pay its debts

12.24 This is the first of the two alternative grounds that enable the court to make a PPP administration order (section 221(1) and (2)). Section 221(6) defines when a PPP company is unable to pay its debts by reference to provisions in the Insolvency Act 1986. Broadly, a company is deemed unable to pay its debts under section 123 of that Act if one of four conditions is satisfied. These are: (a) the company owes £750 or more to a creditor who has served the company with a written demand in the prescribed form requiring the company to pay the sum due, and the company has not paid the sum or secured or compounded for it to the reasonable satisfaction of the creditor within three weeks (the demand is commonly referred to as a "statutory demand"); (b) the company is unable to pay its debts after judgment, and due process (according to the appropriate jurisdiction, in other words, England and Wales, Scotland or Northern Ireland) has been issued to attempt to enforce the judgment and has not been satisfied; (c) it is proved to the satisfaction of the court that the company is unable to pay its debts as they fall due; or (d) it is proved to the satisfaction of the court that the value of the company's assets is less than the amount of its liabilities.

Insolvency of unregistered companies

An unregistered company includes any association and company, **12.25** except a company registered in the United Kingdom under the Joint Stock Companies Acts or under the legislation relating to companies in Great Britain. See in particular section 220(1) of Part V of the Insolvency Act 1986.

An unregistered company is deemed unable to pay its debts under section 222–4 of the Insolvency Act 1986 if one of five conditions is satisfied. These are: if (a) a "statutory demand" has not been satisfied; (b) a debt remains unsatisfied after proceedings have been brought against the company or any member of the company in his character as a member; (c) the company is unable to pay its debts after judgment, and due process (according to the appropriate jurisdiction, in other words, England and Wales, Scotland or Northern Ireland) has been issued to attempt to enforce the judgment and has not been satisfied; (d) it is proved to the satisfaction of the court that the company is unable to pay its debts as they fall due; and (e) it is proved to the satisfaction of the court that the value of the company's assets is less than the amount of its liabilities.

Certificate that it would be just and equitable for the company to be wound up

This is the second of the two alternative grounds that enable the court **12.26** to make a PPP administration order (section 221(1) and (2)). The Secretary of State may receive certain reports or information under provisions that relate to allegations of misconduct in relation to the affairs of the company. The relevant provisions are under the company investigation provisions of the Companies Act 1985 (Part XIV of that Act), the Financial Services Act 1986, the fraud investigation provisions of the Criminal Justice Act 1987 (section 2) and the Criminal Justice (Scotland) Act 1987 (section 52), and the provisions relating to assistance for overseas regulatory authorities in the Companies Act 1989 (section 83).

If it appears to the Secretary of State from the information or report that it is expedient in the public interest that a company should be wound up, he may present a petition for it to be wound up if the court thinks it just and equitable to do so (Insolvency Act 1986, s.124A).

If the Secretary of State does present such a petition, his views must be given special weight. His views may outweigh the opposition of creditors who seek a voluntary winding-up: *Re Lubin, Rosen and Associates Ltd* [1975] 1 All E.R. 577.

The Court's Discretion to Deal with the Petition

12.27 The court's powers under section 9(4) and (5) of the Insolvency Act 1986 are applied to the hearing of a petition for a PPP administration order (section 221(4)). The court must dismiss the petition if satisfied that there is an administrative receiver for the company, unless also satisfied that the person responsible for appointing the receiver consents to the order or certain transactions relating to the appointment of the receiver would be liable to be released, discharged or avoided in certain circumstances (Insolvency Act 1986, s.9(3)).

Subject to that, the court has wide discretion to dismiss the petition, adjourn the hearing (with or without conditions), make an interim order and make any order it thinks fit.

The Requirement to Notify the Mayor

12.28 The court will not wind up a PPP company unless the Mayor is making the winding-up petition or has had 14 days' notice of the petition (section 222).

The Mayor has the opportunity to ask the court to exercise its discretion to make a PPP administration order rather than a winding-up order if the court can be satisfied that the grounds for making such an order are established (section 222(2)).

Voluntary Winding up

12.29 Section 84 of the Insolvency Act 1986 sets out the circumstances in which a company may be voluntarily wound up. Section 223 of the GLA Act imposes additional restrictions on winding up a PPP company. A PPP company cannot be voluntarily wound up without the Mayor having had the opportunity to ask the court to exercise its discretion to make a PPP administration order instead.

A PPP company cannot pass a resolution voluntarily to wind itself up without permission from the Court. The court will not give permission unless the Mayor has received written notice of the proposal and has had the opportunity to ask the court to exercise its discretion to make a PPP administration order rather than give the PPP company permission to be voluntarily wound up.

The Public-Private Partnership Agreement Arbiter ("The PPP Arbiter")

12.30 The PPP arbiter is an independent (sections 225(7) and 226(5)) person appointed by the Secretary of State with various functions relating to PPP agreements. In particular, the PPP arbiter may periodically review PPP agreements (sections 229 and 230). These reviews enable Transport for London in turn to review its priorities and reconsider matters such as the proper price that parties to PPP agreements should be paid.

If no person holds the office of PPP arbiter, the Secretary of State exercises the functions himself (section 227(3)).

The provisions relating to the PPP arbitrator were brought into force on January 12, 2000 (S.I. 1999 No. 3434).

Administration

Financing the PPP arbiter

12.31 The Secretary of State is required to fund certain expenses incurred by the PPP arbiter in fulfilling his or her statutory functions (section 237). These expenses are (a) those sums determined by the Secretary of State as payable to the PPP arbiter by virtue of section 226(2) or (3) (for which, see below under the sub-heading 'Terms of appointment of the PPP arbiter'), and (b) those incurred by the PPP arbiter or by any staff of the PPP arbiter (section 237(1)).

The Secretary of State can recover these costs from London Regional Transport, Transport for London and their subsidiaries (section 237(2)). LRT, TfL and their subsidiaries can in turn recover, insofar as this is provided for in a PPP agreement, their costs from a PPP company (section 237(3)).

Sums received by the Secretary of State under these provisions will be paid into the consolidated fund, which is held by central government. (See the Consolidated Fund Act 1816, s.1.)

Terms of appointment of the PPP arbiter

12.32 The Secretary of State determines the basic terms of appointment of the PPP arbiter (section 226), together with the arbiter's remuneration, travel and other allowances, and either a pension allowance or gratuity or payments towards providing a pension allowance or gratuity (section 226(2) and (3)).

Although the instrument appointing the PPP arbiter will specify the term of his appointment and the terms on which he holds and will vacate office (section 226(1)), the PPP arbiter can only be dismissed for one of three substantial grounds (section 226(5)). Those grounds are: (a) incapacity, (b) misbehaviour, or (c) where the Secretary of State considers that there has been unreasonable delay in the discharge of his functions. This restriction on the grounds for dismissal preserves the independence of the PPP arbiter since any difference of political views between the Secretary of State and the PPP arbiter will not be sufficient reason for dismissal.

The PPP arbiter's staff

12.33 The PPP arbiter may appoint staff, who may discharge functions on his or her behalf (section 227). Staff may take on dual roles if the same person is appointed to be the PPP arbiter and the Rail Regulator (section 228).

Legal liability of the PPP arbiter and staff

12.34 The legal liability of the PPP arbiter and his or her staff and agents is restricted. They are only liable if a person can establish that any acts or

185

omissions were done in bad faith (section 236). In *Roberts v. Hopwood* [1925] A.C. 578, HL at 604, Lord Sumner stated that a public authority's powers were always subject to an implied qualification that they must be exercised in good faith meaning that: ". . . they are giving their minds to the comprehension and their wills to the discharge of their duty . . . ."

The PPP Arbiter's Powers and Duties

12.35 The PPP arbiter will have a duty to act in the way he considers best to achieve three objectives when making binding determinations (under section 229, see below) or advisory directions (under section 230, see below): section 231. Those objectives are:

> (a) if (i) LRT, TfL or a subsidiary of theirs ("the appropriate relevant body") is a party to a PPP agreement and is to pay the price under the agreement, (ii) the appropriate relevant body has notified the PPP arbiter of the resources that it has, or expects to have, available for the purpose of paying the PPP company under the agreement in respect of the requirements imposed, or proposed to be imposed, on a PPP company by or under the agreement, and (iii) in the PPP arbiter's opinion, the proper price to be paid exceeds those notified resources, to ensure that the appropriate relevant body has a proper opportunity to review and amend the requirements imposed, or proposed to be imposed, on a PPP company by or under the agreement;
>
> (b) to promote efficiency and economy (i) in the provision, construction, renewal, or improvement, and (ii) in the maintenance of, the railway infrastructure to which the PPP agreement relates;
>
> (c) to ensure that any rate of return incorporated in the PPP agreement would, in his opinion, and taking into account or ignoring such matters as are specified in the PPP agreement, be earned by a company which is efficient and economic in its performance of the requirements imposed on the PPP company by or under the PPP agreement; and
>
> (d) to enable any PPP company which is a party to the PPP agreement to plan the future performance of the agreement with reasonable certainty.

12.36 The PPP arbiter must consider all these objectives in every case. The only exception is that the PPP arbiter is only obliged to consider the rate of return an efficient PPP contractor is entitled to expect if the agreement (i) contains provision specifying, or for determining, such a rate of return and (ii) states that section 231(4) of the GLA Act is to have effect in relation to the provision.

In the unlikely event that the PPP arbiter should ignore any of the mandatory objectives when making a binding direction, the direction may be challengeable by way of an application for judicial review.

PPP arbiter's directions

12.37   The PPP arbiter has power to give directions on matters referred to him by the parties to a PPP agreement (section 229). When making a direction under this section, he must seek to achieve the objectives set out in section 231, for which see above.

The PPP arbiter must give a direction on any matter that is referred to him if (a) the PPP agreement provides for a matter of that description to be referred to him, and (b) a party to the PPP agreement refers the matter to him. There is no provision describing the method for referring a matter to the PPP arbiter. Presumably, the agreement itself will provide for this.

The PPP arbiter can also give binding directions on any matter ancillary to a matter on which he is required to give a direction. This allows, for example, the PPP arbiter to deal with issues that were not raised in the reference, but which are necessary in order to give effect to the proposed resolution of the matter raised.

The PPP arbiter may wish to exercise his powers of inspection and consultation under section 232 (for which, see below) before giving a direction.

The PPP arbiter must give written notice of the direction to the parties to the PPP agreement.

Although section 229(6) provides for the PPP arbiter's direction to be final and binding on the parties to the PPP agreement and any person claiming under or through them, there are two exceptions to this. First, if the parties to the PPP agreement agree, they can decide that the direction is not final and binding: section 229(6). Second, if the PPP arbiter's decision could be challenged on administrative law grounds, it would be possible for the decision to be quashed.

PPP arbiter's guidance

12.38   The PPP arbiter will have power to issue non-binding written guidance on any matter referred to him jointly by all the parties to a PPP agreement (section 230). The intention is to encourage the parties to a PPP agreement to reach agreement between themselves, without recourse to a binding direction under section 229 or to court proceedings.

When giving guidance, the PPP arbiter must seek to achieve the objectives set out in section 231 (for which, see above). The PPP arbiter may wish to exercise his powers of inspection and consultation under section 232 (for which, see below) before giving guidance.

Ancillary powers of the PPP arbiter

12.39   The PPP arbiter enjoys wide ancillary powers which are to be used to reinforce or enable his specific powers under the GLA Act, rather than to embark on projects wholly unconnected with his or her statutory role. For the purposes of the proper discharge of his functions, the PPP arbiter may inspect railway infrastructure or equipment belonging to or under the control of a party to a PPP agreement, consult bodies or persons in relation to any direction or guidance he proposes to give, and generally to do such things that he considers necessary or expedient (section 232(1)).

The PPP arbiter may require parties to a PPP agreement, their associates and any PPP related third party to provide information that the arbiter considers relevant to the proper discharge of his or her functions. The PPP arbiter must specify or describe the information that he requires (section 233(1)). "Associates" are defined as (a) a parent undertaking of the party, (b) a subsidiary undertaking of any parent undertaking of the party, (c) a subsidiary undertaking of the party, and (d) undertakings in which the party or an undertaking falling within categories (a) to (c) has a participating interest. The terms "parent undertaking", "subsidiary undertaking", "undertaking" and "participating interest" are defined in sections 258–60 of the Companies Act 1985, and essentially relate to the ability of one company to control or influence another.

12.40   The PPP arbiter must "request" the information. If an expression related to the words "notice" or "direction" had been used, the PPP arbiter's request would have to be made in writing (sections 421 and 424). The avoidance of such expressions may imply that the request need not be in writing.

The information must be provided in the form and manner and within such time as is specified in the request (section 233(3)). A person is entitled to refuse to answer a question or to produce a document if he would be entitled to refuse in or for the purposes of proceedings in court (section 233(4)).

There is no direct penalty for failing to provide such information when requested. The first step by the PPP arbiter in enforcing compliance is to serve a notice on a person who has failed to comply with a request for information (section 234).

A person who fails to comply with this notice faces proceedings by the PPP arbiter in the High Court for an appropriate order such as a mandatory injunction ordering him or her to make good the default (section 234(4)). If the court makes such an order, it may also order the costs of the PPP arbiter's application to be borne by the person in default or by any officers of a company or other association responsible for its default (section 234(5)). The court may punish a person who fails to comply with an injunction for contempt of court.

12.41   A person who evades the consequences of compliance with the notice by altering, suppressing or destroying any document he or she was required to produce commits a criminal offence (section 234(3)). The fine in the Crown Court is unlimited. The statutory maximum for a fine imposed after summary conviction is level 5 on the standard scale, currently £5,000 under the Criminal Justice Act 1982, section 37 (as amended).

The PPP arbiter may not disclose information obtained by him under or by virtue of his statutory functions (for example, as a result of an inspection under section 232 or a request for information under section 231 of the GLA Act) during periods in which there is a need to preserve the confidentiality of that information. Unless the disclosure is for one of the statutory purposes set out in section 235 (which relate to matters such as facilitating the carrying out of the functions of the Secretary of State,

Mayor, Transport for London, the PPP arbiter and other statutory bodies), no information relating to the affairs of an individual may be disclosed during his lifetime, and similarly no information relating to a particular business may be disclosed for so long as that business continues to be carried on (section 235(1)). This restriction on disclosure may be enforced by injunction or other civil remedy (section 235(5)).

Chapter 13

ROAD TRAFFIC

13.01 Although traffic regulation law is principally concerned with moving or stationary vehicles, all other types of traffic are also regulated.

A traffic authority is the statutory body that regulates the way in which the public can use highways and other roads to which the public has access. A traffic authority is required to exercise its functions to secure the expeditious, convenient and safe movement of vehicular and other traffic (including pedestrians) and the provision of suitable and convenient parking places on and off the highway. This duty is qualified by the need to have regard to considerations relating to access to premises, amenity, facilitating the passage of public service vehicles and any other matters appearing to the traffic authority to be relevant. (See the Road Traffic Regulation Act 1984, ss.121A and 142(1).)

The general law on road traffic regulation is consolidated in the Road Traffic Regulation Act 1984. In London, that general law has been considerably amended. The GLA Act amends it further.

13.02 When the Greater London Council was abolished, most of its traffic authority functions were transferred to the London borough councils and the Common Council of the City of London (Local Government Act 1985, s.8(2) and Sched.5, Pt II).

The Secretary of State is the traffic authority for roads in Greater London that are trunk roads. Trunk roads are major arterial routes other than motorways (which are "special roads"). They were first created by the Trunk Roads Act 1936, at a time when motorised traffic was becoming an important feature of highways. They are now mainly governed by sections 10, 11 and 19 of the Highways Act 1980. Such roads include those that were trunk roads under the Highways Act 1959 and those that the Secretary of State has since designated (Highways Act 1980, s.329(1)).

Part II of the Road Traffic Regulation Act 1984 made provision for a network of priority routes, known as "red routes", in London. The Traffic Director for London was established in respect of the network (Road Traffic Act 1991, s.52 and Sched. 5).

Contraventions of parking restrictions in London were also decriminalised and dealt with administratively (see the 1991 Act, ss.63–77).

Overview of the New Road Traffic Regulation Regime in London

Transport for London (TfL) is established as a new traffic authority in **13.03** Greater London (Chapter XIV of Part IV and section 271 in particular). Transport for London will be the traffic authority for GLA roads (and side roads, by virtue of section 142(4) of the Road Traffic Regulation Act 1984, inserted by section 292 of the GLA Act): section 271 of the GLA Act, amending section 121A of the 1984 Act.

The London borough councils and the Common Council of the City of London are the traffic authorities for the roads in their areas that are neither trunk roads nor GLA roads.

The functions of the GLA under the Road Traffic Regulation Act 1984 may be exercised by the Mayor acting on behalf of the Authority, except if the function is one expressly conferred or imposed on or exercisable by the Assembly (GLA Act, s.292, inserting section 121C into the Road Traffic Regulation Act 1984). The majority of the provisions relating to road traffic in the GLA Act will be brought into force on July 3, 2000 (S.I. 2000 No.801). The exceptions are: section 272 (GLA side roads), brought into force on January 12, 2000 by S.I. 1999 No. 3434; section 288 (school crossing patrols), brought into force on April 1, 2000 by S.I. 2000 No. 801; and section 291, brought into force on May 8, 2000 for the purposes of enabling the Mayor to give directions to local authorities under section 121B(9) of the Road Traffic Regulation Act 1984 (S.I. 2000 No. 801).

GLA Roads and Side Roads

A GLA road is a road that is designated as such by order of the Secretary **13.04** of State under section 14A of the Highways Act 1980 or by order of the Authority under section 14B of that Act (Highways Act 1980, s.14D, inserted by the GLA Act, s.263). This definition of a GLA road is inserted into the Road Traffic Regulation Act 1984 by section 292 of the GLA Act. See also paragraph 14.02 below.

Similarly, the Secretary of State and the GLA may designate certain roads that connect with GLA roads as GLA side roads: section 124A of the Road Traffic Regulation Act 1984, inserted by section 272 of the GLA Act.

A GLA side road is within the definition of a GLA road (Road Traffic Regulation Act 1984, s.142, amended by the GLA Act, s.292). This means that a road may be designated as a GLA side road if it connects with another GLA side road.

Transfer of Planning and Guidance Functions to TfL

Priority routes and the Traffic Director for London are abolished by section **13.05** 294 and various traffic management powers of the Secretary of State and the Traffic Director for London are repealed because they will no longer be required when the Mayor's transport strategy (section 142, see above) is in force (GLA Act, section 294).

Detailed transitional provisions provide for plans and guidance made under the old provisions and powers to continue for a limited period (GLA Act, s.294).

Any guidance given by the Secretary of State under paragraph 53 of Schedule 4 to the Local Government Act 1985, Part II of Schedule 5 to the Local Government Act 1985 or sections 50 to 63 and 80 of, and Schedule 5 to, the Road Traffic Act 1991 (priority routes, local plans, trunk road plans [and the Traffic Director for London]) will, until superseded by the transport strategy, continue in force and have effect as if it were part of that strategy. The Mayor may modify or revoke it in accordance with the provisions relating to modifications and revocation of the transport strategy (see above—section 294(2)).

The Traffic Director for London's network plan prepared under section 52 of the 1991 Act continues to have effect as if part of the transport strategy until superseded by that strategy. Likewise, the Traffic Director for London's trunk road local plans prepared under section 56 of the 1991 Act continue to have effect as if part of the transport strategy until superseded.

A local plan prepared by a London borough council or the Common Council of the City of London under section 54 of the Road Traffic Act 1991 that has already been prepared or that is in the course of preparation will continue to have effect as if it (a) were part of the transport strategy to the extent that it relates to GLA roads or (b) were a local implementation plan (LIP) (section 145, see above) to the extent that it relates to any other roads, until in either case they are superseded by that strategy or such a plan.

Transport for London's Specific Powers in Relation to Traffic Signs

Traffic Signs

13.06 Transport for London may erect, and has a duty to maintain, traffic signs in connection with GLA roads (section 273, amending the Road Traffic Regulation Act 1984, s.73).

Note that TfL's powers under section 273 can be exercised on roads for which the traffic authority is (a) a London borough council or the Common Council of the City of London, or (b) the Secretary of State, but in the latter case only if the road is not a trunk road (section 273(3), inserting new subsection (1A) into section 73 of the Road Traffic Regulation Act 1984).

Traffic Signs on Walls

13.07 Transport for London may put up traffic signs on walls (section 274, amending the Road Traffic Regulation Act 1984, s.74).

Transfer of the Traffic Control Systems

A traffic control system may provide regulation, instruction, information or **13.08** guidance services to vehicular traffic or pedestrians from installations on or adjacent to the highway. Electronic traffic signals, electronic pedestrian crossings, variable message signs, speed cameras and emergency telephones, together with their associated cables, circuits and computer systems, for example, are all classed as traffic control systems.

The Secretary of State's statutory functions for traffic control systems in Greater London will be transferred to Transport for London for all roads other than trunk roads, and TfL and the Secretary of State may transfer the traffic control systems for the whole of London between each other (sections 275–8).

The London Traffic Control System

The traffic control system for all roads other than trunk roads is known as **13.09** the London traffic control system. This system will be transferred to Transport for London (section 275).

TfL can recover its expenses of operating the London traffic control system, but only insofar as these relate to roads which are neither GLA roads nor trunk roads, from the London borough councils and the Common Council of the City of London. The proportion of these expenses that each of those authorities must pay may be agreed between them and TfL. In default of agreement, TfL is the final arbiter of the amount that each authority will pay, subject to the supervisory jurisdiction of the courts (section 275(3)).

If a London local authority asks TfL to provide new traffic light installations for a borough road, TfL must approve and carry out the work unless it considers there are reasonable grounds for refusing. TfL must also consult the relevant local authority before altering the operating cycle of traffic lights or installing new traffic light installations on a borough road (new section 74A(1) and (6) of the Road Traffic Regulations Act 1984, inserted by section 276).

Devolution of the London Traffic Control System

TfL can agree with a local authority that part of the London traffic control **13.10** system will be transferred to the local authority and the local authority will maintain and operate that part. A local authority may also, with TfL's approval, set up and operate new traffic light installations. In either case, the local authority is treated as the traffic authority for that part of the system or the new traffic light installations: new section 74A(2), (3) and (4) of the Road Traffic Regulations Act 1984, inserted by section 276.

Transfer of the Traffic Control Systems

The traffic control systems for trunk roads, and the separate traffic control **13.11** system for all other roads in Greater London, may be transferred from the

Secretary of State to Transport for London, and vice versa. The power to maintain and operate each system may also be transferred (section 277). They can choose to transfer part or all of the traffic control system. The whole traffic control system could therefore end up in the control of either TfL or the Secretary of State (new section 74B of the Road Traffic Regulations Act 1984, inserted by section 277).

TfL will be deemed to be the traffic authority for a road in Greater London other than a trunk road for the purposes of the provisions of the Road Traffic Regulation Act 1984 that relate to traffic lights (section 278).

Promoting Road Safety and Contributions to Compulsory Schemes Prepared by Local Authorities

13.12 Transport for London may prepare and carry out a programme for promoting road safety and/or to contribute to the compulsory schemes that are prepared by local authorities (GLA Act, s.279, amending the Road Traffic Act 1988, s.39).

TfL will also have a duty to study road accidents on GLA roads that involve vehicles, and to take appropriate measures in response to its findings (GLA Act, s.279, amending the Road Traffic Act 1988, s.39).

Section 1 of the Road Traffic Reduction Act 1997 is amended to take account of the transport strategy roles of the Mayor, the London borough councils and the Common Council of the City of London (section 280). The London local authorities must consider the Mayor's transport strategy and the local implementation plans (LIPs) prepared by London local authorities to implement that strategy (for both of which, see above) when they prepare their reports relating to the levels of road traffic in their areas.

13.13 The London local authorities' reports must: (a) contain an assessment of the levels of local road traffic in their area, (b) contain a forecast of the growth in those levels, and (c) specify either targets for a reduction in the levels of road traffic in their area, or targets for a reduction in the rate of growth in the levels of such traffic (Road Traffic Reduction Act 1997, s.2).

The Road Traffic Reduction Act 1997 was brought into force on March 10, 2000 by. the Road Traffic Reduction Act 1997 (Commencement) (England and Wales) Order 2000 (S.I. 2000 No. 735).

Paying Parking Places on GLA Roads

13.14 A paying parking place is an area of the highway designated by order for use only by such persons or vehicles (or a class of persons or vehicles) authorised by a permit, for which a charge may be made (see section 45(1) and (2) and section 46 Road Traffic Regulation Act 1984).

Designation of Paying Parking Places

Transport for London may designate paying parking places on any GLA **13.15**
road. All local authorities who are not the traffic authority for the road in
question must now obtain the consent of the traffic authority before
exercising the power to designate a parking place under section 45,
whether or not they are a London authority (section 281, amending the
Road Traffic Regulation Act 1984, section 45).

The London borough councils and the Common Council of the City of
London already have power to designate paying parking places on their
roads.

Financial Provisions Relating to Parking Places on Highways

The existing financial provisions relating to parking places on highways are **13.16**
modified to take account of the creation of the Mayor and Transport for
London.

TfL, the London borough councils and the Common Council of the City
of London must all keep accounts of their income and expenditure in
respect of the parking places on the highway for which they are the local
authority (section 282, amending the Road Traffic Regulation Act 1984,
s.55(1)).

At the end of each financial year, any deficit in the account must be
made good out of the general fund. Any surplus can only be applied for all
or any of the following purposes: (a) repaying credits from the general fund
made in the four previous financial years, (b) meeting the cost of off-street
parking, (c) contributing to off-street parking provided by others, and (d)
in certain circumstances, meeting the costs of passenger transport services
and highway or road improvement projects (see the Road Traffic Regulation Act 1984, s.55(4)).

When these provisions are brought into force, there will be two further **13.17**
options on which Transport for London, the London borough councils and
the Common Council may spend any surplus: (e) facilitating the cost of
implementing the London transport strategy, but only insofar as the
transport strategy specifies that the surplus may be applied to that
particular cost, and (f) making contributions to each other.

If a local authority so determines, any amount not applied in any
financial year may be carried forward to the next financial year (Road
Traffic Regulation Act 1984, s.55(3)).

Transport for London, the London borough councils and the Common
Council may form a joint committee under section 101(5) of the Local
Government Act for the purpose of spending surpluses, as if TfL were a
local authority (Road Traffic Regulation Act 1984, section 55(8)).

Reports on a Surplus, Deficit or Carried Forward Amount in the Account

As soon after the end of a financial year as is reasonably possible, TfL, the **13.18**
London borough councils and the Common Council of the City of London

must report to the Mayor (GLA Act, s.282). The report must deal with any action taken by them to make good deficits in the parking places account out of the general fund or to apply a surplus for permitted purposes (Road Traffic Regulation Act 1984, s.55(2)) or to carry forward an amount under section 55(3) of the Road Traffic Regulation Act 1984. This should assist the Mayor to specify, in a future transport strategy (for which, see above), purposes for which surpluses in the account may be spent.

Joint Committees to Appoint Parking Adjudicators

13.19 Transport for London and the London local authorities will be required to establish a joint committee under section 101(5) of the Local Government Act to appoint parking adjudicators, as if TfL were a local authority. The joint committee must be established before September 4, 2000 or such later date as the Secretary of State specifies (section 283, amending section 73 of the Road Traffic Act 1991).

A parking adjudicator is the person to whom a person may appeal against an authority's decision to refuse to accept representations made in respect of charges made in relation to the immobilisation or removal of a vehicle (see sections 71 and 72 RTA 1991). The parking adjudicator has power to require the authority to make a refund in certain circumstances (RTA 1991, section 72(2)).

Regulations made by the Secretary of State (Road Traffic Act 1991, s.73(11)) make provision for the procedure in relation to proceedings before parking adjudicators. The current regulations are the Road Traffic (Parking Adjudicators) (London) Regulations 1993 (S.I. 1993 No. 1202).

The Level of Additional Parking Charges for Roads in London

13.20 Section 284 substitutes new sections 74 and 74A into the Road Traffic Act 1991. Those sections make detailed provision for setting the level of additional parking charges for roads in London.

Under the old section 74(4) Road Traffic Act 1991, the London local authorities had to submit the scheme for additional parking charges to the Secretary of State for approval, and the Secretary of State had a reserve power to set the level of charges by making regulations (former section 74(5) Road Traffic Act 1991). The Mayor now carries out the initial approval and has the default powers, and the Secretary of State will only be involved at the final approval stage (Road Traffic Act 1991, s.74A).

The main differences from the former section 74 Road Traffic Act 1991 are that: (a) TfL will now initially set the charges for GLA roads and trunk roads, (b) the Mayor approves the charges proposed by TfL and the London local authorities, and in default may set the charges by order, (c) the scheme must be published in a form determined by the Mayor, and (d) the Secretary of State may object to charges that he considers excessive, with reserve powers to set the charges by regulations, therefore retaining ultimate control over the level of charges.

Special Parking Area Orders in Relation to GLA Roads or Trunk Roads

A special parking area order provides that offences such as those involving **13.21** the contravention of waiting restrictions, parking in cycle tracks, or parking on a footpath, become decriminalised and replaced by a system of penalty charges (Road Traffic Act 1991, s.76(3) and s.77).

Only TfL may make apply to the Secretary of State for a special parking area order in relation to GLA roads or trunk roads. Only a London borough council or the Common Council of the City of London may do so in relation to other roads (section 285, amending section 76 of the Road Traffic Act 1991).

The Mayor will have power to vary the area covered by a special parking area order: section 286, inserting a new section 76 into the Road Traffic Act 1991. The traffic authority for any road affected will have to consent to the variation and, if all or any part of a Royal Park will be brought within the area, the Secretary of State must consent. The Mayor is not able to include any area that has already been designated in an order of the Secretary of State on grounds of national security. The overall effect should be that the Mayor will be able to decriminalise parking restrictions on almost all GLA roads without having to seek the consent of the Secretary of State under section 76 of the Road Traffic Act 1991.

Responsibility for School Crossing Patrols

A school crossing is a place (a) where children cross roads on their way to **13.22** and from school or from one part of a school to another during the hours 8.30 a.m. to 5.30 p.m., and (b) that is patrolled by a person appointed by a local authority.

From April 1, 2000, responsibility for patrolling school crossings was transferred from the Metropolitan Police to the London borough councils and the eight fringe districts that currently make up the Metropolitan Police District (section 288, amending section 26 of the Road Traffic Regulation Act 1984; S.I. 2000 No. 801).

This brings the regime for the control of school crossings into line with the rest of the country, where local authorities have statutory responsibility. The Common Council of the City of London was already responsible for this in the City of London.

TfL must now be consulted before a school crossing patrol is established over a GLA road (new section 26(4A) of the Road Traffic Regulation Act 1984).

197

Parking Attendants and Traffic Wardens

13.23 Transport for London will be designated as a local authority in respect of the provisions relating to parking attendants (section 289, amending section 63A of Road Traffic Regulation Act 1984). This will allow TfL to provide for the supervision of parking places within Greater London by individuals known as parking attendants (Road Traffic Regulation Act 1984, s.63A(1)).

TfL may arrange with the police authority to employ traffic wardens to act as street parking attendants at parking places provided or controlled by TfL (section 290, amending section 95(4) of the Road Traffic Regulation Act 1984).

The power to prescribe the uniforms to be worn by parking attendants is transferred to the GLA from the Secretary of State (section 289, amending section 63A of Road Traffic Regulation Act 1984). This brings Greater London more into line with the rest of the country, where local authorities decide what uniforms parking attendants must wear.

Notification and Consultation before Exercising Road Traffic Powers

13.24 The London borough councils and the Common Council of the City of London must not exercise their powers under the Road Traffic Regulation Act 1984 so as to affect GLA roads or roads in other boroughs without prior notification to and approval, either explicit or implicit, from the authority for the affected road (section 291, inserting a new section 121B into the Road Traffic Regulation Act 1984).

This provision closely mirrors section 266, which inserts a similar section (new section 301A) into the Highways Act 1980.

The Need for Notification

13.25 London borough councils and the Common Council of the City of London must give advance notification to TfL and each other of work to a road, unless the work will neither affect nor be likely to affect GLA roads or roads outside their area (section 121B(1) and (2)). The Mayor may dispense with the requirement for notification (section 121B (9)).

Lord Whitty, the Under-Secretary of State for the Department of the Environment Transport and the Regions, responded to concerns about authorities using the notification procedure for nearly all works, however minor, and the possibility that authorities would be uncertain about whether notification was required or not. He stated that

"the provisions are modelled on arrangements with which people are familiar—the arrangements for designated roads and priority routes. The concept of 'affect or likely to affect' is well established. . . . when the mayor is in place he will be able to issue guidance on the operation of the provisions." *Hansard* H.L. Vol. 603, col. 652.

The Need for Approval

The work must not go ahead unless TfL or any affected London local **13.26** authority either expressly gives approval, does not object to the proposal within one month of receiving notice of the proposal, or withdraws its objection (section 121B(3)). If an objection from a London local authority cannot be resolved, the GLA can give consent overruling the objection and allowing the proposal to proceed (section 121B(3)(d)). The Mayor may from May 8, 2000 dispense with the requirement for any such express or implied approval: section 121B(9), brought into force for this purpose only by S.I. 2000 No. 801.

Transport for London's Default Powers

If TfL believes a London local authority is proposing to proceed without **13.27** following the notification and approval procedure and considers the procedure is required to be followed, it may direct the authority not to proceed with a proposal until the procedure has been completed (section 291(5)). If a London local authority exercises a power in defiance of the notification and approval requirements, TfL may reverse or modify the effect of the exercise of that power (section 121B (6)).

Consultation in Relation to Royal Parks

The Secretary of State must not exercise his functions in relation to the **13.28** management of roads and traffic in the Royal Parks in such a way as to affect a highway in Greater London unless he has consulted the traffic authority for the highway and Transport for London. Similarly, a traffic authority must consult the Secretary of State before exercising functions in relation to a highway that will affect a Royal Park. A function may be exercised without consultation where this would not be reasonably practicable, but the statutory consultee must be informed as soon as practicable (section 293, inserting a new section 132AA into the Road Traffic Regulation Act 1984).

Note that the duty to consult only arises if the exercise of a particular function does in fact affect the Royal Parks or a highway. It does not arise if the function is merely likely to have such an effect.

Chapter 14

HIGHWAYS

14.01 There is no comprehensive statutory legal definition of the word "highway", but at common law a highway is broadly defined as a way over which all members of the public have the right to pass and repass. Where a highway is maintainable at public expense it is vested in its local highway authority. The Highways Act 1980 identifies the highway authorities who are responsible for the network of highways maintainable at public expense throughout the country.

A highway authority is a statutory body exercising statutory functions in respect of those highways vested in it. Prior to the abolition of the GLC there was, in London, a three-tier hierarchy of highway authorities. The Secretary of State was the highway authority for "trunk roads", the former Greater London Council was the authority for "metropolitan roads" and London borough councils were the highway authority for all other roads. Trunk roads are major arterial routes other than motorways designated as such under the Highways Act 1959. When the GLC was abolished so was the designation of "metropolitan roads". Some were designated trunk roads and the remainder borough roads, resulting in responsibility being split between the Secretary of State and the relevant London boroughs.

TfL as Highway Authority

14.02 Chapter XIII, Part IV of the GLA Act amends the Highways Act 1980 to establish Transport for London (TfL) as a highway authority. One of the purposes of this chapter is to reduce the number of roads designated as trunk roads in London and to transfer responsibility for a newly created strategic London road network to TfL. These roads will be known as GLA roads and upon being so designated by the Secretary of State as GLA roads they will cease to be trunk roads (GLA Act, s.259(3) and Highway Act 1980, s.14A(2) as inserted by the GLA Act, s.260(2)).

The definition of a GLA road (provided by amendments to the Highways Act 1980 made by the GLA Act, s.263) is, within the statutory framework alone, somewhat opaque: a GLA road is one designated as a GLA road (by virtue of sections 14D(1) and sections 2(3), 14A or 14B of the Highways Act 1980 as inserted by sections 259(5) and 263 GLA Act). The practical meaning of a GLA road must therefore be gleaned from other sources. In the White Paper, the government stated that:

"The GLA will acquire responsibility for a strategic London road network. . . . The strategic London road network will include all trunk roads in London. It will not include the M1, M4 and M11 spurs, which are more conveniently managed as part of the national motorway network. . . . [W]e start from the presumption that the strategic London road network should be based upon the primary and red route networks . . . ." (paragraphs 5.33–5.34)

For example, in the City of London,

"[t]he routes that have been designated as the GLA road network are: the existing red route from Bishopsgate to London Bridge, together with the Tower Hill gyratory and Tower Bridge; the route along the northern bank of the Thames; and the A201 northern route which crosses Blackfriars Bridge." *per* Lord Whitty, the Under-Secretary of State for the Department of the Environment, Transport and the Regions, *Hansard* H.L. Vol. 603, cols 641–2.

14–03 The first GLA roads will be designated by the Secretary of State under a new section 14A of the Highways Act 1980. The GLA Roads Designation Order 2000 (S.I. 2000 No. 1117) specifies the highways which became GLA roads on May 22, 2000 for which TfL is the highway authority. Further, pursuant to Greater London Authority Roads (Supplementary Provisions) Order 2000 (S.I. 2000 No.1064) any roads in Greater London which were constructed by an urban development corporation, and to which the public have access are designated as GLA roads and become maintainable at public expense. Any further designation of highways as GLA roads can be made by order by the GLA. The Mayor will initiate such an order. The order must be made with the consent of the highway authority that is losing or gaining jurisdiction over the highway as a result of the order, unless the Secretary of State confirms the order (Highways Act 1980, s.14A, as inserted by the GLA Act, s.261). The authority cannot direct any trunk road or proposed trunk road shall become a GLA road. Such power remains with the Secretary of State (Highways Act 1980, s.14A, as inserted by the GLA Act, s.260).

14–04 The Mayor is under a duty to keep under review the highway system of Greater London (including any proposed highways) together with the allocation of responsibility for that system between the highway authorities in Greater London (Highways Act 1980, s.14B, as inserted by the GLA Act, s.261). Where the Mayor considers it expedient that a highway or proposed highway should become a GLA road or even cease to be a GLA road, the GLA, can by order direct that that highway shall be designated or its designation change accordingly. Where the GLA order that a highway is to cease to be a GLA road that road shall vest in the relevant highway authority, namely the local highway authority for the area, from the date specified in the order. If the GLA order that a highway or proposed highway is to become a GLA road it will become such on the date specified in the order. For any order to have effect it must be made with the consent of the relevant highway authority. In the absence of such consent, the Secretary of State must have confirmed the order. The Secretary of State can modify the order before confirming it. Whether a highway is a GLA road or not can be simply established by producing a certificate to that effect issued by or on behalf of TfL. The certificate shall be evidence of the fact that the road is a GLA road (Highways Act 1980, s.14C, as inserted by the GLA Act, s.262).

TfL is required to prepare and maintain a record of the highways that are GLA roads. The record may consist of a list, a map or both. A copy of this record must be deposited with the GLA and each London borough including the Common Council. These records must be made available for inspection by the public at reasonable times (Highways Act 1980, s.14C as inserted by GLA Act, s.262).

Transfer of Property, Liabilities and Employees for GLA Roads

14.05 Upon a highway or proposed highway becoming, or ceasing to be, a GLA road, the land and other property (including unexpended balances of grants), and all liabilities in relation to the transferred highway (save for any loans or loan charges) shall be transferred to the new highway authority, unless otherwise agreed (Highways Act 1980, s.266A, as inserted by the GLA Act, s.264). The land will be transferred subject to the same covenants, conditions and restrictions as applied to the former highway authority. Land used for storage of materials required wholly or mainly for:

(i) other highways,
(ii) the improvement of frontages of adjoining or adjacent to the highway,

are excluded from such transfer. Materials to be used for the maintenance or improvement of the highway or unexpended balances of loans raised by the former highway authority are also excluded.

14.06 There is no right or liability for work done, services rendered, goods delivered, or money due for payment before the date of transfer. Further, the new highway authority is not liable for damages or compensation for any act or omission before that date, or for the purchase price of any land, or contract to purchase land, completed before the date of transfer.

If there is a dispute between the new highway authority and any other person regarding the property or liabilities transferred by virtue of section 266A of the Highways Act 1980 it must be determined by arbitration (Highways Act 1980 s.266A(7), as inserted by the GLA Act, s.264).

A new section 266B of the Highways Act 1980 provides for the transfer to the new highway authority of the employees needed to maintain a highway that is becoming or ceasing to be a GLA road (GLA Act, s.265). The employees' employment rights are protected by the GLA Act.

Carrying out Works on a Highway

A new section 301A of the Highways Act 1980 inserted by section 266 of **14.07** the GLA Act requires a London borough council and/or the Common Council of the City of London to give advance notification to TfL and other London boroughs, of any exercise of any power under the Highways Act 1980 which will in any way affect, or is likely to affect a GLA road, or a road in that authority's borough (GLA Act, s.266(1) and (2)). The requirement to notify other London boroughs is limited to those boroughs whose roads will be affected or are likely to be affected. The Mayor may dispense with the requirement for notification (Highways Act 1980, s.301A(9)).

Having complied with the notification requirement, the London borough proposing to do the work must obtain the approval of TfL where that work is to a GLA road, or the approval of the relevant London borough in the case where the road is in another borough. If the London borough does not receive any objection to the proposal within one month it can proceed. If there is an objection to the proposal, which is not withdrawn, the GLA or the Mayor on its behalf, may cause a public inquiry to be held and determine whether consent should be given.

If work is done without complying with the notification provisions, TfL **14.08** may reverse the effect of the exercise of the power and recover any reasonable expenses from the London borough council concerned (Highways Act 1980, s.301A(6)). During the passage of the Bill through Parliament Lord Whitty, the Under-Secretary of State for the Department of the Environment Transport and the Regions, responded to concerns about authorities using the notification procedure for nearly all works, however minor, and the possibility that authorities would be uncertain about whether notification was required or not. He stated that:

> "the provisions are modelled on arrangements with which people are familiar—the arrangements for designated roads and priority route. The concept of 'affect or likely to affect' is well established. . . . when the mayor is in place he will be able to issue guidance on the operation of the provisions." *Hansard* H.L. Vol. 603, col. 652.

Royal Parks

A new section 301B is inserted into the Highways Act 1980 by section 267 **14.09** of the GLA Act. This ensures that highway authorities and the Secretary of

State consult each other about their exercise of any of their functions which will affect a Royal Park. In the case of the Secretary of State his duty is limited to the exercise of any of his functions in relation to the management of road and traffic in a Royal Park that will affect a highway in Greater London, but in the case of a highway authority the duty to consult with the Secretary of State relates to any discharge of its functions that will affect a Royal Park.

This duty to consult only arises if the exercise of their function does in fact affect the Royal Parks or a highway. It does not arise if the function is merely "likely" to have such an effect. This is in contrast to the provisions of the new section 301A of the Highways Act 1980 (referred to above).

Road Humps

14.10 Section 268 of the GLA Act creates a special procedure for the construction of road humps in highways in Greater London by amending sections 90A, 90D and 90E of, and inserting a new section 90CA into, the Highways Act 1980.

A road hump is an artificial hump in or on the surface of the highway which is designed to control the speed of vehicles, and includes any other works (including signs or lighting) required in connection with such a hump. It is essentially a raised area of the highway that is intended to make travel at speed less comfortable than slower travel (Highways Act 1980, ss.90F and 329).

Section 90A of the Highways Act 1980 requires the authorisation of the Secretary of State for road humps on a road where the statutory speed limit for motor vehicles is more than 30 miles per hour. As amended, this section permits road humps to be constructed if they fall within new section 90CA of the 1980 Act. This new section enables a highway authority in Greater London to construct road humps, but it can only do so if it serves on the Secretary of State notice containing the requisite details of the proposed hump. The highway authority is required to have regard to any comments made by the Secretary of State before deciding to proceed.

14.11 Regulations made by the Secretary of State under section 90D(4) of that Act may make provision for the construction and maintenance of road humps, but such regulations do not apply to road humps that have been authorised by the Secretary of State or that fall within new section 90CA (see above).

Section 90E(1), Highways Act 1980 is amended by section 268(5) of the GLA Act and new subsections are inserted by section 268(6) of the GLA Act. Section 90E provides that certain road humps are not to be treated as obstructions but as part of the highway and therefore maintainable as part of that highway. The effect of these new provisions is to include those road humps on a highway maintainable at the public expense and falling within new section 90CA (see above).

Traffic Calming Works

Section 269 of the GLA Act creates a special procedure for the construction **14.12** of traffic calming works in highways in Greater London by amending sections 90G and 90I of, and inserting a new section 90GA into, the Highways Act 1980. Traffic calming works are works affecting the movement of vehicular and other traffic for the purpose of promoting safety or preserving or improving the environment through which the highway runs. Commonly, they are constructions such as chicanes that alter the layout of the highway with an effect similar to that of road humps. (See sections 90G, 90I and section 329 of the Highways Act 1980.)

Traffic calming works must either conform to regulations made by the Secretary of State under section 90H of the 1980 Act, be authorised by the Secretary of State or fall within new section 90GA of that Act. This new section only applies to traffic calming works carried out by local highway authorities in Greater London. Where such works are proposed an authority must notify the Secretary of State of the proposed works and provide him with the prescribed details. Before deciding to carry out the works an authority must have regard to any comments the Secretary of State may make. Traffic calming works that conform to the regulations, are authorised or fall within section 90GA shall not be treated as obstructions to the highway but as part of the highway.

Stopping up Orders

Section 270 of the GLA Act introduces Schedule 22 into the Act, which **14.13** contains amendments to the Highways Act 1980 and the Town and Country and Planning Act 1990. This schedule provides for the devolution to London boroughs of powers held by the Secretary of State to stop up or divert highways by amending section 125 of the Highways Act 1980 and sections 247–50, 252–3 and 261 of the Town and Country Planning Act 1990. Where there are objections to the stopping up of a highway the Mayor will decide whether to dispense with the need to hold a public inquiry. These amendments should facilitate development in Greater London as a developer will now be able to seek from the London borough that has approved his development any necessary stopping up order to facilitate that development, rather than having to delay the commencement of development until the Secretary of State has issued a stopping up order.

Chapter 15

NEW CHARGES AND LEVIES

Background to PPP Agreements and the New Transport Charges and Levies

15.01 The Deputy Prime Minister, John Prescott, announced the government's plans for the future funding of London Underground (*Hansard* H.C. Vol. 308, cols 1539–1556). He explained that London Underground Limited will remain as a unified public sector operating company that owns the freehold of the underground system and is responsible for employing train drivers, station staff and line and network controllers. It will enter into between one and three contracts with the private sector for the maintenance and modernisation of the infrastructure of London Underground. The aim is that the assets will be returned to the public sector at the end of the contract in a much improved condition.

The transport sub-committee of the Environment, Transport and Regional Affairs Select Committee conducted an inquiry into the government's proposals and how they would work in practice. Its report recommended that provision should be made to ensure that any gap in funding between income from fares and payments to the contractors did not give rise to undue pressure to increase fares or reduce service levels (London Underground, "7th Report of the Environment, Transport and Regional Affairs Select Committee 1997–8", July 8, 1998 H.C. 715-I). The sub-committee believed that the GLA should have access to additional revenue for spending on public transport from new hypothecated sources of transport-related taxation within Greater London.

15.02 The government responded in October 1998: DETR "The Government's Response to the Report on London Underground of the Environment, Transport and Regional Affairs Select Committee", Cm. 4093 (1998). It referred to plans to hypothecate the revenue from road-user charging and a levy on parking places (which eventually became the workplace parking levy).

The Under-Secretary of State for the Department of the Environment Transport and the Regions, Lord Whitty, explained (when he introduced the Bill to the House of Lords for its second reading) that the money raised by road user charging and the workplace charging levy would be used to fund transport initiatives for a minimum of 10 years:

"Every single penny raised from charging schemes introduced within the first 10 years of the GLA will be ring-fenced for transport expenditure for a scheme's initial period. The expectation is that this period will be 10 years. But the Bill provides a power to allow the Secretary of State to guarantee the hypothecation of the net proceeds for longer than 10 years. This could be particularly valuable if for example the mayor wished to undertake a private finance initiative and the private sector required a guarantee of revenues for longer than 10 years." *Hansard* H.L. Vol. 601, col. 445.

The new powers to charge road users and to raise a levy on parking places reflect these policy statements. The revenues are to be reserved for transport for at least the initial 10 years (section 295 and Schedule 23, and section 296 and Schedule 24 respectively).

The provisions relating to both road user charging and the workplace parking levy came into force on May 5, 2000 except in relation to TfL. They are fully in force from July 3, 2000. See below for the role of TfL in road user charging and the workplace parking levy.

Road User Charging Schemes

Transport for London, the London borough councils and the Common **15.03** Council of the City of London are all given a discretionary power to introduce road user charging schemes (section 295). If a scheme is made by any of these bodies, that body is known as the charging authority (Schedule 23, paragraph 1(1)).

The Mayor may exercise on behalf of the GLA any powers conferred on it in respect of road user charging schemes (Schedule 23, paragraph 2).

A charging scheme may only be made if it appears desirable or expedient for the purpose of facilitating policies or proposals in the transport strategy (Schedule 23, paragraph 3). The scheme must also conform to the transport strategy (Schedule 23, paragraph 5).

Each London local authority will be able to implement a charging scheme in all or part of its area, and in respect of its own roads and GLA roads, although the Secretary of State's consent is required before charges can be imposed in respect of a trunk road. It will also have the power to join with others in a joint charging scheme, and the GLA may require authorities to do so (Schedule 23, paragraph 7).

TfL may administer a scheme for part of London, and will administer any scheme covering the whole of London. A TfL scheme may apply to all roads within the scheme area, although the Secretary of State's consent is required before charges can be imposed in respect of a trunk road. However, the same road cannot be subject to charges by more than one charging authority (Schedule 23, paragraph 9).

Procedure for Making a Road User Charging Scheme

15.04 Consultation and inquiries may be held by the GLA before a scheme is made and, if it so directs, consultation must be carried out by the charging authority. (Schedule 23, paragraph 4). A scheme must be made by order and must be in a form determined by the GLA and approved by it (Schedule 23, paragraph 4). The GLA may modify a scheme order before it takes effect (Schedule 23, paragraph 4).

Equipment for a Road User Charging Scheme

15.05 The GLA may require the charging authority to install and maintain traffic signs in connection with the scheme (Schedule 23, paragraph 4). Charging authorities may install equipment necessary for the operation of a scheme. (Schedule 23, paragraph 14). The GLA can approve the type of equipment to be used, but the Secretary of State can prevent the use of equipment incompatible with national standards and where the incompatibility will be detrimental to those living outside London (Schedule 23, paragraph 29).

Content of a Road User Charging Scheme

15.06 A scheme must identify the area, vehicles and roads to which it applies, the events by reference to which a charge is imposed, the charges to be made under it (Schedule 23, paragraphs 8, 9 and 10), the period it is to remain in force (Schedule 23, paragraph 37) and general proposals by the authority making the scheme for using its share of the proceeds over the next 10 years (Schedule 23, paragraph 19). A scheme cannot impose a charge for keeping a vehicle on a road in a charging area unless it does the same in respect of use of the vehicle in that area (Schedule 23, paragraph 10(2)).

A scheme may provide for concessions from charges to be made (Schedule. 23, paragraph 11). These concessions will be subject to any provisions made by regulations by the Secretary of State that provide for exemptions, reduced rates of charge and limits on charges payable. Such concessions may be applied, for example, in respect of disabled persons.

The GLA may alter the area and roads to which the scheme applies (Schedule. 23, paragraph 9). The GLA may also issue guidance and directions during the operation of a scheme (Schedule 23, paragraphs 33 and 34). No scheme may impose charges in respect of vehicles that are not on a road, or provide for examination of or fitting immobilisation devices to such vehicles (Schedule 23, paragraph 31). The GLA may control the content of schemes by withholding approval from schemes that contain provisions to which it objects (Schedule 23, paragraph 6).

Enforcement

15.07 Regulations may provide for the enforcement of road user charging schemes, and for the resolution of disputes and appeals (Schedule 23, paragraphs 12 and 28). They may also provide that non-payment of a charge will be dealt with administratively, rather than as a criminal matter, and for charges to be recoverable as a civil debt (Schedule 23, paragraph 13).

Regulations may create powers to check compliance with a scheme by examining motor vehicles for display of appropriate documents (such as a permit) or use of appropriate equipment (such as an automatic charging device) (Schedule 23, paragraph 26). They may also create powers to fit immobilisation devices and remove vehicles (Schedule 23, paragraph 27), although note the restriction on using these powers in relation to vehicles that are not on roads (Schedule 23, paragraph 31, above).

A person who uses a false document, or tampers with charging scheme equipment or a vehicle registration plate, with intent to avoid paying a penalty charge or being identified as having failed to pay, commits a criminal offence (Schedule 23, paragraph 25). The maximum penalty is a fine of level 5 on the standard scale, currently £5,000 (Criminal Justice Act 1982, s. 37, as amended) and imprisonment for up to six months. Regulations may provide for simplified procedures for proving such an offence, or contravention of a licensing scheme (Schedule 23, paragraph 30).

Accounts, Revenues and Hypothecation

The GLA, TfL or a London local authority may incur expenses in **15.08** establishing and operating a charging scheme (Schedule 23, paragraph 32). They must keep an account of their income and expenditure in respect of the scheme. They must also keep an account of funds received by them from other authorities' schemes. Deficits in a charging scheme account must be made good out of the general fund (or, in respect of TfL, its gross income), but such funds must be re-credited to the general fund or gross income if the charging scheme goes on to make a profit in the next ten years (Schedule 23, paragraph 15).

The proceeds of charging schemes made within 10 years of the start of the first Mayor and Assembly members' term of office may only be applied for value for money transport purposes by the GLA, TfL, the London borough councils and the Common Council of the City of London. This period is known as the "initial period". The Secretary of State may issue guidance to the GLA, TfL and the London local authorities to help them appraise which purposes will provide value for money (Schedule 23, paragraph 17).

The GLA may require proceeds of charging schemes to be redistributed **15.09** amongst the GLA, TfL, the London borough councils and the Common Council (Schedule 23, paragraph 18).

If TfL, a London borough council or the Common Council makes a scheme, it must prepare an initial 10 year plan and then four year plans for spending its share of the proceeds (Schedule 23, paragraphs 19 and 20). The GLA must also prepare 10 year and four year plans for spending the redistributed portion (Schedule 23, paragraphs 21 and 22). The Secretary of State must approve the 10 and four year plans and the GLA must approve plans made by a London local authority (Schedule 23, paragraphs 19(3) and 20(2)).

Extending the 10 Year Hypothecation Period

15.10 The Secretary of State has discretion to specify a longer initial period than ten years for a particular scheme (Schedule 23, paragraph 16).

After he has consulted the GLA, and assessed the likely proceeds from charges and the potential for spending that money on value for money transport measures, the Secretary of State may make regulations to extend the initial period beyond ten years, or to relax the restrictions on the way in which the money may be spent. The House of Commons must approve such regulations (section 420 and Schedule 23, paragraphs 16 and 17).

Workplace Parking Levy Schemes

15.11 Transport for London, the London borough councils and the Common Council of the City of London may introduce workplace parking levy schemes (section 296).

The Mayor may exercise on behalf of the GLA any powers conferred on the GLA in respect of such schemes (Schedule 24, paragraph 2).

The same premises cannot be subject to more than one scheme at a time (Schedule 24, paragraph 12). Such schemes provide for licensing persons providing workplace parking places at premises in an area designated in the scheme (Schedule 24, paragraph 1). Revenues will be raised through the imposition of licence fees.

The definition of "providing a workplace parking place" embraces a very wide variety of situations. The occupier of premises (as defined for the purposes of non-domestic rates) provides a workplace parking place if he provides at those premises a parking place which is for the time being occupied by a motor vehicle used by defined categories of people. Not only is employee parking covered, but parking by students, agents, suppliers, business customers and others (Schedule 24, paragraph 3).

A licensing scheme may only be made if it appears desirable or expedient for the purpose of facilitating policies or proposals in the transport strategy (Schedule 24, paragraph 6). The scheme must also conform to the transport strategy (Schedule 24, paragraph 8).

Each London local authority will have the power to join with others in a joint charging scheme, and the GLA can require them to do so (Schedule 24, paragraph 10).

Procedure for Making a Workplace Parking Levy Scheme

15.12 Consultation and inquiries may be held by the GLA before a scheme is made and, if the GLA so directs, consultation must be carried out by the charging authority (Schedule 24, paragraph 7). A scheme must be made by order and must be in a form determined by the GLA and approved by it (Schedule 24, paragraph 7). The GLA may modify a scheme order before it takes effect (Schedule 24, paragraph 7). It may also issue guidance and directions during the operation of a scheme (Schedule 24, paragraphs 34 and 35).

Content of a Workplace Parking Levy Scheme

A scheme must identify the area to which it applies, the periods of time for **15.13** which a licence is required, and the charges to be made under it (Schedule 24, paragraphs 11 and 13). The charges must be expressed as a specified sum of money for each licensed unit (Schedule 24, paragraph 13). The scheme must also state the period it is to remain in force (Schedule 24, paragraph 38) and general proposals by the authority making the scheme for applying its share of the proceeds over the next 10 years (Schedule 24, paragraph 25).

A scheme may make provision for the licensing procedure, in other words the procedure for making applications for, granting, issuing, varying and revoking licences (Schedule 24, paragraph 16).

A scheme may provide for concessions from charges to be made (Schedule 24, paragraph 17). These concessions will be subject to any provisions made by regulations by the Secretary of State that provide for exemptions, reduced rates of charge and limits on charges payable. Such concessions may be applied, for example, in respect of disabled persons. The Authority may control the content of schemes by withholding approval from schemes that contain provisions to which it objects (Schedule 24, paragraph 9).

Content of a Licence

A licence must state the name of the licence holder, the premises and the **15.14** maximum number of vehicles that are licensed and the charge for the licence. A licence may be made subject to conditions (Schedule 24, paragraph 14). A licence lasts by default for a year (Schedule 24, paragraph 15).

Enforcement

Regulations may provide for the enforcement of schemes. These may relate **15.15** to liability for charges and penalty charges (Schedule 24, paragraphs 18 and 19), and for the resolution of disputes and appeals (Schedule 24, paragraph 20). They may also provide that non-payment of a charge will be dealt with administratively, rather than as a criminal matter, and for charges to be recoverable as a civil debt (Schedule 24, paragraph 19).

An authorised person may enter premises to ascertain whether the scheme is being contravened or to issue a penalty charge notice (Schedule 24, paragraph 31). A person who wilfully obstructs an authorised person exercising such rights of entry commits a criminal offence (Schedule 24, paragraph 31). The maximum penalty is a fine of level 5 on the standard scale, currently £5,000 (Criminal Justice Act 1982, s.37, as amended). Regulations may provide for simplified procedures for proving such an offence, or contravention of a scheme (Schedule 24, paragraph 32).

Accounts, Revenues and Hypothecation

The GLA, TfL or a London local authority may incur expenses in **15.16** establishing and operating a workplace parking levy scheme (Schedule 24, paragraph 33). They must keep an account of their income and expenditure in respect of the scheme. They must also keep an account of funds received by them from other authorities' schemes. Deficits in a scheme account must be made good out of the general fund (or, in respect of TfL, its gross income), but such funds must be re-credited to the general fund or gross income if the scheme makes a profit in the next ten years (Schedule 24, paragraph 21).

The proceeds of workplace parking levy schemes made within 10 years of the start of the first Mayor and Assembly members' term of office may only be applied for value for money transport purposes by the GLA, TfL, the London borough councils and the Common Council of the City of London. The Secretary of State may issue guidance to the GLA, TfL and the London local authorities to help them appraise which purposes will provide value for money (Schedule 24, paragraph 23).

The GLA may require the proceeds of levy schemes to be redistributed amongst the GLA, TfL, the London borough councils and the Common Council (Schedule 24, paragraph 24).

If TfL, a London borough council or the Common Council makes a scheme, it must prepare an initial 10 year plan and then four year plans for spending its share of the proceeds (Schedule 24, paragraphs 25 and 26). The GLA must also prepare 10 year and four year plans for spending the redistributed portion (Schedule 24, paragraphs 27 and 28). The 10 and four year plans do not come into force until approved by the Secretary of State and, in respect of a plan made by a London local authority, the GLA (Schedule 24, paragraphs 25(4) and 26(2)).

Extending the 10 Year Hypothecation Period

15.17 The Secretary of State can specify a longer "initial period" than ten years for a particular scheme (Schedule 24, paragraph 22).

After he has consulted the GLA, and assessed the likely proceeds from the scheme and the potential for spending that money on value for money transport measures, the Secretary of State may make regulations to extend the initial period beyond ten years, or to relax the restrictions on the way in which the money may be spent. The House of Commons must approve such regulations (section 420 and Schedule 24, paragraphs 22 and 23).

PART D

MISCELLANEOUS PROVISIONS

Chapter 16

THE LONDON DEVELOPMENT AGENCY

Introduction

The Regional Development Agencies Act 1998 (RDA Act 1998) creates **16.01** regional development agencies which are corporate bodies, consisting of not more than 15 members appointed by the Secretary of State. The key underlying objectives of the 1998 Act are, first, to secure a degree of devolution of power from central government to the English regions, and secondly, to improve the economic competitiveness of the regions. One third of an agency is intended to be made up of local councillors in the region, but they are not delegates of their relevant authorities.

The agencies, despite being non-departmental bodies, are accountable to Ministers. The aim of the agencies is to further the economic development and regeneration of their areas, promoting business efficiency, investment and competitiveness, promoting employment, enhancing the development and application of skills relevant to employment in their areas, and contributing to sustainable development in the United Kingdom (RDA Act 1998, s.4).

Part V of the GLA Act amends the 1998 Act to introduce the London **16.02** Development Agency (LDA), and amends a number of the provisions of that Act so far as Greater London is concerned, so that the LDA, together with the GLA, will function as the regional agency for London. The LDA will be an arm of the GLA and will not be established until the Mayor and the Assembly are in place. The responsibility to give strategic direction for economic development and regeneration in London lies with the Mayor, who is assisted by the LDA in drawing up the strategy. The strategy must be in line with national policies and there is an overriding power vested in the Secretary of State to direct the Mayor to revise his strategy where there is a conflict with national policy or if the strategy will, or is likely to, have a detrimental effect. Schedule 25 to the GLA Act introduces further amendments to the 1998 Act that relate to the functioning of the Mayor and the LDA. The Schedule sets out the detailed provisions concerning how the LDA will operate within the confines of the new structure.

The Assembly is responsible for scrutinising the Mayor's strategy and examining the effectiveness of the LDA. The London borough councils, whilst retaining their powers to promote economic development in their areas, will work with the Mayor and the LDA to benefit Greater London

Appointment of Members

16.03 Section 304 of the GLA Act inserts six new subsections into section 2 of the RDA Act 1998 dealing with the appointment of members to the LDA. In appointing members to regional development agencies generally, the Secretary of State must consult with those persons that appear to him to represent the interests of those who live, work, or carry on business in rural parts of the agency's area (RDA Act 1998, s.2(3)(d)). The GLA Act provides that for the purpose of appointing members to the LDA the provisions of section 2 of the RDA Act 1998 applies. That section sets out the criterion for appointing members to the agency, save that understandably it is not necessary to consult with persons who represent the interest of those who live, work or carry out business in rural parts of the agency's area (RDA Act 1998, s.2(6) as inserted by the GLA Act, s.304).

The important change brought about by this amendment to the RDA Act 1998 is that the Mayor is responsible for the appointment of the members of LDA (RDA Act 1998, s.2(7) as inserted by the GLA Act, s.304). The Mayor must ensure that, in appointing the members, there are at least four members of the LDA who are elected members of the London Assembly, a London borough council, or the Common Council of the City of London (RDA Act 1998, s.2(9) as inserted by the GLA Act, s.304). In appointing members the Mayor must ensure that at least half are persons who appear to the Mayor to be persons who have experience of running a business (RDA Act 1998, s.2(10) as inserted by the GLA Act, s.304). The Chairman of LDA designated by the Mayor must also be a person who has experience of running a business (RDA Act 1998, s.2(11) as inserted by the GLA Act, s.304).

Following the establishment of the LDA the Secretary of State will appoint interim members until the Mayor notifies him that his appointments are due to take office. The transitional provisions are set out in the London Development Agency (Transitional Provisions) Order 2000 (S.I. 2000 No.1174) and they will cease to apply once the interim members have ceased to hold office.

Delegated Functions

16.04 The purpose of section 6 of the RDA Act 1998 is to enable any Minister of the Crown to confer functions on an agency by delegation. This section is amended by section 305 of the GLA Act to enable a Minister of the Crown to delegate the function to the Mayor as opposed to the Agency, unless the Mayor consents to such delegation direct to the LDA. The Mayor, subject to authorisation given in accordance with section 38 of the GLA Act, can delegate further functions to the LDA, but any such delegation must be subject to the same conditions as imposed on him by the Minister as part of his authorisation (RDA Act 1998, s.6A(3) inserted by the GLA Act, s.305).

The London Development Agency Strategy

Section 306(1) of the GLA Act inserts a new subsection (4) to section 7 of **16.05** the RDA Act 1998 which states that the duty to formulate, and keep under review, a strategy does not apply to the LDA. A new section is inserted by section 306(2) requiring the LDA to prepare a draft strategy in relation to its purposes to be submitted to the Mayor (RDA Act 1998, s.7A(1) inserted by the GLA Act, s.306(2)). The Mayor is able to give guidance and direction to the LDA in respect of the preparation of this draft strategy (RDA Act 1998, s.7A(6) inserted by the GLA Act, s.306(2)). The Mayor, prior to publishing the "London Development Agency strategy", must consult with the following persons and bodies on the draft strategy:

(1) the Assembly;
(2) the functional bodies;
(3) each London borough council;
(4) the Common Council;
(5) any other body or person whom he considers it appropriate to consult;
(6) such persons as appear to him to represent employers in the agency's area; and
(7) such persons as appear to him to represent employees in the agency's area (RDA Act 1998, s.7A(8) inserted by the GLA Act, s.306(2)).

The draft strategy these persons and bodies will be consulted on will be **16.06** the draft strategy submitted to the Mayor by the LDA, with such modifications (if any) as he considers appropriate (RDA Act 1998, s.7A(3) inserted by the GLA Act, s.306(2)).

After the consultation process the Mayor will publish the strategy as revised, and any reference in the Act to the LDA strategy shall be the strategy as revised (RDA Act 1998, s.7A(9) inserted by the GLA Act, s.306(2)).

The LDA is responsible for keeping the published strategy under review and proposing any revision, and the Mayor can give guidance and direction on reviewing the strategy (RDA Act 1998, s.7A(6) inserted by the GLA Act, s.306(2)).

In exercising any of their functions, the LDA, Transport for London, the Metropolitan Police Authority, and the London Fire and Emergency Planning Authority shall have regard to the strategy (RDA Act 1998, s.7A(5) inserted by the GLA Act, s.307).

Role of the Secretary of State

16.07 New powers have been vested in the Secretary of State in relation to the discharge of the mayoral functions (GLA Act, s.307). A new section 7B inserted to the RDA Act 1998 which enables the Secretary of State to give guidance to the Mayor as to what matters are to be covered by the strategy and the issues to be taken into account in preparing the strategy. The Mayor must have regard to any guidance given by the Secretary of State when preparing his draft strategy (RDA Act 1998, s.7B(3) inserted by the GLA Act, s.307), and where the Secretary of State considers that the London Development Agency strategy is inconsistent with national policy or it will, or is likely to, have a detrimental effect on any area outside Greater London, he can direct the Mayor to make such revision as is necessary to remove the inconsistency or harmful or potentially harmful effect (RDA Act 1998, s.7B(4) inserted the GLA Act, by s.307). National policy is defined as any written governmental policy statement laid before Parliament or published by a Minister. The Mayor is obliged to revise his strategy in accordance with the Secretary of State's direction (RDA Act 1998, s.7B(5) inserted by the GLA Act, s.307), but he is not obliged to consult with the persons or bodies specified in section 7A(8) of the RDA Act 1998 (as inserted by the GLA Act, s.307).

Audit

16.08 Section 308 of the GLA Act amends section 15 of the RDA Act 1998 which provides for the auditing of the regional development agencies accounts. The amendments provide that section 308 does not apply to the LDA, whose accounts are in any event to be audited under the Audit Commission Act 1998, and provides that the LDA is under a duty to send a copy of its audited accounts to the Mayor and the Chair of the Assembly.

Chapter 17

POLICE AND PROBATION SERVICES, FIRE AND EMERGENCY PLANNING, AND CULTURE, MEDIA AND SPORT

Introduction

There are currently 41 police authorities (not including the City of London **17.01** Police and the Metropolitan Police Service) as defined by the Police Act 1996 in England and Wales. Outside London, police authorities are committees, consisting normally of 17 members, of whom nine are members of "relevant councils", five are independent members and three are magistrates (Police Act 1996, ss.2–4 and Scheds 2 and 3). The term "relevant council" refers to the council of a county, district, county borough or London borough the area of which falls within the area of the police authority. Under section 6 of the 1996 Act, it is the duty of every police authority to secure the maintenance of an effective and efficient police force for their area. The authority are required to determine policing objectives in their area with the chief constable (1996 Act, s.7). They must also, under section 8 of the 1996 Act, issue a local policing plan each year and an annual report.

The police force for a police area is under the direction and control of the chief constable who is appointed by the police authority (subject to the Secretary of State's approval) (1996 Act, s.10(1)). Section 10(2) requires that, in the discharge of his functions, the chief constable is to have regard to the local policing plan. Each relevant council must also make arrangements for questions to be put to the police authority and the police authority must make arrangements for the views of local people as to police matters to be obtained (1996 Act, s.20).

Formerly, the Police Authority for the Metropolitan Police District was **17.02** the Secretary of State, under section 76 of the London Government Act 1963 and the Metropolitan Police Acts 1829 to 1963. A 1993 White Paper set out the former government's reasons for not establishing a police authority for London: there was " . . . a special national interest in the work of the Metropolitan Police, both in policing the capital and because of its wider role, for example, in combating terrorism." ("Policing Reform: The Government's Proposals for the Police Service in England and Wales"

Cm. 2281 at pp. 44–45). Instead, an advisory body known as the Metropolitan Police Committee was established in April 1995. It was regarded as a non-statutory non-departmental public body, the main function of which was to be the primary source of advice to the Home Secretary about police matters in London. London local authority associations were critical of the way appointments were made to the Committee.

The 1998 White Paper provides:

> "Unlike other police activities, the MPS (the Metropolitan Police Service) carries out a range of national functions and other tasks which arise from London's role as a capital city, as well as serving the resident community. At present, policing in London, unlike policing elsewhere in England and Wales, is not democratically accountable to the local community. There is no reason why the arrangements for democratic accountability in London should not reflect closely the model of police authorities outside of London, whilst ensuring that those special features of the MPS which justify a difference in approach are identified and addressed. The MPS will be brought into line with other police forces in England and Wales and will in future be overseen by a police authority with a majority of elected representatives."

17.03   As to the special nature of the Metropolitan Police Service in comparison to other police services, see section 96A of the Police Act 1996, added by Schedule 27 to the 1999 Act. It provides that the Metropolitan Police Service has, unlike other police authorities, a special function concerning "the national and international functions of the Metropolitan Police Service" which are defined as "the protection of prominent persons or their residences, national security, counter-terrorism and the provision of services for a national or international service."

The new Metropolitan Police Authority ("MPA"), according to the 1998 White Paper at paragraph 5.143, is to be " . . . an independently constituted authority comprising elected and non-elected members, able to decide in consultation with the Commissioner its own strategy and policing priorities." In that way, the Mayor and Assembly are to have "a close connection with the MPS and help facilitate a London-wide approach to policing in harmony with the Mayor's other policies such as those on transport and economic development". In order to strengthen the relationship between the Mayor and the new authority, the Mayor must include the deputy Mayor amongst the Assembly members appointed to it. At paragraph 5.145 of the White Paper:

> "The Mayor will therefore, through appointments to the MPA, be taking a high level and strategic interest in the MPA's efforts to tackle crime. The Mayor will be able to oversee activity and draw together the efforts of all those London organisations which have a part to play, through his or her influence on the MPA."

In addition to appointments by the Mayor, the Assembly is to have a **17.04** scrutineering role of the new police authority. At paragraph 5.148 of the White Paper:

> "The 1996 Police Act gives powers to councils outside London to summon members of the local police authority to answer questions at council meetings on the discharge of the functions of the police authority. We intend to mirror this statutory provision by giving similar powers to the Assembly in respect of the new MPA. This will ensure that the Assembly has the opportunity to scrutinise the policies and direction being pursued by the MPA."

The New Authority

Under Part VI of the 1999 Act, responsibility for the Metropolitan Police **17.05** Service is transferred from the Secretary of State to a new authority, the Metropolitan Police Authority, with responsibility to secure the maintenance of an efficient and effective police force in the metropolitan area.

Section 310 of the 1999 Act amends section 5 of the Police Act 1996 by inserting new sections, *viz.*, sections 5A to 5C. Under section 5A, there is to be a police force maintained for the metropolitan police district. Section 5B establishes the MPA as a body corporate (unlike police authorities).

The new section 5C provides that the MPA is to have 23 members, although the Secretary of State may by order specify a different number of members which must be an odd number, not less than 17, Before he makes such an order, section 5C(3) requires him to consult the GLA, the MPA and the person or body responsible for appointing magistrates under the Justices of the Peace Act 1997. Further, under subsection (4), an order reducing the number of members may include provision for the replacement of the existing members.

Section 310(2) of, and Schedule 25 to, the 1999 Act inserts Schedule 2A **17.06** into the Police Act 1996. Paragraph 21 of the new Schedule 2A of the 1996 Act provides that any functions exercisable by the Mayor under the Schedule which are largely powers of appointment, are to be exercised by him personally. Under paragraph 1(2) of Schedule 2A where the Police Authority has 23 members, twelve shall be London Assembly members appointed by the Mayor, one of whom must be the Deputy Mayor; seven members are to be independent members appointed, under paragraph 3 of Schedule 2A, by the members of the Police Authority; one independent member appointed by the Secretary of State himself; and four shall be magistrates appointed under paragraph 5 of Schedule 2A. Under paragraph 2(3) of Schedule 2A, the Mayor is required to ensure that, as far as the Assembly members are concerned, his appointments reflect the political balance of the Assembly. A member of the MPA, under paragraph 10 of Schedule 2A, is to hold office for a term of four years unless there has been a shorter term determined by the person or body appointing him.

Section 311 of the 1999 Act amends section 6 of the 1996 Act. Section 6 requires every police authority to secure the maintenance of an efficient and effective police force in their area. That section is amended by the insertion of a new subsection, subsection (5), so that it applies to the MPA as to other police authorities.

17.07 Section 313 of the 1999 Act amends amends section 100J of the Local Government Act 1972 so that the MPA is included in the list of bodies to which Part VA of the 1972 Act applies. Part VA of the 1972 Act deals with access to meetings and documents of certain authorities, committees and sub-committees (see section 58, above). The MPA is included by virtue of the new subsection, section 100J(eza).

Section 314 of the 1999 Act adds section 9A to the 1996 Act so that the Metropolitan Police Service is under the control of the Commissioner of Police of the Metropolis, appointed under another new section, section 9B. Other police authorities, under section 10 of the 1996 Act, are under the direction of the chief constable who is to have regard to the police authority's local policing plan and who is appointed by the police authority subject to the Secretary of State's approval. Under another new section of the 1996 Act, section 9A(2), the Commissioner of Police is also to have regard to the MPA's local policing plan.

The Commissioner and Deputy Commissioner

17.08 Section 315 deals with the office of the Commissioner of the Metropolitan Police and adds a new section, section 9B, to the 1996 Act. This is a special appointment. Under section 11 of the 1996 Act, the police authority appoints the chief constable, subject to the Secretary of State's approval; in contrast, under the new section 9B, the Commissioner of Metropolitan Police Service is appointed by Her Majesty under warrant. Under section 9B(5) of the 1996 Act, no recommendation as to who should be appointed is to be made to Her Majesty until the Mayor has made representations to the Secretary of State about the person to be appointed. Whereas a police authority, under section 11 of the 1996 Act may call upon the Chief Constable to retire (again, with the consent of the Secretary of State and also subject to regulations), the Commissioner holds office at Her Majesty's pleasure. Section 9B(6) of the 1996 Act provides that the Mayor's functions in this regard must be exercised personally.

The White Paper, at paragraph 5.156, suggested that this different approach was required for the appointment of the Commissioner, distinct from a Chief Constable:

"A similar procedure for the appointment of the Commissioner of Metropolitan Police will be introduced for London. This will, however, be modified to take account of the need to protect the national interest, the international obligations of the MPS and the presence of a democratically elected Mayor. The Mayor and the Commissioner will need to be able to work together in the best interests of London and the Mayor will be given a statutory right to comment on the short list of candidates submitted to the Home Secretary by the MPS."

Section 316 of the 1999 Act adds section 9C to the 1996 Act which deals **17.09** with the functions of the office of Deputy Commissioner of Police for the Metropolitan Police Service.

The statutory rank of Deputy Commissioner under section 9C of the 1996 Act is new; previously, when the Commissioner was unable to perform his duties, a designated Assistant Commissioner would exercise them for him. As in the case of any other deputy, such as the Deputy Mayor or Deputy Chair of the Assembly, the Deputy Commissioner can exercise any or all of the powers and duties of the Commissioner but only when there is a vacancy in the officer of Commissioner or with the consent of the Commissioner. The Deputy Commissioner, in addition, can only exercise the Commissioner's functions where there is a vacancy in the office of Commissioner, for a maximum period of three months.

Section 315 of the 1999 Act inserts section 9D into the 1996 Act which deals with the appointment of the Deputy Commissioner. He is to be appointed in much the same way as the Commissioner of Police. The main difference is that the Secretary of State need only have regard to representations made by the Commissioner.

Section 318 adds section 9E into the Police Act 1996. This new section deals with the removal of the Commissioner or Deputy Commissioner. The MPA, having obtained the approval of the Secretary of State may call upon the Commissioner of Police (or Deputy Commissioner) to retire in the interests of efficiency or effectiveness. Under section 9E(2) of the 1996 Act, however, the MPA must first consult with the Commissioner (or Deputy Commissioner).

Assistant Commissioner

Section 319 of the 1999 Act inserts section 9F into the Police Act 1996, **17.10** which provides for the appointment, removal and functions of the office of the Assistant Commissioner of the Metropolitan Police. Under the new section, the Assistant Commissioner is appointed, by the MPA with the approval of the Secretary of State, by the local police authority. His functions are to be determined by the Commissioner. Subsections 9E (1) to (3) of the 1996 Act, above, dealing with removal, apply.

Under the Greater London Authority Act (Commencement No. 6 and Preliminary Arrangements for the MPA) Order 2000 (S.I. 2000 No. 1095), the MPA assumed its functions as from July 3, 2000. Initial standing orders for the first meeting of the MPA were made by the clerk to the MPA.

The Metropolitan Police District

17.11 Section 323 of the 1999 Act amends section 76 of the London Government Act 1963 so that the metropolitan police district includes Greater London, excluding the City of London, Inner Temple and the Middle Temple. Section 76 of the 1963 defined the boundaries of the Metropolitan Police District so as to include parts of Essex, Hertfordshire and Surrey. These "fringe" areas outside Greater London were Epsom and Ewell, Hertsmere and Spelthorne (wholly within the Metropolitan Police District) and Broxbourne, Elmbridge, Epping Forest, Reigate and Banstead and Welwyn Hatfield (partly within the Metropolitan Police District).

This section replaces that definition so that the Metropolitan Police District is reduced in area and consists only of the 32 boroughs. The effect is that local councils, the police and the Crown Prosecution Service will no longer have to work with two different police forces as they did under the old boundary.

Probation Services

17.12 Sections 1 and 2 of the Probation Service Act 1993 provide for the establishment of probation service areas. Under the 1993 Act, there is an inner London probation area made up of two or more petty sessional division areas as determined under section 2 of the 1993 Act; and, in all other cases, probation areas are coterminous with the local petty sessions area. Section 2 provides that the Secretary of State may by order make provision for combining any two or more petty sessional areas into one probation area; and, as to inner London, he may make provision in an order for combining into one area all of the petty sessional areas of the inner London area. Section 326 of the 1996 Act, however, extends the Secretary of State powers by allowing him to combine all of the petty sessional areas of Greater London into one probation area.

The London Fire and Emergency Planning Authority

17.13 The purpose of Part VII of the 1999 Act is to ensure that fire and emergency planning comes within the overall responsibility of the Mayor; that the old London Fire and Civil Defence Authority should be re-constituted as a new independent authority called the London Fire and Emergency Planning Authority ("LFEPA"), responsible to the Mayor; and that the new authority should be the "fire authority" for the purposes of the Fire Services Act 1947 in the Greater London area.

Fire authorities outside London, under section 4 of the Fire Services Act 1947, are the non-metropolitan county councils in England, and joint fire and civil defence authorities for the metropolitan counties. In Wales, they are county and county borough councils.

A unitary council in a non-metropolitan area will prima facie become the fire authority but a joint authority may be established by the Secretary of State by order under section 21 of the Local Government Act 1992. Non-metropolitan county councils who are also fire authorities may also form voluntary schemes to combine their fire services, under section 5 of the 1947 Act. The Secretary of State may also require combination schemes to be made between authorities, under section 6 of the 1947 Act. Such combination authorities are bodies corporate and consist of representatives of the constituent authorities.

17.14 Each fire authority is required to make arrangements for fire fighting and to secure that there is an efficient fire fighting service under section 1 of the 1947 Act.

Under the Civil Defence Act 1948, the designated Minister may prescribe by regulation the functions of local authorities in respect of civil defence. If the authority fail to comply with regulations, the Minister may carry out the functions himself or transfer them to another authority. The Civil Defence (General Local Authority Functions) Regulations 1993 (S.I. 1993 No. 1812) provided that it is the function of non-metropolitan county councils to develop civil defence plans for their areas. District councils are under a duty to assist county councils in the preparation of the plan. Authorities may perform civil defence functions for emergencies and disasters which are not related to hostilities under the Civil Protection in Peacetime Act 1986.

In London, the previous fire authority was the London Fire and Civil Defence Authority, being a joint authority established under section 27 of the Local Government Act 1985 and it consisted of the members of elected members of the London borough councils and the Common Council. Under the 1999 Act, the LFCDA is to be reconstituted and placed within the responsibility of the GLA. The new body is to be known as the London Fire and Emergency Planning Authority (1999 Act, s.328(2)). The reconstitution day is July 3, 2000 (under the Greater London Authority Act 1999 (Commencement No. 5 and Appointment of Reconstitution Day) Order 2000 (S.I. 2000 No. 1094).

17.15 Note that the Mayor's responsibilities are limited to appointing members of the new authority and setting its budget. Schedule 23 to the 1999 Act contains further provisions about the new body. Under Paragraph 1(1), it is to consist of 17 members, nine of whom are to be Assembly members appointed by the Mayor, and the remainder representatives of the London borough councils appointed by the Mayor on the nomination of the borough councils. As in paragraph 2(3) of Schedule 2A to the Police Act 1996 which deals with appointments to the MPA, the Mayor, under paragraph 1(2) of Schedule 23 to the 1999 Act, is required to ensure that his appointees reflect the political balance of the Assembly—as are each of the London boroughs concerning their nominated members. Under paragraph 1(5), the Secretary of State may by order vary any of the numbers specified in paragraph 1(1) but he must consult with the Mayor, the Assembly, the GLA and every London borough council.

Section 332 of the 1999 Act adds a new subsection to section 104 to the Local Government Act 1972, the effect of which is to ensure that the provisions of this Act concerning disqualification from being elected Mayor or a member of the Assembly apply to the LFEPA. Section 333 amends section 146A of the 1972 Act. Section 146A provides that certain bodies such as a police authority and the Service Authority for the National Crime Squad are to be treated as a local authority for the purposes of most of the provisions of the 1972 Act. This now includes the new London Fire and Emergency Planning Authority.

Culture, Media and Sport

17.16 Part X of the 1999 Act deals with the functions of the Authority concerning culture, recreation and sport. All main authorities have extensive powers to provide recreational facilities, including indoor and outdoor facilities, and water sports. The Authority, however, will not provide services but co-ordinate them or assist in co-ordinating them. According to the White Paper, at paragraph 5.188, the Mayor is to play an important role in London's cultural and sporting life. In particular:

> "The Mayor will be expected to play an active part in making appointments to publicly funded London organisations and, in some cases, to control either all or part of their funding."

The White Paper proposed the establishment of a "Cultural Strategy Group" for London, consisting of representatives of the major London cultural bodies. It was to have a highly influential but not necessarily determinative role in the creation of the Mayor's strategy. The group and the Mayor would co-ordinate London-wide cultural events, initiatives and policies.

Section 370 of the 1999 Act establishes the Cultural Strategy Group For London as a body corporate, the main function of which is to provide advice to the Mayor concerning his culture strategy under section 371 and such other functions as may be conferred on it. Schedule 29 to this Act provides for the constitution of the Cultural Strategy Group. Under paragraph 1, the Group is not to be regarded as enjoying any Crown status or immunity and nor are its members to be considered agents of the Crown or civil servants.

17.17 The Group may enter into transactions which are calculated to facilitate or are incidental to the discharge of its functions and it may acquire and hold land for the same purposes. Paragraph 2 provides that the Group shall consist of no fewer than 10 but no more than 25 members. They are all to be appointed by the Mayor in such a ways as he considers to be representative of bodies concerned with relevant matters or as have knowledge, experience or expertise relevant to the Group's functions.

Under section 376 (1) of the 1999 Act, the Group is to formulate a draft strategy and submit it to the Mayor. The Mayor shall then prepare and publish his "culture strategy". Section 376(3) defines this strategy as the document submitted to him by the Cultural Strategy Group but with such modifications as the Mayor thinks appropriate. The Cultural Strategy Group, additionally, is to keep the Mayor's strategy under review and submit proposals to revise it. The definition of the matters which might come within the Culture Strategy, in subsection (5), is extremely wide. The are defined to include:

(1) arts, tourism and sport;
(2) ancient monuments and sites;
(3) other important buildings and sites;
(4) museums and galleries;
(5) library services;
(6) archives;
(7) treasures and antiquities; and,
(8) broadcasting, film and other media.

It is important to note that, unlike local authorities, the GLA has no **17.18** power to control or regulate any of the above matters or provide any services with respect to any of them. For example:

(1) local authorities under section 144 of the Local Government Act 1972 have powers to encourage people to visit their areas for recreational or health purposes;
(2) they can also provide recreational facilities under section 19 of the Local Government (Miscellenaous Provisions) Act 1976;
(3) they may arrange or contribute towards the expenses of doing anything which it is necessary or expedient for the provision of entertainments;
(4) authorities which are library authorities in their areas are under a duty to provide a comprehensive and efficient library service (Public Libraries Act 1964, s.7);
(5) at the request of the owner, principal authorities can assist in or undertake or contribute towards the cost of, preserving and maintaining ancient monuments (Ancient Monuments and Archaeological Areas Act 1979, s.24).

Sections 376(6) and (7) of the 1999 Act empower the Mayor to set a deadline for the draft strategy with which the Group must comply. The Mayor is, by section 376(3), not required to endorse the Group's draft strategy and may present his own modified version. If so, then, by section 376(8), he must consult the bodies listed in section 42 above as well as the Group.

Section 377 of the 1999 Act empowers the GLA to provide assistance for **17.19** the purpose of any museum, gallery, library, archive or other cultural institution. Main authorities, and in two-tier areas, county councils, are library authorities under the Public Libraries and Museums Act 1964. Under section 7 of the 1964 Act, they are required to provide a comprehensive and efficient library service in their areas. The same authorities have a power to provide and maintain museums and art galleries within their areas or elsewhere. Bearing in mind the special nature of many libraries and museums in London, this section appears to be directed at non-municipal types of libraries and museums.

Under section 39 of the 1999 Act, the Mayor may delegate functions to the functional bodies subject to the exception in subsection (6)(c). Section 380 of the 1999 Act allows the Mayor to delegate functions under this Part of the Act to the same functional bodies but, in addition, to the Cultural Strategy Group. This section has a similar structure to section 39. Under section 380(6), the Mayor cannot delegate this power to delegate, or his power to make byelaws concerning Trafalgar and Parliament Squares; and, under section 380(7), he can only delegate his duty to formulate a culture strategy to the Deputy Mayor or to a member of staff of the Authority.

Tourism Functions

17.20 Under section 378 of the 1999 Act, the Authority has specific tourism functions. These include:

(1) the encouragement of people to visit London;
(2) the encouragement of people outside of the United Kingdom to visit the United Kingdom and London; and,
(3) to encourage the provision and improvement of tourist facilities.

This section is modelled on section 144 of the Local Government Act 1972 under which local authorities may (as distinct from being bound by a duty to) " . . . encourage persons to visit their area for recreation, health purposes or to hold conferences . . . ". They also have the power " . . . to provide or encourage any other person of body to provide facilities for conferences, trade fairs and exhibitions or encourage any other person or body to improve any existing facilities for those purposes." Further, under section 144(2) of the 1972 Act, an authority may "contribute to any organisation approved by the Secretary of State for the purposes of this subsection and established for the purpose of encouraging persons to visit the United Kingdom or any part thereof." There is no definition of "encourage" in the 1972 Act, but section 144(1)(a) of the 1972 Act states that the authority may encourage "by advertisement or otherwise". Note also section 144(6): an authority may "provide financial or other assistance" to bodies having the same general function as that of the Authority.

17.21 Under section 378 of the 1999 Act, however, the GLA is not merely empowered to encourage visitors and the improvement of facilities for visitors and tourists; it is under a duty to do so. This may be seen to be an indication of the importance given by Parliament to tourism as part of the

London economy. Further, under section 378(3) of the 1999 Act, the GLA has had expressly conferred upon it incidental and ancillary powers to its tourism powers. There is also, in section 378(3) a clearer definition of what the GLA's encouragement function is to consist of: publicity, advisory and information services, and research. The GLA may also carry out these activities outside the United Kingdom. By virtue of section 378(5), it is not intended that the Authority is to become a main tourist board for, or of, London, as this subsection requires it to have regard to the desirability of co-operating and consulting the Secretary of State and any Tourist Board. Section 378(6) of the 1999 Act is in similar terms to section 144(3) of the 1972 Act. It gives the GLA the power to provide financial assistance to any person or organisation with similar functions as those set out in section 378. Under section 379, the GLA is under a duty to advise any Minister, the British Tourist Board and the English Tourist Board about tourism in London.

Trafalgar Square and Parliament Square

Sections 383 to 386 provide for the transfer of day-to-day responsibility for **17.22** Trafalgar Square and Parliament Square from the Secretary of State for Culture, Media and Sport to the GLA. Both Squares are to remain Crown land. The Mayor is responsible for their repair and maintenance and for controlling and licensing their use.

PART E

PLANNING AND ENVIRONMENTAL FUNCTIONS

Chapter 18

PLANNING

Introduction

Part VIII of the GLA Act amends the Town and Country Planning Act **18.01** 1990 ("TCPA") by establishing the Mayor's planning functions and incorporating his planning powers within the planning system. It is intended that the Mayor's powers will have a major role to play in improving the economic, social and environmental well-being of Londoners by promoting sustainable development through his strategies for transport, economic development and regeneration, spatial development and the environment. It is important to note from the outset that the Mayor and the Assembly are not local planning authorities ("LPAs") for the purposes of the TCPA, so the current LPAs for Greater London area remain the same. However, unlike the Secretary of State, the Mayor is not in any capacity superior to the existing LPAs that function in Greater London. How they discharge their various duties under the TCPA will, however, be affected by this Part of the 1999 Act.

By way of overview, the Mayor, the Assembly, the London boroughs and **18.02** the Secretary of State will each have to act in the following separate ways to provide the strategic context for London boroughs' planning activities. The Mayor is responsible for:

- producing a spatial development strategy ("SDS") for Greater London;
- ensuring that any revision or amendment of a unitary development plan ("UDP") by a London boroughs generally accords with the SDS;
- following consultation on planning applications of strategic importance, directing LPAs to refuse an application on strategic grounds; and
- in consultation with the London boroughs, setting up a scheme to monitor the implementation of the SDS.

The Assembly's functions in the planning context involves:

- responding to the draft SDS;
- carrying out investigations into particular planning policy issues; and
- scrutinising the Mayor's performance in the discharge of his duties and the exercise of his powers.

The London boroughs' responsibilities have been extended by the Act to:

- require them when reviewing or altering their UDPs to adopt such amendments to, or to replace, the existing plan with a development plan that is in general conformity with the SDS;
- consult with the Mayor on applications that are of strategic importance in accordance with the regulations of the Secretary of State.

18.03 The Secretary of State's role is enhanced in that he will not only be able to direct the Mayor regarding the SDS to protect national or broader regional interests, but he is able to regulate which planning applications must be referred to the Mayor for consideration and those he can direct an LPA to refuse. Pursuant to his powers under the TCP Act as inserted by the GLA Act the Secretary of State has made the Town and Country Planning (Mayor of London) Order 2000 (S.I. 2000 No. 1493) ("the Order"), and the Town and Country Planning (London Spatial Development Strategy) Regulations 2000 (S.I. 2000 No. 1491) ("the Regulations"). Both the Order and Regulations are effective from July 3, 2000. The Order provides that applications of potential strategic importance (as defined in the Order) must be sent to the Mayor, and that he is able to direct the notifying LPA that it be refused. The Regulations regulate on the form and content of the SDS; the procedure to be followed from the preparation to publication of the SDS and its relationship with UDPs. Both the Order and the Regulations are discussed in more detail below, together with the draft circular "Strategic Planning in London".

The Spatial Development Strategy (sections 334–343)

18.04 One of the most important and far reaching planning functions vested in the Mayor is the duty to prepare and publish the SDS. This new concept in planning is not a development plan for Greater London, but it offers a common spatial framework for all the Mayor's strategies and policies (*i.e.* spatial development, transport, London Development Agency, waste management, air quality, ambient noise, biodiversity and culture). It also provides a framework for the development and land use policies for London contained in UDPs. As the SDS provides the general framework for the future planning of London, it is dominant over the other strategies prepared by the Mayor. Its importance is reflected by the fact that it is only this strategy the Secretary of State has reserved power to require the

Mayor to make, review or alter the SDS, and regulate those matters that should be included in it or the procedure to be followed. As far as the other strategies are concerned the Secretary of States powers are more limited.

Form and Content of SDS

Sections 334 to 338 of the GLA Act set out the form of this new strategic **18.05** planning guidance, and the procedure to be adopted by the Mayor from its preparation to publication. The Regulations stipulate the form and content of the SDS; the documents to accompany the SDS, and the procedure to be followed by the Mayor in preparing, withdrawing, publishing, making, reviewing, altering, or replacing the SDS, which will be applicable to the discharge of the Mayor's duty to review (GLA Act, s.339). The Regulations apply to the whole area of the Authority, but the Secretary of State has power to provide differently for different parts of Greater London. There is a significant overlap between the Regulations and those relating to structure plans (Town and Country Planning (Development Plan) Regulations 1991 (as amended) (S.I. 1991 No. 2794). The SDS must contain a reasoned justification for the Mayor's strategy for spatial development in Greater London, separate to the SDS (Regulations, art. 4(1)) and the SDS will contain a diagram illustrating the Mayor's strategy for spatial development in London, which does not need to be on a map base (Regulations, art. 5(1)).

The SDS will contain policies for the development and use of land in the **18.06** capital, though the policies must be of "strategic importance" to London. There is no definition of "strategic importance" but the draft circular provides that such matters should be of more than local importance and not concern issues more appropriately dealt with in a UDP. The SDS may also contain policies relating to part of Greater London, *e.g.* policies for particular parts of the capital such as regeneration corridors, central London or the River Thames. The SDS may identify broad areas of particular strategic importance as opposed to opportunities for individual sites. The success of the SDS will depend on the ability of the Mayor to adopt broad policies capable of implementation during the period of strategy (proposed to be 15–20 years) and avoiding detailed policies that are more appropriately reflected in a UDP.

In preparing, reviewing or altering the SDS the Mayor is under a duty to **18.07** have regard to his general duties (GLA Act, s.41); the regional context; the national context, and the European context. The Mayor must have regard to the following matters when carrying out such an exercise:

- principal purposes of the Authority (section 41(4)(a) — see also the GLA Act s.30);
- the effect the SDS will have on the health of the persons in Greater London (GLA Act, s.41(4)(b)(i));
- the effect the SDS will have on the achievement of sustainable development in the United Kingdom (GLA Act, s.41(4)(b)(ii));

- the need to ensure that the strategy is consistent with national policy and international obligations (GLA Act , s.41(5)(a));
- the need to ensure consistency between the strategies of the Mayor (GLA Act, s.41(5)(b) — see also GLA Act, s.41(1))
- the resources available for the implementation of the strategy (GLA Act, s.41(5)(c));
- the desirability of promoting and using the River Thames safely, in particular for the provision of passenger and freight transport services (GLA Act, s.41(5)(d));
- any regional planning guidance issued by the Secretary of State that is relevant to or affects an area that adjoins Greater London (GLA Act, s.342(1)(a));
- such other matters as may be prescribed by the Secretary of State (GLA Act, s.342(1)(b)).

18.08 The last two matters are additional to those matters the Mayor is generally obliged to have regard to in the preparation or revision of any of his strategies (section 41(4)) (see paragraph 3.32 above). In the Regulations it is proposed that the Mayor will be required to have regard to the following:

- any policy statement of the Secretary of State relating to the recovery and disposal of waste in England under section 44A of the Environmental Protection Act 1990;
- the objectives of preventing major accidents and limiting their consequences;
- the need

    (a) in the long term, to maintain appropriate distances between establishments and residential areas, areas of public use and areas of particular sensitivity or interest; and
    (b) in the case of existing establishments, for technical measures in accordance with Article 5 of Directive 96/82 on the control of major-accidents involving dangerous substances so as not to increase the risk to people.

Reference to national policies will include Planning Policy Guidance notes ("PPGs"), relevant circulars and any statement of planning policy. Further, any reference in planning policy to LPAs will be taken to include reference to the Mayor. The relevant regional guidance to which the Mayor must have regard to is the Regional Planning Guidance for London (RPG3) and Regional Planning Guidance for the South East (RPG9). It is the intention that until the final version of the SDS is published RPG3 will remain extant.

18.09 The draft circular states that the SDS should take into account the European Spatial Development Perspective ("ESDP"), the Community Initiative on Transnational Co-operation on Spatial Planning

("INTERREG") and other European and transnational programmes and instruments relating to spatial planning.

The detail of the SDS is a matter for the Mayor. The SDS should address all issues of strategic importance to the capital with a spatial dimension, and the draft circular advises this would include policies concerning:

- sustainable development;
- transport;
- economic development, regeneration and social inclusion;
- housing;
- the natural and open environment;
- waste;
- the Mayor's other environmental strategies;
- Town centres and major retail, leisure and other trip-generating development;
- Major cultural and community facilities;
- the central area: London's capital and world city roles; and
- the River Thames.

The SDS should, in clear and concise terms, set out the policies **18.10** supported by a reasoned justification, and identify those policies relating to development and land use that are to be reflected in the UDPs. It is proposed that the SDS should also include targets and milestones against which the SDS can be measured. In order to measure its performance the Government intends to provide a framework on Best Value principles.

The Government also considers that the principles of managing the production of development plans, as set out in PPG 11 and 12, should be applied to the preparation of the SDS. The view is that this will ensure the publication of a strategy that is up-to-date and relevant, though when compared with the process involved from preparation to adoption of a structure plan, it is not difficult to envisage the final SDS being adopted only after some considerable time and deliberation.

Public Participation

Public participation in the preparation of the SDS is provided for in section **18.11** 335 of the GLA Act. It is similar to the form followed by LPAs in the preparation of structure plans under the TCP Act. The Mayor must first prepare a draft SDS. After the SDS has been drafted, but prior to publication, the Mayor is not only under a duty to make it available to the Assembly and the functional bodies, but he must also consult them (GLA Act, s.335(2)(c)). This is to help secure consistency between the Mayor's different strategies. The Act defines "functional bodies" in section 424(1) as the following:

- Transport for London;
- the London Development Agency;
- the Metropolitan Police Agency;

- the London Fire and Emergency Planning Authority.

18.12 Following consultation with the Assembly and the functional bodies the Mayor must prepare a draft of his proposed SDS and make it available at the principal office of the GLA and such other places within Greater London as the Mayor considers appropriate (Regulations, art. 7(1)). Notice of the proposed SDS must be announced by advertisement, which will also specify the time period within which representations must be made, which is a period of not less that 12 weeks ending on the date specified in the notice, or where the Mayor proposes a minor alteration to the SDS, six weeks from the date of the notice (Regulations, art. 7(6) and (7) respectively)

A copy of the draft SDS must be sent to:

- the Secretary of State;
- every London borough council;
- every County Council, District Council whose areas adjoin Greater London and are affected by the proposed SDS;
- those persons or bodies prescribed by regulation;
- any other person or body considered by the Mayor to be appropriate (section 335(3)).

The Regulations also require the Mayor to send a copy of the SDS to the Countryside Agency and the Nature Conservancy Council for England, the Environment Agency and the Historic Buildings and Monuments Commission for England (Regulations, art. 7(5)).

18.13 In determining the bodies to which, or the persons to whom, it is appropriate to send a copy of the SDS, the Mayor must include those bodies he has identified as being appropriate to be consulted on the exercise of the Authority's power to do anything which is considered will further any one or more of its principal purposes (GLA Act, s.32(3)), namely those voluntary bodies whose activities benefit the whole or part of Greater London; bodies which represent the interest of different racial, ethnic or national groups in Greater London and bodies that represent the interests of persons carrying on business in Greater London.

The Mayor must send out with all copies of the SDS a statement setting out that representations may be made to the Mayor (section 335(5)). The Regulations provide that the period for making representations is not less than 12 weeks (six weeks in the case of a minor alteration to the SDS) after the Mayor gives public notice that the SDS is available for inspection, *i.e.* starting with the date on which notice is given in a newspaper (article 7(8)). Any person, including those served with a copy of the proposed SDS, can make representations, but any representations must be made in writing and addressed to the Mayor at the address indicated in the notice (Regulations, art. 7(9)).

18.14 Following the expiry of the period within which representations may be made, the Mayor must consider any representations he receives (GLA Act, s.335(2)(e)). He is not required to consider those objections that are received out of time (Regulations, art. 7(11))

As a proposed SDS might well be a material consideration to be taken into account in a planning decision, the Mayor is able to withdraw the proposed SDS at any stage prior to its publication (GLA Act, s.336). On its withdrawal, the Mayor must withdraw the copies that have been made available for inspection, and give notice to the Assembly; each of the functional bodies; all those persons, bodies and Councils notified under section 335(3) of the GLA Act, and every body which, or person who, made representations in accordance with the regulations. If the Mayor exercises this power to withdraw the proposed SDS, it does not affect his duty under section 334(1) of the GLA Act to prepare and publish a SDS, and he must recommence the process of preparing a new SDS.

Examination in Public

Following the conclusion of the consultation exercise and consideration of **18.15** the representations made in accordance with the Regulations, the Mayor must cause an examination in public to be held before he can publish the SDS, unless directed otherwise by the Secretary of State (GLA Act, s.338). It is expected, as in the case for structure plans, an examination in public will not be held when only minor or uncontentious objections are proposed to an existing SDS. The Secretary of State will appoint the person or persons (hereinafter "the Panel") to conduct the examination in public. The Mayor is required to send to the Panel a copy of all the representations made in accordance with the Regulations, who will, in consultation with the Mayor, determine what matters ought to be examined. The only criterion for assessing which matters are to be examined at the hearing is that the matters must be ones which affects the consideration of the SDS, *i.e.* strategic objections (GLA Act, s.338(4)).

No person has the right to be heard at the examination in public (GLA Act, s.338(6)). Only the Mayor and those invited by the person or persons conducting the examination in public (EIP) may take part at the hearing (GLA Act, s.338(7)).

Under Article 8 of the Regulations the procedure proposed reflects that **18.16** currently employed in EIPs for structure plans. As the framework within which the SDS is examined reflects that followed in adopting a structure plan, it seems likely that any such regulations would reflect the guidance given to LPAs in Annex C of PPG12. It is the intention that the examination in public should provide an informal opportunity for the discussion and testing in public of the justification for selected policies and proposals; it will not be a hearing of objections, nor need it cover every aspect of the proposals. The examination in public is a statutory inquiry for the purposes of section 1(1)(c) of the Tribunals and Inquiries Act 1992, but is not an inquiry for any other purpose of that Act.

The costs of holding the examination in public, including the fees and expenses of the person or persons appointed to conduct the examination in public, will be borne by the GLA. This does not cover the costs of those invited to the hearing to make representations on strategic matters identified as affecting the consideration of the SDS.

At the conclusion of the examination in public, the Panel will report to the Mayor. The Regulations provide that the Panel's written report must be publicly available within eight weeks of it being received (article 8(9)). The Mayor must take it into account before publishing the SDS, but where he does not accept any Panel recommendation he must state his reasons (article 9(2)).

Publication

18.17 Before the Mayor is able to publish the SDS, he must have considered any representations made in accordance with the regulations, or if no such representations have been made, until the 12 week period (or six weeks in the case of minor alterations) for lodging representations has expired (GLA Act, s.337). Further, where an examination in public has been held, the Mayor must not publish the SDS before the Panel appointed to conduct the inquiry has reported to the Mayor. The Secretary of State is empowered to make regulations under section 343 prohibiting the publication of the SDS without further steps being taken (GLA Act, s.337(5)).

The Secretary of State can, at any time prior to publication of the SDS, give the Mayor a direction requiring the removal of an inconsistency or an amendment to avoid any detriment to the interest of an area outside Greater London (GLA Act, s.337(6)). This power can only be exercised if the Secretary of State considers that it is expedient to issue such a direction for the purpose of avoiding any inconsistency with current national policies or relevant regional planning guidance, or any detriment to the interests of an area outside Greater London.

18.18 Earlier drafts of the Bill referred to "relevant regional planning guidance", but the Act omitted reference to "regional". This oversight was corrected by the Greater London Authority (Miscellaneous Amendments) Order 2000 (S.I. 2000 No. 1435) by the insertion of "regional" after "relevant" in section 337(6)(a) of the GLA Act. Thus, the Secretary of State in deciding whether it is expedient to direct the Mayor to remove, for example, an inconsistency in the SDS, will consider any regional planning guidance he has issued so far as it relates to an area which includes or adjoins Greater London.

Once a direction has been issued, the Mayor will only be able to publish the SDS if he satisfies the Secretary of State that he has modified it to make it conform to the direction, or if the direction is withdrawn. Once the SDS has been published it becomes operative from that date.

Monitoring and Data Collection

18.19 The Mayor is under a duty to monitor the implementation of the SDS and the UDPs for each London borough; and to monitor and collect information about matters relevant to the preparation, review, alteration, replacement or implementation of the SDS (GLA Act, s.346). This duty overlaps with the duty under section 339(1) of the GLA Act to review matters affecting the SDS. The Mayor is also required to review matters which may be expected to affect the development of Greater London or the planning of its development, and those other matters that are relevant to the content of the SDS (GLA Act, s.339(1)). By imposing a duty on the Mayor to so monitor and collect information, the Secretary of State can decide whether he needs to issue a direction requiring the Mayor (where a review has not already been activated), within such time as may be specified in the direction, to prepare and publish such alterations to the SDS as he may direct, or prepare and publish a new SDS to replace the existing one (GLA Act, s.341(2)).

Review, Alteration and Replacement

The Mayor's duty to review the SDS from time to time goes hand in hand **18.20** with his duties to review matters which may be expected to affect the development of Greater London or the planning of its development (GLA Act, s.339), and to monitor the implementation of the SDS and of the UDPs of each London borough council (GLA Act, s.346(a) and (b)). The Mayor must also have regard to those matters contained in section 41(4) of the GLA Act (see paragraph 3.32 above). The Mayor may identify a need to amend or replace the SDS. If the Mayor does not of his own initiative review the SDS as a result of monitoring the prevailing conditions for the development of Greater London and its planning framework, the Secretary of State can direct him to review the SDS or such part of it as he may specify in his direction (GLA Act, s.341(2)).

It is in the context of this framework that the Mayor will not only prepare but will also review his SDS. In developing proposals for altering or replacing the SDS the same consultation procedures and other provisions apply as for the original strategy, *i.e.* sections 334 to 338 of the GLA Act.

Where the Act refers to the SDS, such reference is to the SDS as altered or any new SDS replacing a previous one (GLA Act, s.346(4)). Prior to the alteration to or replacement of the SDS, the Mayor's proposals, unless withdrawn, may be material considerations for the determination of planning applications and therefore can be taken into account by the Mayor when deciding whether to issue a direction to a LPA to refuse an application.

Notification of Views to Surrounding LPAs

Section 348 of the GLA Act imposes a wide ranging duty on the Mayor to **18.21** inform a potentially large number of bodies of his views concerning any matters of common interest, whether general or specific, that relate to the planning and development of Greater London or those areas in the vicinity of the Authority. The Mayor must inform all LPAs for areas in the vicinity of Greater London, and any body on which those authorities are represented, of his views. He may advise such other bodies as he considers should be informed (GLA Act, s.348(1)). As the role of the Mayor is to provide a strategic planning overview, his policies and proposals will have an effect outside Greater London. Where his views, whether general or specific, relate to planning or development in those areas outside Greater London, the Mayor can inform those authorities or bodies on which they are represented of his views (GLA Act, s.348(2)). The Mayor is also under a duty to consult with the London borough councils about the exercise of his functions from time to time (GLA Act, s.348(3)). Where any body on which the GLA is represented assists the Mayor in discharging his functions under this section, the Mayor may defray their expenses (GLA Act, s.348(4)).

Implication on Development Control

18.22 At first sight the Act does not give the Mayor the power to determine individual planning applications, but the TCPA (in particular sections 12, 13, 15, 21, 26 and 336) is amended by section 344 of the GLA Act to give the SDS statutory force within the planning policy framework for Greater London, and enables the Secretary of State to give the Mayor the power to direct refusal of planning permission in certain specified cases.

Even though the SDS does not form part of any development plan for Greater London, as defined by section 27 of the TCPA, it does provide the framework within which London borough councils are to prepare and alter their UDPs. Any UDP must generally conform to the SDS for the time being in force (TCPA, s.12(3C) as inserted by the GLA Act, s.344(2)). As a result the SDS will affect any determination by a London borough as a LPA under the TCPA, as acquiring authority under the Land Compensation Act 1961 and as highway authority under the Highways Act 1980.

As far as the determination of planning applications is concerned, the Order makes the Mayor one of the statutory consultees for planning applications of strategic importance and vests in him the power to direct refusal of any application on which he is notified.

Unitary Development Plan

18.23 Section 12 of the TCPA sets out the requirements imposed on London borough councils in preparing UDPs. A UDP consist of two parts, Parts I and II. Part I of the plan consists of a written statement formulating the LPA's general policies in respect of the development and use of land in its area, which includes policies on the conservation of the natural beauty and amenity of the land; the improvement of the physical environment; and the management of traffic. In formulating Part I of the development plan, the LPA is required to have regard to:

- any regional or strategic planning guidance given by the Secretary of State to assist in the preparation of the plan;
- current national policies;
- the resources likely to be available and such matters as prescribed by the Secretary of State.

Section 344(2) of the GLA Act imposes a new requirement on all London borough councils, namely that they must now prepare a plan, or an alteration to an existing plan, that conforms with the SDS in force at the time of its adoption.

Part II of the UDP translates the general planning strategy set out in Part I into more detail, for example land-use proposals for local areas. Part II must not only generally conform with Part I, but it must now also generally conform with the SDS (GLA Act, s.344(3)).

Public Participation

Section 13 of the TCPA sets out the extent to which the public is entitled **18.24** to participate in the preparation of the unitary plan. Before the content of a UDP is finally determined, LPAs are required by virtue of regulation 10 of the the Town and Country Planning (Development Plan) Regulations 1991 to consult with a list of consultees that includes the Secretary of State, and to consider any representations made by them before finally determining the content of their proposals. A new subsection (TCPA, s.13(1A)) provides that all London borough councils are required to obtain a written opinion from the Mayor that its proposals are in general conformity with the SDS before they can place the plan on deposit (GLA Act, s.344(4)). A London borough can apply for the Mayor's written opinion in writing and such request must be accompanied with a copy of the relevant UDP (Regulations, art. 13(1)). The Mayor must give his opinion within the period which representations may be made to the LPAs with respect to the UDP, *i.e.* within six weeks beginning with the date of first publication of the LPA's notice in a local newspaper of the deposit of the UDP (Regulations, art. 13(2)). This goes further than a duty to consult, which is implied by this requirement, but it does not mean that the LPA is prevented from depositing their plan in the absence of such written opinion.

Where the Mayor is of the opinion that the proposed unitary plan is not **18.25** in general conformity with the SDS, then his response to an application for a written opinion of general conformity shall be treated as an objection to the unitary plan (GLA Act, s.344(5)). The normal course of calling an inquiry to hear objections to the deposit draft plan will follow, and ultimately a decision will be made by the LPA as to whether to adopt the plan as originally prepared or as modified so as to take into account any objections or any other material considerations. However, since the

Secretary of State has extensive powers under the TCPA to require LPAs to modify proposals before adoption, to call them in for his own approval, and to issue a holding direction whilst he determines whether to call-in the plan, he can ensure general conformity in the planning policy framework. If no such action is taken any aggrieved person can question the validity of the UDP by making an application to the High Court under section 287 of the TCP Act.

Adoption of Unitary Development Plan by a Local Planning Authority

18.26 Under section 15 of the TCP Act, a London borough council is not permitted to adopt a unitary plan unless Part II is in general conformity with Part I. This section has been extended by the insertion of a new requirement prohibiting a LPA from adopting a unitary plan unless Parts I and II generally conform with the SDS (GLA Act, s.344(6)). Where the LPA has obtained the written opinion of the Mayor that the pre-deposit plan is in general conformity with the SDS, then so long as there is no significant policy change, the LPA can rely upon that opinion. In any event, at the point of adoption, the Secretary of State has extensive powers to ensure that no LPA attempts to adopt a plan that fails to comply with the statutory requirements, including this new requirement.

Greater London: Conformity with Spatial Development Strategy

18.27 Section 21A has been inserted in the TCP Act by section 344(7) of the GLA Act which requires LPAs in Greater London, when proposing to make, alter or replace a unitary plan, to make a "permitted assumption". This is defined in section 21A(2) as an assumption that a proposed alteration or modification to the SDS, or a proposed new SDS to replace an existing SDS, has become operative even though the Mayor has not published it. Therefore, an LPA must prepare its policies in light of the SDS as proposed to be amended, not in conformity with the published SDS. Where an LPA make a "permitted assumption," it must be included in any copy of a plan or proposal that it has served on the GLA.

LPAs are not entitled to make a "permitted assumption" after they know that the proposed alterations or new SDS have been withdrawn. The Mayor has the power to withdraw a proposed SDS at any stage prior to publication (GLA Act, s.366(1)).

Directions to Refuse Applications for Planning Permission

18.28 Section 344(9) of the GLA Act introduces an important and potentially far reaching power that has been conferred on the Mayor. Section 74 of the TCP Act has been amended to enable the Secretary of State to prescribe by a development order the circumstances when the Mayor can, subject to such conditions as prescribed, direct a London LPA to refuse an application for planning permission of prescribed description in any particular case. This power has been exercised in the making of the Order.

The Order establishes four categories of planning applications that are deemed to be applications of potential strategic importance and therefore applications on which the Mayor must be notified, unless he has advised the authority in writing that he does not wish to be consulted pursuant to the Order. These applications are set out in the Schedule to the Order and are as follows:

- Large scale development, *e.g.* development which comprises or includes the provision of more than 500 homes, flats, or houses and flats;
- Major infrastructure, *e.g.* a railway station;
- Development which may affect strategic policies, *e.g.* development which would be likely to result in the loss of more than 200 houses, flats, or houses and flats;
- Development on which the Mayor must be consulted by virtue of a direction of the Secretary of State.

The duty to notify the Mayor of an application of potential strategic **18.29** importance applies to all applications for planning permission, except those applications for permission to develop without compliance with conditions previously attached (*i.e.* applications under section 73 of the TCP Act), and applications for renewal of planning permission where the previous planning permission was granted pursuant to an application received by the LPA on or before July 2, 2000 (Order, Sched. 1, para. 1). If an LPA receive an application for development which they consider forms part of a more substantial development on the site or on the adjoining site, then they shall treat it as an application for the permission for the more substantial development (Order, Sched. 1, para. 2).

In addition to sending the Mayor a copy of the application, the LPA is prevented from determining such an application unless it also sends to him a copy of the representations received, the officer's report on the application and a statement that the LPA propose to grant permission together with any conditions they will impose.

Following receipt of this documentation, the Mayor has 14 days with **18.30** which he can direct the LPA to refuse the application, or notify them that he is content for permission to be granted. Where the Mayor is minded to direct an LPA to refuse an application, he is under a duty to have regard to the development plan and the SDS (as altered or replaced (GLA Act, s.341(4))) so far as material to the application (TCP Act, s.74(1C) as inserted by the GLA Act, s.344(9)). The Order provides that if the Mayor considers that the grant of planning permission would be contrary to the SDS or prejudicial to its implementation or otherwise contrary to "good strategic planning in Greater London" then he may direct a LPA to refuse the application (Order, art. 5(1)). In the context of assessing whether an application is contrary to "good strategic planning" the Order (Order, art.5(2)) requires the Mayor to have regard to the following matters so far as material to the application:

- the principal purposes of the GLA;
- the effect the permission would have on:

  - the health of persons in Greater London, and
  - the achievement of sustainable development in the United Kingdom;

- national policies and such international obligations as the Secretary of State may notify to the Mayor for the purposes of section 41(5)(a) of the GLA Act;
- any regional planning guidance issued by the Secretary of State so far as related to an area which includes or adjoins Greater London;
- the desirability of promoting and encouraging the use of the River Thames safely, in particular for the provision of passenger transport services and for the transportation of freight;
- any statement which contains the Secretary of State's policies in relation to the recovery and disposal of waste in England and which is made under section 44A of the Environmental Protection Act 1990;
- the objectives of preventing major accidents and limiting the consequences of such accidents; and
- the need:

  (i) in the long term, to maintain appropriate distances between establishments and residential areas, areas of public use and areas of particular natural sensitivity or interest, and

  (ii) in the case of existing establishments, for additional technical measures in accordance with Article 5 of Council Directive 96/82 on the control of major-accident hazards involving dangerous substances so as not to increase the risks to people.

18.31   The Mayor's duty in exercising development control powers does not reflect the same duty imposed on all LPAs under section 54A of the TCP Act, namely, that a planning application must be determined in accordance with the development plan unless material considerations indicate otherwise; although in practice the power of the Secretary of State to call in applications for his own determination, or to award costs against the Mayor (GLA Act, s.345), should prevent any conflict arising.

LPAs are not permitted to allow applications on which the Mayor has been notified until the period of 14 days has elapsed or the Mayor has notified the LPA that he is content for planning permission to be issued. Where the Mayor directs refusal an LPA is bound by the direction, unless the Secretary of State has directed otherwise (Order, art. 5(8)). Where the

Mayor direct an LPA to refuse an application, any direction must be accompanied with a statement of reasons, and a copy of that refusal and statement of reasons must be served on the Secretary of State (Order, art. 5(4) and (6)). The Mayoral power to direct refusal is akin to the Secretary of State's power under the Town and Country Planning (General Development Procedure) Order 1995 (S.I. 1995 No. 419) to call in an application for his own determination, and then refuse to grant permission having called it in.

Any conflict between the Mayor and an LPA on an application of **18.32** potential strategic importance may be resolved by the Secretary of State making the decision on the application. For example, where a London LPA wishes to approve an application for planning permission contrary to its UDP, which has to be notified to the Secretary of State and the Mayor at the same time, the Mayor must act within 14 days as opposed to the 21 days enjoyed by the Secretary of State (*cf.* Order, art. 4 and Town and Country Planning (General Development Procedure) Order 1995 (S.I. 1995 No. 419), art. 20). This extra period of time for the Secretary of State will enable him to take into account the views of the Mayor before deciding whether to intervene, and ensures that the decision on a particular application accords with the plan-led planning system within which both applicants and LPAs now operate.

The planning system as amended by the GLA Act does permit the Secretary of State and the Mayor to come to different conclusions on strategic planning policies in relation to an application for permission. The above scenario, however, demonstrates that the Secretary of State has ultimate control over how the Mayor discharges his functions, since he can call in the application and approve it even where the Mayor directs an LPA to refuse it.

The responsibility for determining planning applications remains with **18.33** the LPA, and where it has not been called in by the Secretary of State the applicant may exercise his right of appeal against a decision to the Secretary of State under section 78 of the TCP Act. There is no right of appeal against the issuing of a direction to refuse by the Mayor, and the LPA is under a duty to refuse on receipt of such a direction. The only direct method of challenging any such direction is by way of judicial review. In the absence of such a challenge, the applicant can appeal to the Secretary of State against the refusal to grant planning permission, at which stage the merits of the application are examined in the context of the reasons for refusal. In such a case the decision notice of the LPA would reflect the Mayor's reasons for issuing the direction.

The Act amends the TCP Act to enable the Secretary of State, in certain circumstances, to recover his costs from the Mayor and award the costs of an appeal against the Mayor (GLA Act, s.345). This ensures that where the Mayor has acted unreasonably in directing a refusal of permission, an applicant on appeal may be able to recover his costs from the Mayor as opposed to recovery from the LPA (who are under a duty to refuse on receipt of such a direction from the Mayor).

The Secretary of State is empowered to modify any provision of this Act that relates to an appeal under section 78 of the TCP Act following a refusal to grant planning permission, pursuant to a direction requiring refusal (TCP Act, s.74(1B)(c)). In this context, the Secretary of State will be particularly concerned with any provision relating to appearance by parties at an appeal and costs.

Recovery of Costs at Local Inquiries

18.34 Where a local inquiry is held by the Secretary of State to hear an appeal against a decision to refuse to grant planning permission, and that refusal was as a result of the Mayor's direction pursuant to article 5 of the Order, the Secretary of State can recover his costs from the Mayor and award against him such costs incurred by other parties who attend the inquiry as a result of the LPA's decision. The Secretary of State is only able to award costs if the following criteria are satisfied:

   (i) the LPA for a London Borough have refused to grant planning permission;

  (ii) that refusal is in compliance with a direction made by the Mayor under the Order;

 (iii) and there is an appeal to the Secretary of State under section 78 (GLA Act, s.322B(1)).

Section 320 of the TCP Act provides that the Secretary of State may cause a local inquiry to be held for the purposes of the exercise of any of his functions under the TCP Act. A local inquiry to hear an appeal against a refusal to grant planning permission is an inquiry for the purposes of section 320 of the TCP Act. The Secretary of State may recover from the local authority or such other party to the inquiry as he directs his costs incurred in relation to that inquiry (Local Government Act 1972, s.250(4) to (5)). This power to recover costs incurred has been enlarged to cover local inquiries held as a result of the Mayor's direction to refuse. Section 322B as inserted provides that where a local inquiry is held under such circumstances section 250(4) and (5) of the Local Government Act 1972 shall be treated as if substituted by section 322B(5) and (6) of the GLA Act respectively.

18.35 The effect of this substitution enables the Secretary of State may recover his costs in relation to such an inquiry:

  (i) from the Mayor if he is not a party at the inquiry and the Secretary of State decided that the Mayor acted unreasonably in making the direction which was acted upon by the LPA, or

 (ii) where the Mayor is a party or if the Secretary of State does not decide to recover the costs from him, from the LPA or other party as he may direct.

The Secretary of State may certify the level of costs and any certified amount must be paid by the Mayor, LPA or other party to the inquiry. Any costs not paid can be recovered summarily by the Secretary of State as a civil debt.

Further, the Secretary of State may also make orders as to the costs of the parties to the inquiry, and to and by whom those costs are to be paid. Section 322B(6), as substituted, provides that the Secretary of State may order the Mayor to pay the costs of the other parties to the inquiry, but only if he was not a party to the inquiry and the Secretary of State decides that he acted unreasonably in making the direction which resulted in the appeal against the refusal.

Not all appeals against the decision of the LPA to refuse to grant **18.36** planning permission result in a local inquiry. Any applicant can have his appeal to the Secretary of State determined by written representations or following an informal hearing. Under section 322(2) of the TCP Act the Secretary of State has the power, by virtue of section 250(5) of the Local Government Act 1972, to award costs in proceedings that give rise to a hearing so that costs at even an informal hearing are capable of being recovered. It follows that at informal hearings to which this section applies, the Secretary of State has the power to award costs against the parties, which may include the Mayor if he is not a party to the inquiry and the Secretary of State decides that he acted unreasonably in making the direction which resulted in the appeal against the refusal. The same would apply where an inquiry has been arranged but is subsequently cancelled.

If the Secretary of State makes an inter parties award of costs such an order may be made an order of the High Court on application by the party named in the Secretary of State's decision, and those costs will not be recoverable until such an application has been made.

Duty of Functional Bodies

Section 424(1) of the GLA Act defines functional bodies as being the **18.37** following:

1. Transport for London
2. the London Development Agency
3. the Metropolitan Police Agency
4. the London Fire and Emergency Planning Authority

Each body in the exercise of its statutory duties is required to have regard to the policies and proposals contained within the published SDS. As these bodies are involved in the early consultation process in preparing the proposed SDS (section 335(1)) they will have had significant input to the SDS as published and therefore will be fully aware as to how it will affect their functioning.

London Planning Advisory Committee (LPAC)

18.38 Section 349 of the GLA Act abolishes the joint planning committee for Greater London, known as the London Planning Advisory Committee (LPAC), initially set up under section 5, Local Government Act 1985 and preserved by section 3 of the TCP Act. This was an advisory committee established after the abolition of the Greater London Council, and its statutory duty was to advise LPAs in Greater London on matters of common interest relating to planning and development of Greater London, and to inform the Secretary of State and other LPAs in the vicinity of London of the views of the London authorities about such matters and how those matters affected those areas in the vicinity of London. The committee also had a limited power to contribute towards the costs of those LPAs and bodies on which they were represented.

As the Mayor has now been vested with the responsibilities that were the function of LPAC, the committee is redundant.

Chapter 19

ENVIRONMENTAL FUNCTIONS

Introduction

The Mayor, under Part IX of the Act, is required to prepare a wide range **19.01**
of documents relating to environmental policy. These are as follows:

- the state of the environment report;
- the London Biodiversity Action Plan;
- the municipal waste management strategy;
- the London air quality strategy; and
- the London ambient noise strategy.

Of these documents, the one likely to receive the highest profile is the
state of the environment report. This report draws upon the policies and
proposals contained in the strategies and action plan, and brings together
all the disparate parts of environmental reporting within London, providing a central environmental data resource (GLA Act, s.351).

The Secretary of State has an important role to play in the exercise of
the Mayor's functions in this respect, in that he can issue directions, both
general and specific, with which the Mayor must comply. The functional
bodies, namely, Transport for London, the London Development Agency,
the Metropolitan Police Authority, and the London Fire and Emergency
Planning Authority, must have regard to the Mayor's strategies when
exercising any of their functions (GLA Act, s.373).

The State of the Environment Report

The Mayor is required to prepare a report known as the "state of the **19.02**
environment report" (GLA Act, s.351(1)), which will describe the state of
the capital's environment through a range of specified indicators which are
either prescribed or left to be identified by the Mayor where appropriate
(GLA Act, s.351(3)). The report does not form part of a strategy for the
purposes of this Act, although it will present reliable information in the
public domain and inform the debate on the environment, which may in
turn precipitate a change in emphasis or even direction in the Mayor's

strategies. The report must contain information under the following specific environmental headings so far as they are relevant to Greater London, though the Mayor may add other information where he considers it is appropriate:

- *Air quality and emissions to air, including in particular emissions from road traffic.* The report is likely to draw upon the London air quality strategy. This strategy contains proposals and policies implementing the Secretary of State's national air strategy prepared pursuant to section 80 of the Environment Act 1995, and aiming to achieve the air quality standards and objectives as prescribed by Air Quality Regulations 1997 (S.I. 1997 No. 3043). It also contains information about current and future air quality in Greater London, the measures to be taken by the Authority, Transport for London, and the London Development Agency to implement the strategy, and the steps the Mayor will encourage other persons or bodies to take to implement the strategy (GLA Act, s.362(3)). The Mayor is under a duty to produce the London air quality strategy (GLA Act, ss.362 to 369) and the report will assess and report on the state of the capital's air quality and emissions to the air in the context of the strategy.
- Road traffic levels.
- Water quality and emissions to water.
- Ground water levels.
- Energy consumption and the emission of substances which contribute to climate change.
- Land quality.

19.03
- *Biodiversity.* This part of the report is likely to draw upon the London Biodiversity Action Plan produced by the Mayor (GLA Act, s.352), and assess the capital's environment in this context. The Action Plan contains information about the ecology, the wildlife of Greater London and its habitat, together with any proposals for and commitments to the conservation and promotion of biodiversity.
- *Production, minimisation, recycling and disposal of waste.* This part of the report is likely to draw upon the "municipal waste management strategy" prepared by the Mayor under section 353 of the Act, and assess the capital's environment in the context of the policies and proposals contained in the strategy for the recovery, treatment and disposal of municipal waste, or such other proposals and policies concerning waste as the Mayor considers appropriate.
- *Noise.* The Mayor is under a separate duty to publish the "London ambient noise strategy" (GLA Act, s.370) which not only sets out information about ambient noise levels in Greater London and their impact on those living and working in Greater London, but also assesses the impact on the Mayor's strategies prepared under section 41(1) of the Act on those levels, and summarises the action taken or to be taken for the purpose of promoting a reduction in the levels.

- Natural resources.
- Litter.

The Mayor must publish his state of the environment report within **19.04** three years from the day of the first election (GLA Act, s.351(2)(a)) and any subsequent report must be published within four years beginning with the date of publishing the previous state of the environment report (GLA Act, s.351(2)(b)).

Before this report is produced the Mayor must consult with the following bodies about the contents of his report:

- the Environment Agency;
- each London borough council;
- the Common Council; and
- any other person the Mayor considers appropriate to consult (GLA Act, s.351(4)).

Once published the state of the report must be kept for a period of six years from the date of publication (section 351(7)) for inspection, free of charge and at reasonable hours, at the principal offices of the Authority (section 351(5)). A copy of the report, or any part of the report, must be provided to any person during the six-year period upon payment of a reasonable fee (section 351(6)).

London Biodiversity Action Plan

Biological diversity, or biodiversity, is the variety and variability of all **19.05** species of plants, animals and micro-organisms on earth, as well as the ecosystems they compose. International conventions are often one of the principal forces behind new environmental legislation. The most recent notable international development was the United Nations Conference on Environment and Development (UNCED)—the "Earth Summit"—at Rio de Janeiro in June 1992. The Convention on Biological Diversity, promoted at the Summit, was ratified by the United Kingdom on June 3, 1994, and provides the framework for developing the role of the Mayor in formulating the London Biodiversity Action Plan ("the Action Plan"), as part of the national strategy for biodiversity, to promote biodiversity in Greater London.

The Action Plan must contain information about:

- the ecology of Greater London;
- the wildlife of Greater London and its habitat;
- any proposals for the conservation and promotion of biodiversity within Greater London; and

- any commitments made by the Nature Conservancy Council for England, the Countryside Agency, and the Environment Agency regarding conservation and promotion of biodiversity within Greater London (GLA Act, s.352).

19.06   The Mayor must obtain the agreement of the Nature Conservancy Council for England (*i.e.* English Nature), the Countryside Agency, and the Environment Agency to his proposals for conservation and promotion of biodiversity before publishing his Action Plan (section 352(2)(c)). English Nature, established under the Environmental Protection Act 1990 ("EPA"), advise the Secretary of State on nature conservation issues, with specific responsibilities for advising on species and habitat protection, the dissemination of knowledge about nature conservation, the support and conduct of research into nature conservation, and safeguarding of protected sites (see the EPA, s.132). The Countryside Agency has responsibilities in relation to the preservation and enhancement of natural beauty in England and the provision of recreational activities, including rights of way. It is these amenity functions which distinguish it from English Nature. The Environment Agency has the majority of powers in relation to pollution control and in discharging its functions under the EPA, its principal aim and objective is to protect and enhance the environment, taken as a whole, and to attain the objective of achieving sustainable development.

19.07   In preparing the Action Plan the Mayor must have regard to any plans relating to biodiversity prepared by any London borough council, or the Common Council, and to any guidance issued by the Secretary of State stating what matters he is to take into account in preparing the Action Plan, which will invariably include any written statements of national and international policy (GLA Act, s.352(4)). When he has prepared the Action Plan he must then consult with the Nature Conservancy Council for England, the Countryside Agency, and the Environment Agency (GLA Act, s.352(3)). The Mayor will have to take into account any responses received through the consultation process and, if any of the proposals are not supported by any or all of the bodies consulted, then those proposals cannot form part of the Action Plan. Where the Action plan is revised following consultation, the Mayor must publish the Plan as revised (GLA Act, s.352(5)).

Once the Action Plan has been published, the Mayor can revise it at any stage, but he must carry out the same process of considering the relevant plans on biodiversity prepared by London borough councils or the Common Council, and have regard to any guidance the Secretary of State may issue on revising the Action Plan. Where the Plan is revised, any reference in the Act to the London Biodiversity Action Plan, shall be taken to mean reference to the published Plan as revised (GLA Act, s.352(6)).

The Municipal Waste Management Strategy

The Environmental Protection Act 1990, as amended by the Environment **19.08** Act 1995 ("EA"), provides the backdrop for waste management in England and Wales. The EPA established three classes of waste authority: waste regulation authority, waste disposal authority and waste collection authority (EPA, s.2). Waste regulatory functions are now vested in the Environment Agency. In London, the waste disposal authorities are the West London, North London, East London and West Riverside Waste Authorities (comprising of members from the constituent councils), the Common Council, and, otherwise, the London borough councils (EPA, s.30(2) and S.I. 1985 No. 1884). The waste collection authorities in London are the London borough councils, the Common Council, the Sub-Treasurer of the Inner Temple and the Under Treasurer of the Middle Temple (EPA, s.30(3)). The EPA provides the legislative framework for waste management and provides that responsibility for waste management lies with waste disposal and waste collection authorities. For the purposes of sections 353 to 359 of the Act, which set out the mayoral functions regarding waste, any reference to waste authorities means waste collection and waste disposal authorities (GLA Act, s.360(2)). The Environment Agency regulates the discharge of these functions.

The Mayor is under a duty to prepare and publish a document known as **19.09** the "municipal waste management strategy" (GLA Act, s.353(1)). Municipal waste is defined as any waste in the possession or under the control of a body which, or a person who, is a waste collection authority for Greater London, or a body which is a waste disposal authority in Greater London (GLA Act, s.360(2)). Waste is to be construed in accordance with section 75 of the EPA (GLA Act, s.360(2)). The original definition of waste was formally amended by the EA 1995 to incorporate the new definition of waste found in the Waste Management Licensing Regulations 1994 (S.I. 1994 No. 1056). Waste is now defined as "any substance or object in the categories set out in Schedule 2B to [the Environmental Protection Act] which the holder discards or intends or is required to discard" (EPA, s.75(2)). The "holder" is "the producer of the waste or the person who is in possession of it", and the "producer" is the person whose activities produce waste or any person who carries out pre-processing, mixing or other operations resulting in a change in the nature and composition of the waste.

This new definition was introduced to implement the provisions of the **19.10** E.C. Waste Framework Directive 75/442 (as amended in particular by Directive 91/156). There are therefore two elements to the definition of waste:

(i) there must be a material substance or object that comes within any of the categories listed in Schedule 2B; and

(ii) the substance or object must have been or intended to be discarded by its holder.

If both elements are satisfied then the item is waste for the purposes of the "municipal waste management strategy".

The Strategy

19.11 Up to 80 per cent of London's waste is transported by road to landfill sites in Kent, Essex and Bedfordshire. Essex County Council has stated that it intends to ban imported waste and Bedfordshire County Council is currently reviewing its position. In response to the need for a review of London's waste management arrangements, the Mayor's "municipal waste management strategy" must set out policies and proposals that integrate the various options for the "recovery, treatment and disposal of the municipal waste, or such other policies or proposals as the Mayor considers appropriate" (GLA Act, s.353(2)). In the context of sections 353 to 359 "recovery" means not only the recovery of materials from waste, but obtaining energy from waste. Both "treatment" and "disposal" are to be construed in accordance with the EPA, s.29(6). "Treatment" as defined provides that waste is treated when it is subjected to any process, including making it reusable or reclaiming substances from it. "Disposal" is defined as any of the operations listed in Schedule 4 to the Waste Management Licensing Regulations 1994 (S.I. 1994 No. 1056), which includes a wide range of activities ranging from tipping of waste above or below ground to its release into the sea. It is clear that the "municipal waste management strategy" will contain policies and proposals that are far reaching, covering every aspect of managing the municipal waste produced by Greater London. The municipal waste management strategy is a strategy to which sections 41 to 44 of the Act apply.

19.12 In formulating his policies and proposals relating to municipal waste the Mayor must have regard to the national waste strategy prepared by the Secretary of State and any other guidance given to him by the Secretary of State, for the purpose of implementing that strategy and relating it to the content of his own strategy. The Secretary of State's national strategy, which he is under a duty to prepare by virtue of section 44A of the EPA, can comprise one or more statements containing his policies in relation to the recovery and disposal of waste in England and Wales. A draft national waste strategy was published as a white paper, entitled "Making Waste Work—A Strategy for Sustainable Waste Management in England and Wales", Cm. 3040. This sets out the government's aim of securing the sustainable management of waste. There are three objectives: (a) reducing the amount of waste produced; (b) identifying the best use of the waste that is produced; (c) minimising the risk of immediate or future environmental pollution and harm to human health by adopting the most appropriate waste management practices. This duty to produce a national strategy replaces the duty that was imposed on waste regulatory authorities to produce a waste disposal plan. At present there is no National Waste Strategy, and this white paper is simply advisory.

The Mayor, when preparing his strategy, must also have regard to the **19.13** plans prepared by the waste collection authorities in Greater London (GLA Act, s.353(3)). It is a duty of each waste collection authority as respects household and commercial waste arising in its area to prepare a waste recycling plan setting out arrangements made and proposed to be made both by the authority and by any other persons for dealing with such waste by separating, baling or otherwise packaging it for the purpose of recycling it (EPA, s.49(1)).

The Mayor's policies and proposals must work within this framework providing a strategic lead on municipal waste in London and setting out sustainable practices for the management of the waste produced in Greater London.

Procedural Steps

Once the Mayor has prepared or revised the "municipal waste manage- **19.14** ment strategy" the Act sets out a number of procedural steps that he must take before publishing it. He must consult with the specified bodies (GLA Act, s.353(5)), or such other body as he considers it appropriate to consult, save that such a body must be concerned with the minimisation, recovery, treatment or disposal of municipal waste (GLA Act, s.353(5)(e)). The specific bodies who must be consulted are as follows:

- the Environment Agency,
- the waste disposal authorities in Greater London, and
- any waste disposal authority that adjoins any part of the boundary of Greater London.

The waste disposal authorities for Greater London are those identified by **19.15** section 30(2)(b) of the EPA as described above. Following receipt of the consultees' responses, the Mayor can review his strategy, if he considered it necessary to do so, and then proceed to publish the strategy as revised (GLA Act, s.353(6)). The Mayor is able to revise his strategy at any time, but he must follow the same procedural steps as he followed in preparing the initial strategy.

It is the "municipal waste management strategy" that provides the strategic lead on municipal waste in Greater London, and to which all waste disposal and collection authorities must have regard. The strategy is always the strategy as revised, except where the context otherwise requires (GLA Act, s.353(7)).

Duties of Waste Authorities

The Act requires all waste disposal authorities and waste collection **19.16** authorities to have regard to the municipal waste management strategy in the exercise of any function under Part II of the EPA (GLA Act, s.355).

Part II of the Environmental Protection Act sets out the framework which endeavours to regulate waste throughout its life cycle from the point of production to its final disposal. The Mayor's strategy will mirror this framework providing all waste disposal authorities and waste collection authorities with the strategic lead in discharging their functions. Even though the Mayor is not a waste authority with power to control the collection or disposal of waste, he not only gives the waste authorities direction through his strategy, he may also give directions to these authorities where to do so is necessary to secure implementation of his strategy (GLA Act, s.356).

Directions by the Secretary of State

19.17 The Secretary of State can at any stage give a direction to the Mayor about the context of the municipal waste management strategy, where he is satisfied that it or its implementation is likely to be detrimental to any area outside Greater London, or the policies contained in the Secretary of State's national waste strategy (pursuant to section 44A of the EPA) requires that a direction is given to ensure that any new policies are implemented (GLA Act, s.354(1) and (2)). This is a discretionary power that can only be exercised after the Secretary of State has consulted with the Mayor (GLA Act, s.354(3)(b)). Where such a direction is issued, the Mayor is under a duty to comply with it (GLA Act, s.354(4)). The possibility of a direction being given may highlight a need for the Mayor to conduct a review of the whole or part of the strategy. If he needs to revise his strategy to comply with the Secretary of State's direction, he must follow the statutory requirements set out in section 353 of the GLA Act.

Directions by the Mayor

19.18 The Mayor's power to direct, where it is necessary to do so to secure implementation of his strategy, is limited to the acts of the waste disposal authorities and the waste collections authorities in Greater London. It is akin to the Secretary of State's power to give a binding direction to the Environment Agency in relation to the terms and conditions that must, or must not, be included in waste management licences (Environmental Protection Act, s.35(7)), and the power to give binding directions relating to the modification (Environmental Protection Act, s.37(3)) and/or the suspension and revocation of such licences (EPA, ss.38(7) and 42(8)).

Parliament has made provision for the period prior to publication of the first municipal waste management plan. Pending publication, for the purposes of exercising the mayoral power to issue a direction under section 356 of the Act the Mayor will only be able to issue such a direction where it would otherwise be detrimental to the implementation of the national waste strategy prepared by the Secretary of State under section 44A (GLA Act, s.360(5)).

The Mayor can only issue a direction under section 356 of the Act, whether it be a general or specific direction after consultation with the authority on whom it is to be served (GLA Act, s.356(4)). This does not restrict the exercise of the power, it only imposes a precursor to the exercise of the power in itself. Where the waste authority receives a direction from the Mayor it is under a duty to comply with the direction (GLA Act, s.356(5)).

Waste Contracts

The only restriction in the exercise of the Mayor's power to direct an **19.19** authority in the exercise any of its functions is that he cannot issue a direction where an authority would be required to terminate a waste contract before the expiry of its term, or the direction would require the authority to act in a way that would result in a breach of any term of a waste contract (GLA Act, s.356(2)). A waste contract is defined by the Act as a contract which includes or is to include provision relating to municipal waste made by a waste authority in the discharge if its duties under Part II of the EPA (see paragraph 19.10 above for definition of "municipal waste").

Where a waste authority is required to comply with the public procure- **19.20** ment regulations in awarding a waste contract, and in compliance with those regulations the authority has sent the second information notice relating to the award of that contract to the Official Journal of the European Communities, the Mayor is prohibited from issuing a direction requiring the authority in the exercise a function under Part II of the EPA in relation to the awarding of a waste contract (GLA Act, s.356(3)). The public procurement regulations are the Public Works Contracts Regulations 1991, the Public Services Contracts Regulations 1993, the Public Supply Contracts Regulations 1995, and the Utilities Contracts Regulations 1996 (section 360(2)).

Despite these restrictions on the exercise of the power to direct, the Mayor does have power to obtain information from waste authorities relating to existing and proposed waste contracts (see sections 357 and 358). The overriding requirement is that any such direction must be necessary to secure the implementation of the municipal waste management strategy (GLA Act, s.356(1)).

Information about Existing/New Contracts

In order to exercise the power to direct an authority in the exercise any of **19.21** its functions the Mayor needs to have all the relevant information available regarding the waste contracts awarded and those to be awarded.

Waste disposal authorities are responsible for the formation of the privatised waste disposal companies which are in turn responsible for the disposal, keeping or treatment or collection of waste (EPA, s.32). Any contract awarded for such activity to a waste disposal contractor, which must be contracted out by the authority, is not only subject to the procedure set out in Part II of Schedule 2 to the EPA, but also to the E.C. public procurement regime. E.C. procurement Directives, as incorporated in domestic Regulations (Public Works Contracts Regulations 1991 (S.I. 1991 No. 2680), Public Services Contracts Regulations 1993 (S.I. 1993 No. 3228), Public Services Contracts Regulations 1995 (S.I. 1995 No. 201)—all as amended) is additional to domestic law, and is designed to co-ordinate national procedures for the award of public contracts in order to remove trade barriers.

19.22   Sections 357 and 358 of the GLA Act set out the duties imposed on waste authorities to notify the Mayor of the prescribed matters relating to waste contracts (GLA Act. s.357(1)), and provide information, if so required. Before the end of the period of 21 days from the date on which section 357(1) of the GLA Act comes into force, every waste authority is under a duty to notify the Mayor of the date on which the term of any waste contract they are party to is due to expire (GLA Act, s.357(1)).

By way of a separate duty, but without prejudice to the above duty to notify the Mayor (GLA Act, s.357(3)), a waste authority, at least two years but not earlier than three, before the date on which the term of a waste contract is due to expire must notify the Mayor of the date on which the term is due to expire (GLA Act, s.357(2)). Further, if at any stage before a waste contract is due to expire a waste authority proposes to terminate the contract or amend it, or if it receives notification from another party to the contract that it is to be or is terminated or amended, then the Mayor must also be notified (GLA Act, s.357(4)).

The purpose of notifying the Mayor is to enable him to consider whether he wants to direct that he be provided with more information (GLA Act, s.357(5)). The information provided also enables him to decide whether the arrangements for entering into a new contract, its terms or any amendment or proposed amendment to the existing contract would be detrimental to the implementation of the municipal waste management strategy.

19.23   It is important to note that there is a duty to provide the Mayor with all the information that is available in the waste authority's possession (GLA Act, s.359(1)). Section 359 sets out two situations where information is exempt from the information the authority is under a duty to provide, namely:

- information which has been provided to the waste authority by another person and that person has imposed a requirement that the information must remain confidential;
- information, the disclosure of which would put the waste authority in breach of any public procurement regulations applicable to the contract in question.

If, at the time the information is provided, the waste authority notifies the Mayor that it is of the opinion that the information is confidential information or exempt information (as defined by section 100A(3) and section 100I of the Local Government Act 1972), the Mayor is under a duty not to disclose that information, except to the staff appointed by the Mayor or the Assembly, who may only disclose it to other members of staff appointed by the Mayor or the Assembly (GLA Act, s.359(2)). This duty also applies to information provided by the waste authority in relation to new contracts under the duty outlined in section 358 of the Act.

The duty to provide the Mayor with all the available information in the waste authority's possession similarly applies both to existing and new contracts.

Where the waste authority is awarding a new waste contract as opposed **19.24** to amending an existing contract the Mayor has the power to direct an authority to provide him with information in order that he can determine whether the award of the contract would be detrimental to the implementation of the municipal waste management strategy (GLA Act, s.358). Where the public procurement regulations apply, and notice in respect of the contract must be sent to the official Journal of the European Communities in accordance with the relevant regulations, the Mayor must be notified of the waste authority's intention to send the said notice, which must not be sent until 56 days have lapsed from the date the Mayor was notified (GLA Act, s.358(1)). These procedural steps must also be followed where the public procurement regulations do not apply (GLA Act, s.358(2)). Where the Mayor issues a direction under section 358 the waste authority must comply with it (GLA Act, s.358(4)).

Parliament has made provision for the period prior to publication of the first municipal waste management plan. Pending publication, as in the case with any direction under section 356 of the Act, the Mayor will only be able to direct under section 357 and/or section 358 of the Act where there would be detriment to the implementation of the national waste strategy prepared by the Secretary of State under section 44A of the EPA (GLA Act, s.360(5)). Where the Mayor gives such a direction the waste authority must comply with his direction (GLA Act, ss.357(6) and 358(4)).

Waste Recycling Plans

Section 49 of the EPA establishes the duty that waste collection authorities **19.25** must investigate what arrangements can practically be made for recycling household and commercial waste. Authorities are required to prepare waste recycling plans which must be available for the public to inspect.

Section 361 amends this section to require the waste collection authority to send a copy of the draft waste recycling plan to the Mayor before finally determining the content of the plan or any modification to an existing plan. The Mayor is obliged to consider the draft plan and is able to give directions to the authority with which the authority must comply. The Mayor, like the Secretary of State, can issue directions to the waste collection authority specifying the time by which the authority must perform its duty and if such a direction is issued the authority must comply with it (EA 1995, s.49(7A) inserted by the GLA Act, s.361(5)).

London Air Quality Strategy

19.26 The main controls on atmospheric pollution are to be found in the Environmental Protection Act which establishes a two-tier system of controlling emissions into the atmosphere from certain prescribed industrial processes: "Integrated Pollution Control" (IPC) for the most seriously polluting processes; and "Local Authority Air Pollution Control" (LAAPC) for others. The statutory nuisance provisions of the Environmental Protection Act and the Clean Air Act 1993 are also relevant. However, by far the most important step taken to improve air quality, reducing and controlling pollutants in the atmosphere was the introduction of the national air quality strategy under section 80 of the Environment Act. The Secretary of State is under a duty to publish his strategy which must contain policies with respect to the assessment or management of air quality. The strategy must also contain policies for implementing E.C. and international objectives.

A key tool for delivering the national air quality strategy is the system of Local Air Quality Management introduced by the Part IV of the Environment Act. Local authorities are placed under a duty to achieve, at a local level, the national air quality strategy. Each authority is under a duty to carry out a review of the quality and likely future quality of air in its area, and an area identified as not achieving or likely to achieve the air quality standards and objectives must be designated as an air quality management area. Upon declaring such an area the local authority must draw up an action plan identifying measures to achieve the objectives.

19.27 In this context the Mayor is required to prepare and publish a London air quality strategy (GLA Act, s.362(1)). This strategy must contain the Mayor's policies and proposals for implementing the National Air Quality Strategy and any regulations made under section 87 of the Environment Act (specifically, the Air Quality Regulations 1997 (S.I. 1997 No. 3034)). The Mayor may also set out other policies and proposals relating to the improvement of air quality in Greater London as he considers appropriate (GLA Act, s.362(2)). The London air quality strategy must contain information on the following issues:

- not only the current but the likely future air quality in Greater London;
- the steps to be taken by the Authority, Transport for London and the London Development Agency in implementing the strategy; and
- the measures which other persons or bodies are to be encouraged by the Mayor to take for the purpose of implementing the strategy.

19.28 The Mayor must not only have regard to those matters prescribed by the Air Quality Regulations 1997 (S.I. 1997 No. 3043), but he must have specific regard to the reviews conducted by local authorities in Greater

London pursuant to section 82 of the EA. Where the air quality standards or objectives are not being achieved the local authority will establish an air quality management area. If any area has been designated as an air quality management area, the Mayor must also take this into account when preparing his strategy. Further, where an area has been designated as an air quality management area by order of a local authority pursuant to section 83 of the EA, the Mayor shall take into account the local authority's written plan (known as an "action plan") which sets out how it seeks to achieve the air quality and standards for the area (GLA Act, s.362(4)). For these purposes any reference to 'local authority' has the same meaning as in section 91(1) of the EA, namely, any unitary authority, district council, so far as it is not a unitary authority, the Common Council of the City of London, and the Sub-Treasurer of the Inner Temple and the Under-Treasurer of the Middle Temple (GLA Act, s.366).

The Mayor must consult with the Environment Agency and any local **19.29** authority whose boundary adjoins any part of the boundary of Greater London when preparing his strategy. Following the consultation process the Mayor may revise his strategy, if appropriate, and then publish the strategy. If the Mayor considers that revision is necessary, or should be directed by the Secretary of State to revise it, he must have regard to the same matters and follow the same procedure. Once again, he can direct any local authority in Greater London to provide him with information, advice and assistance he requires to revise the strategy (GLA Act, s.365(1)).

Any reference to the London air quality strategy is reference to the strategy as revised (GLA Act, s.362(7)).

Duties of Local Authorities in Greater London

As discussed above, Part IV of the EA sets out the strategic and local **19.30** framework for national air quality. When undertaking local air quality management or discharging any other duty under Part IV of the EA local authorities in Greater London must also have regard to the London air quality strategy (GLA Act, s.364).

Directions by the Secretary of State

Where the Secretary of State considers that the London air quality strategy **19.31** or its implementation would be detrimental to any area outside Greater London, or that a direction is required concerning the content of the strategy to ensure implementation of the National Air Quality Strategy, then he may give the Mayor such a direction (GLA Act, s.363(1)). Any direction pursuant to this power may be general or specific, but can only be exercised after consultation with the Mayor (GLA Act, s.363(3)). The Mayor cannot resist the direction, save by challenging it by way of judicial review. If compliance with a direction requires a revision of the strategy then such a revision must be carried out.

Mayoral Powers

19.32 The Mayor can direct a local authority in Greater London to provide him with such information, advice and assistance as he may require to prepare or revise the London air quality strategy (GLA Act, s.365(1)). Again, such a direction may be general or specific, but once the direction has been issued the local authority must comply with it and provide the Mayor with the required information, advice and/or assistance.

The EA is amended by sections 367 to 369 of the Act. Where a local authority fails to, or to properly, implement the provisions of Part IV of the Environment Act the Secretary of State had the power to direct them to do so. Section 85 of the EA is amended by the Act to remove that power from the Secretary of States so far as Greater London is concerned and vests it in the Mayor (GLA Act, s.367).

19.33 The Mayor now has the power to direct any local authority in Greater London to implement the provisions of Part IV of the EA. The Mayor can only issue a direction after he has consulted with the local authority concerned (EA, s.85(4A) as inserted by the GLA Act, section 367(3)). In deciding whether to issue a direction the Mayor must have regard to any guidance issued by the Secretary of State with respect to, or in connection with, the exercise of any of the powers conferred, or the discharge of any of the duties imposed on local authorities under Part IV (EA, s.88(1)).

Section 85(5) of the EA as amended by section 367(4) of the Act means that the Secretary of State cannot give any direction to local authorities in Greater London requiring them to take steps for the implementation of any obligations of the United Kingdom under Community Treaties or any international agreement to which the United Kingdom is a party. The Mayor is able to revise his strategy to give effect to any new Community Treaties or any international agreement, to which all local authorities in Greater London are under a duty to have regard when exercising their powers under Part IV of the EA (GLA Act, s.364) in default of which the Mayor can direct accordingly.

Where the Mayor gives a direction to any local authority under section 85 of the EA he is required to send a copy of any direction to the Secretary of State.

19.34 The EA is further amended by section 368 of the Act by the addition of a new section, section 86A. This new section provides that where a local authority is in the course of preparing an action plan for the purpose of achieving air quality standards and objectives in the area designated by the plan, the Mayor shall, within the relevant period, *i.e.* from the date of effect of section 368 to December 2005 (Air Quality Regulations 1997 (S.I. 1997, No. 3043), reg. 3), submit to the authority proposals for the exercise of his powers in pursuit of the achievement of air quality, standards and objectives. Where he submits proposals to a local authority under section 86A of the EA, he must state the time or times within which he proposes to implement each of the proposals. The action plan must include a statement of any of the proposals submitted to the authority by the Mayor and the time or times as set out in the Mayor's statements.

Schedule 11 to the EA is also amended by section 369 of the Act. This Schedule sets out the consultation requirements where a local authority exercises its functions in relation to an air quality review, an assessment under section 82 (local authority reviews) and section 84 (duties of local authorities in relation to designated areas) of the EA, or the preparation of any action plan or any revision of an action plan. Paragraph 2 of this Schedule sets out the people and bodies that must be consulted, and by the newly inserted sub-paragraph (2A) of paragraph 1, Schedule 1 requires a local authority in Greater London, and those authorities whose areas are contiguous with Greater London, to also consult the Mayor when exercising the above functions.

London Ambient Noise Strategy

There has been a series of legislative moves to tackle the problems caused **19.35** by noise. The EPA established the concept of statutory nuisance (EPA, s.79), which has been refined and added to by the Noise and Statutory Nuisance Act 1993 and the Noise Act 1996. Where noise emitted from premises is at a level so as to be prejudicial to health or a nuisance, or the noise that is prejudicial to health or a nuisance is emitted from or caused by a vehicle, machinery or equipment it amounts to a statutory duty and places the burden on the local authority to take action to secure the abatement of that nuisance (EPA, s.80).

Sections 370 to 372 of the Act deal with the Mayor's duties and powers in the context of noise. These in no way remove from the local authorities the responsibility for localised neighbourhood noise issues which may amount to a statutory nuisance.

Section 370 of the GLA Act imposes a duty on the Mayor to prepare and **19.36** publish a document known as the "London ambient noise strategy". This document must consist of:

- information about the ambient noise levels in Greater London and the impact of such noise levels on those living and working in Greater London;
- an assessment of all the Mayor's strategies on the ambient noise levels; and
- a summary of the action taken, or proposed to be taken to promote a reduction in the ambient noise levels in Greater London and reduce the impact on those living and working in Greater London.

Ambient noise is defined as noise that relates to transport, including **19.37** road traffic, rail traffic, aircraft and water transport, and such other sources of noise, which includes vibration, considered by the Mayor to be appropriately included in the strategy (GLA Act, s.370(3)). Where the noise emits from a fixed industrial source, that noise can be included in the matters dealt with by the strategy regardless of whether it falls within the four categories of noise that are expressly excluded from the ambit of the strategy. These four categories of noise are as follows:

- noise emitted from construction sites as the local authority has power under section 60 of the Control of Pollution Act 1974 to serve notice imposing requirements which includes specifying the level of noise and the hours of operation;
- noise caused by the operation of a loud-speaker in a street whether or not the operation would be in contravention of section 2(1) of the Control of Pollution Act 1974;
- noise at work which is the duty of the employer to control under the Health and Safety at Work, etc. Act 1974; and
- noise emitted from premises or emitted from or caused by a vehicle, machinery or equipment in a street. This is to be given the same meaning as found in section 79 of the EPA (GLA Act, s.370(5)). The only exceptions to this exclusion is noise caused by aircraft other than model aircraft and noise made by traffic. As the noise generated by aircraft is expressly excluded from the definition of statutory nuisance, so this Act includes such noise within the definition of ambient noise thereby enabling it to be incorporated in the Mayor's strategy.

19.38   When the Mayor prepares a London ambient noise strategy he must consult with the Environment Agency (GLA Act, s.370(6)), and where he revises it he shall publish it as revised (GLA Act, s.370(7)). For the purposes of this Act, any reference to the London ambient noise strategy will mean reference to the strategy as revised (GLA Act, s.370(8)). The strategy is a strategy for the purposes of sections 41 to 44 of the Act.

Aviation Noise—Aerodromes

19.39 Section 371 of the Act provides that the Mayor will be advised by any person who provides air navigation services of

- any proposed alteration of any route used regularly by civil aircraft before arrival at, or departure from, any aerodrome;
- any proposed addition of any route;
- any substantial alteration proposed to be made to procedures used for managing the arrival of civil aircraft at any aerodrome,

if the proposed alteration or addition will have a significant adverse effect on the noise caused by aircraft in Greater London. "Noise", for the purposes of this section, includes vibration. An alteration to a route used regularly by civil aircraft includes an alteration to the altitude at which the aircraft regularly fly (GLA Act, s.371(3)). Where a person who provides air navigation services falls within one of the above three grounds he must consult the Mayor about the proposed alteration or addition where it is reasonably practicable to do so (GLA Act, s.371(1)).

Section 35 of the Civil Aviation Act 1982 provides that the person managing an aerodrome designated for the purposes of that section by the Secretary of State shall provide those persons or bodies identified in the section adequate facilities for consultation with respect to any matter concerning management or administration of the aerodrome which affects the interests of those persons or bodies. Section 372 amends that section by adding that for any local authority in Greater London, the Mayor must be afforded the same facilities for consultation on behalf of the Authority.

INDEX